Philosophy of Education for Our Time

Philosophy

*of Education
for Our Time*

FREDERICK MAYER

PROFESSOR OF PHILOSOPHY
UNIVERSITY OF REDLANDS

NEW YORK
THE ODYSSEY PRESS · INC ·

COPYRIGHT 1958
BY THE ODYSSEY PRESS, INC.
ALL RIGHTS RESERVED

PRINTED IN THE UNITED STATES

First Edition

TO
Mrs. Everett MacDonald
with deep respect and devotion

PREFACE

OF ALL THE SUBJECTS OF STUDY philosophy of education can be the most important. It clarifies the function of our schools, it illuminates the basic areas of knowledge, and it attempts to frame the objectives and goals toward which our educational system is—or should be—moving. It is significant not only for the student and the teacher but for all those who are concerned with the future of civilization.

All of us occasionally wonder about the destination of our pilgrimage. Where are we going? What is our destiny? What are our most important accomplishments? How can education help us to lead a happier and more constructive life? It is important to know not only the concepts of educational philosophers, but also how their ideas can make our own lives more meaningful. Basically, education is a subjective process and thus factual knowledge is only a prelude to individual creativity.

We are witnessing today an unparalleled expansion of education. Within a few decades twice as many students will attend our primary and secondary schools, and our universities will be crowded as never before. Millions more will take part in adult education. Some educators view this expansion with alarm, but they forget that it may provide a unique opportunity to spread enlightenment and a rational way of life. Genuine education is not just for the few; it is reserved not merely for the elite; it is valuable for all—the young and the old, the rich and the poor. If our society is to have lasting greatness,

PREFACE

ignorance must be overcome, and this can be done only when education becomes a total process and a total concern.

The danger is that we may merely repeat the slogans and the ideas of the past. As science and technology advance, so our educational insights must change. What was creative in the 1920's may be static in the 1950's and 1960's. We cannot rely on one philosophy or on one man. There is no infallible prophet in education just as there can be *no absolute voice of spirituality*. Educational philosophy is the biography of the moment; not a reflection of eternal truths.

I have attempted in this book to outline a new philosophy of education. It follows in the tradition of Jefferson, Emerson, and James and is based upon faith in reason and unwavering humanitarianism.

I want to express, above all, my thanks to Aldous Huxley and Albert Schweitzer; also to Richard Neutra, Dean Ernest Colwell, Dr. Clarence Linton, Dr. Merritt M. Thompson, Dr. Floyd H. Ross, and Professor Gordon Atkins. I owe much to the inspiration of Dr. Lawrence E. Nelson, Dr. David Poston, Dr. Gilbert Becker, Dr. Alvin Haag, Dr. William Parker, Dr. Vernon Tolle, and especially to Dr. George Armacost. In the preparation of the manuscript I have had the valuable assistance of Mr. E. Frank Lee, Miss Celestine Labat, Miss Lorraine Lenz, Miss Alvina Gissler, and Miss Jean Heard.

Frederick Mayer

CONTENTS

Part One The Foundations

I. A Philosophy for Our Times 3

II. Education for Wisdom 15

III. God and Education 26

IV. Jefferson and the Ideal of Freedom 41

V. Emerson and the Quest for Spirituality 53

VI. Dewey and the Ideal of Uncertainty 68

VII. The Dilemmas of American Education 80

Part Two Philosophy in Action

VIII. Aspirations and Conduct 93

IX. The Spark of Creativity 106

CONTENTS

X. The Ideals of Teaching 119

XI. The Teacher and Society 129

XII. Moral Values in Education 143

XIII. The Goals of Education 154

XIV. The Quest for the Good Life 166

XV. The Problem of Truth 175

XVI. Man, Freedom, and Culture 185

XVII. This I Believe 195

Glossary of Names 199

Glossary of Terms 217

Selected Bibliography 223

Index 227

PART ONE

The Foundations

I. A PHILOSOPHY FOR OUR TIMES

Philosophy and Education

WE ARE LIVING in an age of technicians. The advance of scientific machinery has been so great that we tend to be more concerned with application than with theory, with practical issues rather than long-range ideals. Some thinkers like Spengler believe that philosophy in such an age is only a footnote to futility. Yet the danger exists that we may be seduced by methodology, that, as Santayana said, we may redouble our efforts because we have lost our aims.

Man's dilemmas

Quantitative expansion may be a doubtful good for civilization. We can build more automobiles, more refrigerators, more television sets, and politically, our power may increase all over the world, yet these accomplishments may be insignificant. For a great material civilization is never an end in itself, it is only a prelude to the life of reason. *The realm of matter thus is the overture to the realm of spirit.*

A sober view of history should convince even the most enthusiastic proponents of materialism that power has within itself the seeds of its own destruction. Did not Lord Acton say that power corrupts and absolute power corrupts absolutely? The great saints of mankind from Jesus to Schweitzer have taught us that real power is inward, not external, qualitative, not quantitative. The great educators from Socrates to Whitehead have shown that the greatest adventure of man lies not in the political or economic realm, but in the realm of *ideas.*

The creative spirit

The great need of our time then is for a creative view of man, yet according to Scheler:

> In no other period of human knowledge has man ever become more problematic to himself than in our own days. We have a scientific, a philosophical, and a theological anthropology that know nothing of each other. Therefore we no longer possess any clear and consistent idea of man. The evergrowing multiplicity of the particular sciences that are engaged in the study of men has much more confused and obscured than elucidated our concept of man.[1]

We need philosophy not as a technical study, but as an aid to illuminate the problem of man, to give meaning and coherence in an age in which change and flux reign supreme.

Without a creative philosophy we will be like Harry Street in Hemingway's masterful short story *The Snows of Kilimanjaro.* All his life Harry Street had tried to become an outstanding writer. He had tried a life of excitement and adventure, he had seen wars and revolutions. He had married a wealthy woman, who could give him material security. But he was unhappy, for he felt that he had sold his soul and that he had missed the most important part of life: creativity. Now he was dying in Africa. Now he felt he really had the ability to write, to describe the fundamental emotions of life. As he felt the unyielding touch of death, he knew it was too late. He had lived the unexamined way of life, and he had to pay the penalty.

Like Harry Street we all have to make significant choices. Philosophy and education aid us to make our choices more intelligently and more rationally, to see the consequences of our actions. We have to decide: What type of persons will we be? What will be our vocation? What will be the values we shall stress most? And what shall be our central purpose?

[1] Max Scheler, *Die Stellung des Menschen im Kosmos,* pp. 13ff.

A PHILOSOPHY FOR OUR TIMES

In the *Upanishads* we read that most individuals are dominated by the veil of unreality, the veil of Maya; they mistake appearance for reality, illusion for truth, and change for permanence. This means a life of desperation and futility, guided by the passions of the moment. The wise men, according to the *Upanishads*, will stress the essential self, the *Atman* which is beyond space and time and which is part of the unitary structure of the universe.

This view may lead to a rather static concept of the self; like the universe the ultimate nature of the self remains a mystery. And, as Kant indicated in *The Critique of Pure Reason*, fundamental paradoxes—paralogisms—result when we try to define the essence of selfhood. The self just as society is in a state of change. But man has awareness of awareness. He is conscious of the change within and without, subjectively and objectively, and through philosophy and education he can frame tentative goals and objectives towards which all change can be directed.

The meaning of philosophy

Philosophy thus is an intensely *personal* matter. It begins with a sense of alienation. If we lived in a perfect Utopia, few of us would be philosophically minded. But since we live in an imperfect society and a world in which death plays a prominent role, we feel the chasm between ideal and actuality, hope and realization, expectancy and fulfillment. The anti-climactic and tragically incomplete nature of life lead to philosophic wonder. We live in a dual world: the world of experience, of our senses, the realm of immediacy, and the world of our dreams and hopes, the realm of ideals. Can the two worlds meet?

Some philosophers like Plato establish a sharp contrast between experience and ideas. Some religious thinkers, like Augustine, speak even of two cities: The City of God and the City of men; both are involved in a constant state of conflict and warfare. Other thinkers like James, Dewey, and Kilpatrick see the unitary aspects of life and avoid the dualism of experience and the transcendental realm. To them ideals are not patterns of absolute perfection, but goals and objectives implicit in action.

THE FOUNDATIONS

Ideal and actuality

Still, our philosophic pilgrimage begins with a recognition of contrast. Wherever we look we see an enormous distance between Utopia and actuality. Permanence is dissolved in the stream of time. As we read in the *Rubáiyát*:

> Oh, threats of Hell and hopes of Paradise!
> One thing at least is certain—*this* life flies;
> One thing is certain and the rest is Lies;
> The Flower that once has blown forever dies.

This is not an invitation to cynicism; on the contrary, skepticism is a preliminary purge. It illuminates *false* hopes and expectations. Without a knowledge and an understanding of our limitations, we tend to lack, as Russell indicates, a sense of cosmic piety. We set up our own self as the standard of reality and as the ultimate value.

To recognize our limitations should not lead us to despair and anguish. To be sure, as Pascal shows, man is suspended between the infinite and the infinitesimal; he is constantly threatened by nothingness. As we become philosophically aware, we realize that no achievement is final, no triumph absolute, no glory complete, no victory ever-lasting. We recognize the profound insight of Camus' philosophy, especially in *The Plague* and *The Stranger*. Are we not all condemned to perish? Are we not all like prisoners awaiting final execution?

This is only one side of the story. By the use of intelligence and education we overcome the limitations of mortality, we participate in a process which goes beyond immediacy. We feel the comradeship of millions of others, who are fellow pilgrims seeking for truth and enlightenment. We are inspired by a power which transcends our own individuality. We begin to realize that man is the measure of things and that he can control the world both within and without. Did not Bacon say that knowledge is power? Has not the progress of modern science substantiated the faith of Bacon?

Still we must not go to the extreme of foolish optimism. We have been much more successful in the control of nature than in the understanding of the self. *Our technology dwarfs our ideas.* We are proud to drive the latest model car, but many of our ideas go back to the beginning of civilization. We are proud of novelty in technology and often ashamed of novelty in our thinking. We exist simultaneously in the twentieth century A.D. and in the twentieth century B.C. Our machines are part of the present, but in our ideas we are often conscientious objectors to the present.

We are only too conscious of the fact that civilization produces enormous neuroses. One of the most illuminating books by Freud deals with the topic of *Civilization and Its Discontents*. The struggle between our emotional drives and the restraints of civilization has been intensified in our own time. Entire nations like Germany under Hitler and Italy under Mussolini have deserted the pathways of civilization and have returned to the jungle of extreme nationalism, bellicose imperialism, and irrational authoritarianism. We should realize that if we look upon history under the aspect of astronomy we are only a few seconds away from the jungle.

Towards maturity

A mature view of philosophy thus sees the precarious nature of life. Irrationality has a thousand different manifestations; prejudice exists in myriad forms. *Often education is only a rationalization for our animal faith.* Often education only systematizes our biases; many times education is only a scientific superstructure built upon the swampland of superstition.

Philosophy and education thus are tools of enlightenment. They indicate that man cannot live by absolutes; *that life is an exercise in uncertainty, that yesterday is not the criterion and standard for tomorrow.* We may want to escape to a timeless realm of perfection, but such an escape is impossible. Did not St. Francis already realize that salvation is a social matter? What good is individual perfection in an age of Hiroshimas and concentration camps? Smugness thus is as dangerous in education and philosophy as in the spiritual life.

A mature philosophy ought to have fruitful consequences; it ought to result in action. Contemplation for the sake of contemplation may be an intellectual form of narcissism. For man is part of society, and the welfare of society determines to a great extent his own destiny.

THE FOUNDATIONS

Education is the practical test of our philosophic theories. In the educative process we see the consequences of our ideas and ideals. The schoolroom thus is the link between actuality and aspiration, hope and fulfillment.

The Importance of Educational Thought

Weaknesses

Yet contemporary education often neglects philosophic ideals. Certain cults have developed which extol an irrational way of life. For example, there are those who favor activity for the sake of activity. They feel that just doing anything is a sign of educative growth. They believe that all subjects have the same value and thus they equate typing with poetry, and flower-arrangement with history, and basketweaving with social studies. Other educators are so concerned with methodology that they neglect long-range goals. *They teach technique without vision, mechanical perfection without philosophic understanding.* Still other educators are overwhelmed by the importance of tests and measurements and, like the logical empiricists, they feel that what cannot be measured has no value and significance in education.

All these viewpoints are valuable when held in a moderate spirit; when they become the ends and goals of education, they tend to give a one-sided foundation to the educative process.

Function of theory

Philosophy in education unifies the various fields and attempts to overcome the distance between the arts and the sciences, values and facts. Philosophy not only criticizes our fundamental assumptions, but gives coherence to the entire intellectual enterprise. Philosophy is interested not merely in the present, but in the day after to-morrow. Philosophy, thus, has a certain utopian tendency; it points to the future, to the unrealized potentialities of mankind.

The influence of philosophers upon education must not be underestimated. We have only to think of the impact of Dewey, Kilpatrick, and Hutchins upon our own civilization. We are guided by a few fundamental ideas, by what Whitehead calls the climate of opinion. When ideas change, they represent a profound revolution, not only in the intellectual realm but also in the realm of society.

There are those who believe that sociological determinism is all important in history and life. For example, they would say that Dewey was so influential in twentieth century education because he represented the down-to-earth, pragmatic spirit of American industrialism and because his ideas were designed for mass education. Russell thus speaks of Dewey as the intellectual apostle of the philosophy of power, expressed in economic terms by American business. Such a view is rather superficial. The great philosopher may be a product of his times; subconsciously, his ideas may reflect the dominant currents of his culture, but his work redirects and redefines the aims of civilization and education. Dewey thus may have been the voice of the human dynamic spirit of American civilization; at the same time his work and his influence led to a change in the *direction* of American civilization.

The great thinker gives form to change. His personality, his ideals, his beliefs become part of history, and education is different and more profound because of his existence. An idea has a temporal and spatial history just like society; when an idea is applied creatively and constructively, it can change the course of history.

Dewey's influence

Let us take the idea of democracy as an example. Before Dewey, democracy in education implied merely a theoretical faith. The concept of democracy was negative. A certain amount of freedom was given to the teacher, but it was often denied to the student. W. T. Harris thus thought that discipline and effort should guide education.

Now Dewey in such work as *Democracy and Education*, *My Pedagogic Creed* and *School and Society* indicates that democracy is the essence of education. Just as democracy in politics stresses the sovereignty of the individual, so the schoolroom should stress the sovereignty of the student. Education becomes not a preparation for adult existence, but education is equated with life. Democracy ceases to be a statement of theoretical ideals and becomes a way of action and behaving. The idea of freedom expands through the self-expression of the student and through a more humane concept of teaching. The school ceases to be a mere intellectual center, it becomes a *community center*. In short, the great thinker, like Dewey, indicates the range of possibilities. He sees fundamental relationships, and his ideals are applied in the classroom. Ultimately, his faith leads to the *reconstruction* of education and philosophy.

History and Education

In certain periods of history sharp intellectual breaks can be detected. For example, medieval philosophy symbolized a pronounced difference in emphasis from classical thinking. Instead of a stress upon man, the emphasis was upon God. Philosophy became the prelude to theology. In the Renaissance this direction was reversed and instead humanism became the fundamental philosophy. Humanism, especially in Erasmus, Ramus, Montaigne, Rabelais, Colet, Ficino, Pico della Mirandola, Vives, and Reuchlin, stressed the centrality of reason, the importance of this world, and neglected the Beyond.

The same difference in emphasis can be seen in the work of Peirce, James and Dewey. With the development of pragmatism absolutes cease to be the center of philosophy. The philosopher-king leaves his ivory tower, and he enters society and attempts to clarify social problems and social issues. He tries to apply the scientific method—open-mindedness, a tentative spirit, hypothetical solutions, and rigorous verification—to all areas of life.

Tradition and novelty

Traditional philosophies are not overthrown; they just appear to be of *less consequence* to our generation. History is extremely generous when it comes to the obsolete. Side by side, we find the old and the new, the functional and the impractical, tradition and experimentation. Perhaps, as Santayana said, we do not refute our predecessors, we just bid them good-bye. Still we can be certain that we shall meet the old philosophies again, for the perennial issues of thought appear again and again in various disguises. Thus the conflict between Dewey and Hutchins reminds us of the struggle between the Eleatics who, like Hutchins, believed in permanence and Heraclitus who, like Dewey, stressed change.

This does not imply that novelty is an illusion. On the contrary, certain periods of history produce qualitative as well as quantitative changes. Still, perennial problems remain with us like the problem of change and permanence, relativism and absolutism. A mature philosophy, it should be pointed out, will see both permanence and change. To view life only in Heraclitean or Bergsonian terms, to see only flux may lead to instability and activism, and may create rootless human beings. On the other hand, to be a slave to permanence is to become fossilized, a serf to tradition and an alien to our own time. The flow of time is irreversible; we cannot recover the past; we can only see it as an aspect of the present.

The type of philosophy we hold will determine, to a great extent, the educational system we support. Thus in Athens education was mainly in the hands of philosophers. The life of reason was extolled. The student was taught that contemplation was the goal of life and that scientific application was unworthy of a free man. In the Middle Ages the concept of *hierarchy* dominated both philosophy and education. In education it implied that only a few could be taught and that *faith* was more important than reason. In the Renaissance, as philosophy became more universal, and as knowledge was expanded both in the literary and in the scientific realm, education included the middle class and had a more secular basis.

Importance of American education

In the United States, with the development of a democratic philosophy of education, universal schooling became part of our national ideology. Equal educational opportunity became the goal towards which we strive. The American experiment in education thus is of great historical significance. It may ultimately be even more important than the American contribution to technology. The great

THE FOUNDATIONS

change of our time is not symbolized by the Russian Revolution of 1917 or the Nazi revolt of 1933, but by the development of free universal public education.

The critic might say that this is a rather romantic viewpoint. He may point to Public School No. 402 in a large city. Are not the youngsters ill-disciplined; the teachers under-paid, with a narrow background; and the administrators autocratic? Where is the brave new world of education? Let us realize that our experiment in public education is of recent origin. We have just started; we are conscious of its shortcomings, but it offers a solid hope for the future. It points the way to survival, to a tower beyond futility.

We are living in climactic times. We are suspended between dawn and disaster. Perhaps the choice of our times is Public School No. 402, or Hill 402, the type of hill described so eloquently by Ernie Pyle in his *Brave Men*. Ernie Pyle describes the storming of the hill and how the tide of battle flowed on. When he saw the hill, it was surrounded by a strange atmosphere of unreality. The country-side was quiet; in the distance artillery fire could be heard. The evidences of struggle were still apparent, abandoned machine-guns, helmets, and the bodies of men who would never march again. They would be praised by historians and politicians, many fine words would be said about their sacrifice, but they would not hear them. Ernie Pyle was struck above all by the *finality* of their sacrifice.

In the future, Hill 402 would be just an insignificant incident. Atomic destruction would dwarf all previous violence. It would represent a nightmare beyond human comprehension; it would be the climax of destruction, the ultimate in man's inhumanity to man.

Public School No. 402 may be a rather feeble defense against destruction when seen from the perspective of the present. But it offers a formidable basis for the future, a foundation for our aspirations, and a bridge to a better to-morrow.

Questions and Topics for Discussion

1. What are the dangers of a technological civilization?
2. Why is the adventure of ideas so important?

3. What is the significance of Hemingway's *The Snows of Kilimanjaro*?
4. Why is philosophy ultimately a personal matter?
5. What is Pascal's view regarding man's position in the universe? What is your own view?
6. How can education be a tool of enlightenment?
7. Discuss the statement, "Education is the practical test of our philosophic theories."
8. Why is it important to have a philosophical viewpoint in education?
9. How does a great thinker influence civilization? Do you believe that civilization is shaped by great men or by social institutions? Justify your answer.
10. How did John Dewey influence American civilization?
11. What are the educational implications of pragmatism?
12. Do you believe that history is a cycle or that it produces genuine novelty?
13. In what ways is education determined by the social environment?
14. Why is the American experiment in public education of such vast significance?
15. What, in your opinion, are the limitations and advantages of the U. S. public school system?
16. Discuss the statement of Pascal: "The last proceeding of reason is to recognize that there is an infinity of things which are beyond it."
17. What, in your opinion, are the main differences between Oriental and Western thinking? How do these differences influence educational institutions?
18. List the values which are most important to you and explain their significance.
19. What to you is the nature of the crisis of our age?

Selected References

BERKSON, I. B., *Preface to an Educational Philosophy*, 1940.
BODE, B., *Fundamentals of Education*, 1931.
BRAMELD, T. B., *Patterns of Educational Philosophy*, 1950.
BROUDY, H. S., *Building a Philosophy of Education*, 1954.
BRUBACHER, J. S., *Eclectic Philosophy of Education*, 1951.
CUNNINGHAM, W. F., *Pivotal Problems of Education*, 1940.
DEWEY, J., *Democracy and Education*, Ch. 24, 1916.
———, *Sources of a Science of Education*, 1931.
FITZPATRICK, E. A., *Readings in the Philosophy of Education*, 1936.
HEMINGWAY, E., *Short Stories*, 1942.
HORNE, H. H., *The Democratic Philosophy of Education*, 1935.

THE FOUNDATIONS

Hutchins, R. M., *The University of Utopia*, 1954.
Kilpatrick, W. H., *Philosophy of Education*, 1951.
———, *Source Book in the Philosophy of Education*, 1934.
Mueller, G. E., *Education Unlimited*, 1949.
Mumford, L., *Faith for Living*, 1940.
Ortega y Gasset, J., *Toward a Philosophy of History*, 1941.
Pyle, E., *Brave Men*, 1944.
Russell, B., *Education and the Modern World*, 1932.
Schweitzer, A., *The Philosophy of Civilization*, 2 parts, 1923.
Sorokin, P. A., *The Crisis of Our Age*, 1941.
Wynne, J. P., *Philosophies of Education from the Standpoint of the Philosophy of Experimentalism*, 1947.

II. EDUCATION FOR WISDOM

Lags in College Education

FORMAL EDUCATION is not the equivalent of wisdom. It is amazing how much we do not learn in school. We can be exposed to four years of college and our degree may only indicate faithful attendance and our ability to memorize. We may obtain a doctorate of philosophy, without any philosophic insight and with a narrow culture. Often the Ph.D. represents merely knowledge of a narrow field held by a narrow individual in a narrow manner.

Studies made of our college graduates indicate that too few read serious books after graduation. They are somewhat like H. M. Pulham, Esquire, who at the beginning of Marquand's story was reading *The Education of Henry Adams*, and at the end was still not finished with it. We do too much "athletic" reading in college. Reading thus becomes like cod-liver oil, we know that it is good for us; but we do not like it nevertheless. No wonder that Plato becomes the prelude to the comic page, and Santayana the overture to Gorgeous George on television.

Babbitt as an example

The partial failure of education can best be seen in *Babbitt* by Sinclair Lewis. Babbitt is a college graduate who has gone to a state university. He has taken mostly "useful" subjects; he is remarkably misinformed. After college he did not read serious books; instead he received his opinions from the editorial page of his newspaper. To Babbit, college was important because it improved his social position; in this way he could look down on those who had not gone to college. Education aided him in making a better living. He had no tolerance for non-essential subjects; they were for the highbrows. And no one could consider Babbitt a highbrow.

Still Babbitt looked up to Howard Littlefield, his neighbor. Littlefield was a Phi Beta Kappa who could quote statistics for hours, and whose mind had an amazing capacity for facts. But he never examined his basic assumptions. To him world history was the story from neolithic times to Zenith and Howard Littlefield. His values were conditioned by the idols of the time. Like Babbitt, he measured knowledge in material terms. He would readily sell his soul to the highest bidder.

Babbitt's son hated school with religious fervor. He hated especially Latin. He looked down upon his teachers who made so little money, and who had no understanding for the desires of youth. He wanted adventure, not knowledge. School to him was a miniature jail.

Babbitt's daughter had gone to finishing school and this fact had "finished" her education. She had been exposed to Freud, Darwin, and Nietzsche, and she could discuss these writers at length without understanding them. She was remarkably ignorant after sixteen years of formal education. Still this did not prevent her from being snobbish and looking down on those who had not gone to college.

Limitations of Knowledge

Importance of humility

Education, to be fruitful, should be based upon the realization of our ignorance. As Montaigne said in *Apologie de Raimond Sebond*:

> Let man make me understand by the force of his reason, upon what foundations he has built those great advantages he thinks he has over other creatures. Who has made him believe that this admirable motion

of the celestial arch, the eternal light of those luminaries that roll so high over his head, the wondrous and fearful motions of that infinite ocean, should be established and continue so many ages for his service and convenience? Can anything be imagined so ridiculous, that this miserable and wretched creature, who is not so much as master of himself, but subject to the injuries of all things, should call himself an emperor of the world, of which he has not power to know the least part, much less to command the whole?[1]

Nicholas of Cusa said that knowledge moves from human to divine ignorance. As we start our process of inquiry, we find a world of chaos; as we end, chaos still remains, but there is order and coherence in it. Science advances by upsetting the equilibrium which the world of our common sense establishes. To the genuine scientist, as Poincaré points out, all facts are problems, all dogmas assumptions, and all truths hypotheses. Not to be certain of our conclusions, not to hold our views in a rigid manner indicates a mature philosophy of life and history. Does not the theory of evolution indicate the omnipresence of change? Is not intellectual rigidity a sign of regression?

Like Kant we often establish categories of experience and then try to coerce life to fit into these preconceived concepts. Durkheim indicates that no universal *a priori* categories exist; they are products of our social environment, merely auxiliary concepts by which experience is classified. We forget that categories are not things-in-themselves; they are merely symbols of experience through which we try to establish order and unity. Life goes beyond the categories of knowledge, for life offers infinite possibilities, a combination of a multitude of essences, of which our mind knows only a few. Existence itself is an exercise in limitation; knowledge as the reflection of existence must recognize its fallible structure.

All this implies humility, a frank recognition that our merits may be accidental. It means that we recognize our debt to the past, that the process of learning is greater than the individual.

For knowledge is cumulative. We build upon the foundations of yesterday. No theory develops in a social vacuum. Thus Einstein's

[1] Montaigne, *Essays*, II chap. ixx.

theory of relatively depended on the development of non-Euclidean geometry; Einstein benefited greatly from the reading of Mach and Kant. In earlier times Copernicus was stimulated by his knowledge of the pre-Socratic thinkers, who had challenged the geocentric view of the universe.

Gestalt psychologists like Wertheimer, Lewin, and Köhler are correct when they point to pattern as the fundamental fact of existence. The whole does determine the structure of the parts. Our achievements, in part, are products of the *Zeitgeist*, the spirit of our times.

Humility implies both a recognition of the importance of reason and what Santayana calls "the wisdom of the heart." *Thus we see knowledge, not as a possession, but as a process; not as an entity, but as a quest; not as an achievement, but as an adventure.*

Humility implies a recognition that our views may be mistaken and that our philosophy is subject to change. When we study the views of the great philosophers we see how their ideas changed. Take Nietzsche, as an example: In his youth he was dominated by the ideas of Schopenhauer; in his more mature years by Wagner; later by Voltaire, and just before his insanity by the ideals of Zoroaster. In his early years he was extremely nationalistic, in his later years he tried to be a good European. All this may imply inconsistency to the academic historian, but does it not actually mean that Nietzsche was a mirror of his times, and that he subordinated consistency to sincerity?

Dangers of dogmatism

I do not believe, then that there is one philosophy or one theory of education. If there were only one true philosophy, how could it encompass all the shades and varieties of experience? How could it account for the pluralistic structure of the world? How could it be reconciled with the fact of empirical diversity? Dogmatism in philosophy is usually a sign of provincialism. We mistake our own tribe for the universe, our own conclusions for the ultimate truth; we set up, in Toynbee's words, the ephemeral self for the eternal self.

The dogmatist in philosophy, education, and religion usually suppresses part of the evidence. He sees more similarity than variety. He forms preconceived conclusions and then sees to it that the facts fit his conclusions. He approaches the book of the world with a veil consisting of his own ego-centricity. His greatest weakness is that he is unwilling to *learn*. He views life from the standpoint of finality, not in an exploratory spirit.

Note how different the scientific spirit is from that of dogmatism. The genuine scientist sees the flux of life. He acknowledges his debt to other researchers, he indicates that his conclusion is tentative, and he shows further areas of exploration and inquiry.

The consequences of philosophy

Does this imply that all philosophies are completely relative? Does this mean the elimination of value judgments? Does this attitude stand for complete skepticism? The answer is no: Philosophy can be judged by its consequences, ideal and actual; by its capacity to enrich and to sustain life; and, above all, by its contribution to the enlightenment of man. We can ask such questions as the following: Does the philosophy we hold lead to an affirmative view of life? Is it designed for the few or the many? Will it expand or narrow civilization? Is it in accordance with scientific ideals or does it support a pre-scientific view of life?

The importance of philosophy thus cannot be overestimated. We all have a rendezvous with philosophy; only some of us live merely by custom and tradition; some exist on a vegetative, but not on a rational level. *The result is a life of noisy futility.*

The philosopher, like the teacher, has a grave responsibility. He can either advance or retard civilization. His voice may aid the forces of destruction or the forces of creativity. Unfortunately, too many thinkers in modern times, like Spengler, Pareto, and Heidegger, have become willing adherents to totalitarianism; others, like many logical empiricists, have developed a cult of irresponsibility. They have been overwhelmed by the scientific method and so concerned with linguistic problems that they have left the social area to demagogues and fanatics.

THE FOUNDATIONS

Values of Educational Philosophy

Philosophy for educational leaders

Administrators especially can benefit from a deeper philosophical view of life. Too often they are interested merely in buildings, rather than teachers, and too often they develop autocratic tendencies. I talked to a junior-college administrator a short time ago who said that he believed in democracy in education. I had to smile, for his faculty lived in a state of virtual serfdom; his office was inaccessible to the ordinary professor; teachers had to bargain with him to get a raise. He conducted faculty meetings like a dictator. Apparently, he did not realize the dualism between his pretension and actuality.

Too many educational organizations have no central purpose, or, if they do, it is an inferior one. Too often the curriculum centers around the athletic stadium. In some enterprising colleges, Ph.D.'s are now given in mortuary science. *Some universities apparently are a collection of buildings in search of a soul.*

The reading matter of some administrators is the telephone book, as Adler pointed out. This may be an exaggeration, but it describes the intellectual wasteland so prevalent among some educational leaders. This results in the cult of expediency, and in looking upon educational institutions as business organizations. The task of education is not merely to reflect life, but to create new patterns of existence.

Yet, we should not be too hard on administrators. By nature, many of them tend to be timid, and they are invariably afraid of adverse public criticism. A dean one time said to a new faculty member: "Now remember, I just don't want any trouble!"

School boards and boards of trustees can contribute much to the advancement of education. In the past, they have often yielded to pressure groups, and they have frequently been guided by economic determinism. They have saved money foolishly by underpaying teachers. This has been a contributing cause to the wholesale exodus of instructors from the teaching profession. To pay a teacher less than a mechanic or a plumber indicates a disrespect for knowledge. The more we promote a fair recognition of the teaching profession, the more we expand the democratic way of life. Democracy, it must be remembered, depends on the cultivation of reason; it rests on intelligent choice which is best promoted through great teachers and great administrators.

The teacher and educational theory

A mature and profound philosophy of education is especially needed by the teacher. Too often the teacher is intellectually sterile, too often he does not keep up with current research and does not expand his cultural background. In many cases the learning of subject matter becomes the goal of education. Students are reduced to numbers; the relationship between them and the teacher tends to be on a mechanical basis.

Philosophy can give the teacher a more profound *vision* of the possibilities of education. He can be inspired by great thinkers like Comenius, Pestalozzi, Froebel, Hutchins, and Dewey. Philosophy can make education more pleasurable and profound. Ultimately, what matters in education is the relationship between teacher and student. The teacher should ask himself the following questions: Am I really reaching the student? Am I creating constructive attitudes? Am I an unforgettable event in the life of the student?

Kierkegaard, the great Danish thinker, said that as we reduce life to its essentials only two realities remain: Man and God. In attempting to find salvation Kierkegaard was not concerned with the externals of religion; the spiritual life to him was an intensely personal matter. This existential philosophy can be applied to education. Beyond the subject matter, beyond competence, are basic attitudes; beyond extra-curricular activities is the relationship between teacher and student. Both want to be educated. The teacher has a headstart, his experience is more profound, he has learned more facts, but his education is never complete. If he rests upon his laurels, if he regards his achievements in a complacent manner, he ceases to be a teacher, and he becomes a *pedant*—an intellectual version of arrested evolution. The learning process in education must be reciprocal;

otherwise education becomes a monotonous soliloquy on the part of the teacher.

The teacher should not take his knowledge too seriously. Nature can be a better guide than the textbook. Here he can learn from Walt Whitman:

When I heard the learn'd astronomer,
When the proofs, the figures, were ranged in columns before me,
When I was shown the charts and diagrams, to add, divide, and measure them,
When I sitting heard the astronomer where he lectured with much applause in the lecture-room,
How soon unaccountable I became tired and sick,
Till rising and gliding out I wander'd off by myself,
In the mystical moist night-air, and from time to time,
Look'd up in perfect silence at the stars.[2]

Students and philosophy of education

Students, like teachers, can greatly benefit from a constructive philosophy of education. Vital choices are made by students on the basis of inadequate evidence. To be more specific, in high school they often select a business course because it tends to be easier. Some of the most brilliant students do not go to college because they are seduced by easy money and are impatient to get out of school. Yet immediate success may prove to be ultimate failure.

Many students in college do not receive an education because they take snap courses. Frequently, they follow their interests too closely. Thus a business administration major tends to avoid liberal arts courses; a liberal arts student will avoid scientific courses; and the student majoring in art will not be interested in economics. Yet a "chance encounter" with a different field may change the entire intellectual life of the student.

When the student enters college, he is confronted by a host of possibilities. Should he concentrate upon studying or should he devote most of his time to the social life? What should be the balance of curricular and extra-curricular activities? What should be his attitude toward athletics? Should he work his way through college?

[2] "When I Heard the Learn'd Astronomer."

EDUCATION FOR WISDOM

Should he join a fraternity or not? All these problems cannot be settled merely on the basis of expediency, for they demand philosophic analysis.

Scheduling also plays an important part in the student's life. Many students avoid 8-o'clock and afternoon classes. Robert Hutchins confessed that he took a class in English at 12:00 at Yale because the professor was a popular teacher, so much in demand in New York that usually at 12:20 he left New Haven and departed for the lucrative lecture field in New York.[3]

Parents and the educative process

Parents, also, should formulate a creative philosophy of education. In the nineteenth century parents often acted like minor dictators. They stressed obedience and rigid conformity on the part of their offspring. Thus they developed a sharp dualism in family relationships. They set themselves up as patterns of perfection, while they regarded their children as being sinful and wayward. Today we often go to the other extreme. Many parents thus give too much freedom to their youngsters and encourage an over-abundance of self-expression. Neither authoritarianism nor laissez-faire is ideal in education, rather we should strive for a spirit of mutuality and genuine understanding between parents and children.

Parents, even grandparents, can have an unforgettable educational influence upon the life of their offspring. One of my friends, who is an assistant superintendent in Arizona, tells about the influence of his grandmother, whose schooling consisted only of six grades.

My grandmother lived with my parents, and during my earlier days was my tutor and friend. In the long summer evenings in Indiana, she and I would sit in the big lawn swing listening to each other. Of course, many of the conversations were stories of her youth, of the little log school she had attended, of the complete family life on a farm in the 1870's. In those pre-McCormick days all members of the family—mother, girls, and boys—were enlisted in the farm corps, for planting the corn, for cultivating, for cutting and binding the wheat, for the carnival of threshing, and for the autumnal task of harvesting the corn. Spelling contests—'spelldowns'—were important events in her school life.

[3] Cf. Hutchins, *Education for Freedom*, p. 7.

THE FOUNDATIONS

What did she teach that is important, meaningful even today? The prime lesson I learned was the pioneer habit of work—the naturalness of hard work, of manual work. She never forgot the boredom and heartlessness of an overload of this kind of work, but she never really regretted that she had worked in the fields. This made the land hers—nature was her friend, and it was only unfortunate that friendship can at times be overbearing.

The lasting lesson does not necessarily have to be an expensive, dynamic one. Pictures of childhood come back in varying degrees of vividness, but most clear to me was the incident of the ice-cream 'kerplunk.' All of our family were visiting in a near-by town one summer afternoon, stopping for the treat of a 'bought-ice-cream-cone.' By the perverseness of gravity, or perhaps by the determination of fate, my cone turned in my hand, and the ice-cream fell to the ground. Before my tears could fall, she handed me her cone, with a 'Here, let's trade.' A little lesson, but so impressive to me in its gesture of kindness, sympathy, consideration for another.

My most impressive teacher, my first real teacher, one who directed me toward teaching without knowing it in the summer twilight sessions of pre-school years, was this grandmother whose schooling went only through six grades.

Questions and Topics for Discussion

1. Why is formal education not the equivalent of wisdom?
2. Why is *Babbitt* such a significant book from an educational standpoint?
3. Why is Montaigne important? What did he say about human ignorance? Do you agree or disagree with him? Why?
4. Why should we not be certain of our conclusions?
5. Are scientific laws absolute or relative? Justify your answer.
6. Can there be *one* philosophy of education?
7. Is our educational philosophy only a reflection of emotional biases? Explain your answer.
8. Compare the scientific spirit with that of dogmatism.
9. How can we evaluate a system of philosophy?
10. How can administrators benefit from educational philosophy?
11. Why does the class-room teacher need a mature philosophy of education?
12. How can parents benefit from a creative educational viewpoint?
13. What attitude do you favor in bringing up children? Defend your viewpoint.

14. Compare and contrast the nineteenth century attitude regarding the upbringing of children with that of our own time.
15. Do you feel that we are producing another lost generation in our colleges?
16. According to your own viewpoint, what are the most important values of a college education?
17. Do you believe that education has improved or declined in the 20th century? Justify your answer.

Selected References

ADAMS, H., *The Education of Henry Adams*, 1908.
ALLPORT, G., *Personality*, 1937.
ASHLEY MONTAGU, M. F., *The Direction of Human Development*, 1955.
BERGSON, H., *Creative Evolution*, 1944.
BROWNELL, B., *The College and the Community*, 1952.
CASSIRER, E., *An Essay on Man*, 1944.
CURTI, M., *The Social Ideals of American Educators*, 1935.
FROMM, E., *The Sane Society*, 1955.
HENDERSON, S., *Introduction to Philosophy of Education*, 1947.
JOHNSON, G., *Some Ethical Implications of a Naturalistic Philosophy of Education*, 1947.
LEWIS, S., *Babbitt*, 1922.
MARITAIN, J., *Education at the Crossroads*, 1943.
MARQUAND, J., *H. M. Pulham, Esquire*, 1941.
MONTAIGNE, M. E., *The Education of Children*. (Translated by L. E. Rector.) 1899.
PETERS, C. C., *Foundations of Educational Sociology*, 1932.
RUGG, H., *Foundations for American Education*, 1947.
STANLEY, W. O., *Education and Social Integration*, 1953.
THAYER, V. T., *Public Education and its Crisis*, 1954.
WARD, H. H., *Democracy and Social Change*, 1940.

III. GOD AND EDUCATION

Religious Foundations

The Puritans

AMERICAN EDUCATION owes a great debt to the religious environment in which it developed. The Puritans, who were instrumental in the establishment of the American system of education, came to this continent in the faith that a *new* commonwealth would be created, dedicated to God and to a rigorous way of life.

It is difficult to be neutral regarding the influence of Puritanism upon the American character. Thinkers like Mencken have regarded the Puritan temperament as the greatest obstacle in the creation of an enlightened commonwealth. Santayana in the *Last Puritan* showed that culture could not prosper in an atmosphere of moral imperatives and moral restrictions. Did not Puritanism indicate a lack of sophistication? Did not Puritanism lead to an agonized conscience? Did not Puritanism view the world in a provincial manner? Other thinkers, like Townsend in his *Philosophical Ideas in the United States,* and Perry in *Puritanism and Democracy,* have been more friendly to the Puritan ideal of life. Townsend even claimed that Jonathan Edwards, the great Puritan thinker, was the foremost philosopher ever produced in the United States.

Theological considerations

To understand Puritan ideals, we should be conscious of their *theological* background. The ghost of Calvin cast a heavy shadow upon Puritan thought. Calvin, who for many years had been moral dictator of Geneva, believed that man is innately sinful, and that we are all involved in Adam's rebellion against God. Man, according to Calvin, is naturally depraved; his pride and his self-assertion were responsible for his fall from grace. Life itself is a pilgrimage full of sorrow and turmoil. To enjoy it would be folly, for man's destiny is in the *Beyond*. To achieve the infinite glories of heaven is the goal of man's pilgrimage. The vision of final salvation gave meaning to the struggles of the saints, to their torments and sufferings on earth. Yet Calvin made it quite clear that only a few would go to Paradise, while the majority of mankind would perish in hell-fire.

The early New England textbooks were full of moralistic material. For example, in one selection the fate of the sinner was compared with fate of the virtuous person. The sinner apparently had a wonderful time on earth; he enjoyed the pleasures of the flesh; but after death his body burned in an everlasting hell. While the virtuous man, whose life on earth had been one of deprivation, now enjoyed the glories of heaven and he was satisfied that justice had been done in the damnation of the sinner. Jonathan Edwards must have impressed both the youngsters and the adults in his congregation when he preached on such topics as "Sinners in the Hands of an angry God." Had not God's mercy been outraged? Was not God provoked by the waywardness of mankind? Was not the life of the sinner held by a slender thread over hell-fire? Was not hell an ever-present possibility?

God was regarded as being perfect by Calvin and Edwards, whereas man's imperfection was stressed. The sovereignty of God contrasted with the weaknesses of man. And God's justice would not tolerate a violation of the moral commandments. From the beginning of time God had *predestined* those who were to be saved and those who were to be damned.

This view of theological determinism did not create a fatalistic attitude on the part of the Puritan. For who could be certain he was saved? Who could understand the mysteries of Providence? Who could know with complete assurance he was one of the saints? To be sure, there were certain indications of divine election. To believe in the tenets of Calvinism, to lead a virtuous life, to support the preachers, to attend church regularly, to make the Bible the center of existence, to avoid gambling, drinking, and lewd women, to work hard and honestly—all these activities were symbols of a vigorous faith, and presumably would lead to salvation, but no one could guarantee salvation. *God determined the fate of the saints and the sinners.* Actually, according to Calvin, all were eligible for hell-fire, because of their pride and their waywardness, but God in his mercy had decided to spare the minority.

The Puritan teacher

The task of the teacher in the Puritan commonwealth was to train the student in rigorous virtue. Was not the teacher a representative of God? Was it not the teacher's task to drive the devil out of the student? Education was to be hard and painful, otherwise it would lead to an Epicurean way of life. Flogging was used regularly; the physical punishment of students was harsh. All this was justified on theological grounds, so that the student would avoid a life of sin.

The Puritans had an enormous faith in the value of *work*. To loaf, to live a parasitical existence would lead to a life of waywardness. Tawney has shown clearly the connection between Puritanism and capitalism. Both systems glorified work, both believed that the virtuous man would be successful, both felt that lack of success indicated a useless existence. The Puritan felt that contemplation for the sake of contemplation was sinful, life was evaluated in activistic terms. "We are saved by doing" was the keynote to Puritanism.

This does not imply that the system of education established by the Puritans was utilitarian. Harvard's main purpose at first was to train ministers. The Bible was the center of the curriculum. The main ideal of Puritan education was to train citizens so that they could understand the Bible and thus avoid the temptations of the

GOD AND EDUCATION

devil. One of the favorite books of the Puritans was Increase Mather's *An Essay for the Recording of Illustrious Providences*. It showed the providence of God, who had guided his faithful from the beginning of history. The book was full of miracles, which were accepted as actual occurrences by the ordinary believer. The Puritan teacher was not a scientist, but a man of faith; he taught his students to accept the revelations of the Bible, and that nature was only a prelude to the kingdom of God.

Intolerance

The most disconcerting aspect of the Puritan temperament was its intolerance. Quakers, Catholics, and freethinkers were regarded with profound suspicion. They were frequently persecuted in Puritan Boston. The witchcraft craze is one of the darkest spots in American history. The Puritans believed that witches were agents of the devil. Cotton Mather, one of the most fanatical preachers, urged constant vigilance against witches on the part of his congregation. When several witches were executed, he used that occasion to give a sermon on the providence of God. School children, who attended the execution of witches, were told by their teachers that witchcraft represented the power of evil and that they were to report to their elders anyone who might be suspected of practicing such a villainous activity.

Intolerance has been a constant threat in American education. Fear of unorthodox ideas has continued throughout the course of American history. In times of crisis the American teacher is scrutinized by the community. Conformity is the great ideal; heresy is to be avoided. The study by the Lynds of *Middletown* and *Middletown in Transition* indicates the prevalence of Puritanism in the small community and the dislike of new ideas. Such a spirit encourages censorship. In our own time the forces urging censorship are well-organized. Like the Puritans, they believe in categorical standards, and that they are the guardians of righteousness and public morality. Usually, the period of hysteria does not last long; the witchcraft craze lasted only a few years and afterwards many Puritans repented the excesses. Ultimately, in American history, social coercion has never been completely successful, because freedom is a persistent ideal in American culture.

The Puritan concept of liberty was limited. Freedom did not imply separation of state and church, liberty to seek the truth, freedom of inquiry. The Puritans were convinced they had the *key* to truth. No wonder that liberals like Roger Williams and Anne Hutchinson were persecuted and had to flee to Rhode Island, which was so liberal in Puritan times that it was called "Rogue's Island."

Freedom of opinion did not prevail in the Puritan classroom. Objectivity was regarded as an inferior method of teaching. The instructor was required to live up to the tenets of the community. Before he could teach, his morals and religious ideals were scrupulously inspected. If he became a heretic, he was not allowed to continue his instruction. His task was to inspire his students with the advantage of a godly way of life, so that they would avoid independent thinking, and be obedient to their preachers.

Evaluation of Puritan teachings

This does not imply that Puritan teaching was shallow and dominated by a revivalistic trend. On the contrary, the instructor, especially in college, demanded a high-level of performance. A knowledge of the classics was the foundation of Puritan education. Conclusions were often based on the Aristotelian syllogism; a rigorous logic was used to prove the advantages of a God-centered way of life.

The disadvantages of this type of teaching are quite apparent. It tended to create a narrow individual who could see only one side of a problem. Education became too formal and too provincial. The study of the sciences was neglected. Did not science for the sake of science alienate man from God? Was not revelation more important than scientific reasoning?

Yet, indirectly, Calvinism, as Sarton points out, prepared the way for scientific reasoning and a scientific methodology. For Calvinism held that the external world is guided by laws and that man cannot change the structure of the universe. Science, likewise, accepts a faith in the law-abiding nature of the universe; only science is interested in the *mechanistic* rather than the purposeful structure of the external world.

Decline of Puritan education

If world history, as Toynbee asserted, is dominated by the rule of challenge and response, the ultimate decline of Puritan education can be traced to its failure to respond to the challenge of the middle class. As life in the United States in the eighteenth century acquired a more secular basis, as the power of capitalism expanded, parents wanted a more practical education for their children. After all, Latin and Greek would be of secondary importance to the future businessman. Exact and detailed knowledge of the Bible would be excellent assets in the ministry, but of secondary value in public life. Furthermore, the westward expansion of America changed educational standards. The pioneer who conquered the wilderness and who fought the Indians was usually uninterested in theology; he wanted an emotional type of religion and an educational system which stressed the ideals of freedom and equality.

The Triumph of Deism

Basic beliefs

The intellectual force that supplanted Puritanism in the eighteenth century was Deism. The Deists like Ethan Allen, Paine, and Franklin believed in a rationalistic interpretation of religion and life. They felt that traditional religion had been too authoritarian and had stressed dogma and revelation rather than common sense. Traditional religion had neglected science and had over-emphasized theology. The basic tenets of Deism were not atheistic; on the contrary, the Deists believed that God exists, but the God of the Deists was far more merciful and rational than the God of Edwards and Calvin. He demanded virtue and right doing rather than slavish obedience.

THE FOUNDATIONS

John Locke

Here the influence of John Locke became especially important. John Locke in his *Essay Concerning Human Understanding, Two Treatises on Government, Letters Concerning Toleration,* and *Some Thoughts Concerning Education* constructed a new basis for philosophy. Locke was the insistent opponent of absolutism in all spheres—especially in religion, politics, and education. He was distrustful of fanaticism, of men who are carried away by their "enthusiasm." He demanded a *reconstruction* of philosophy, for we are to realize that we are limited and that we do not have a monopoly on wisdom. Most of our disputes, according to Locke, arise from a misunderstanding of language; we are overwhelmed by technical terms; we do not clarify our meanings; we mistake the word for the object which it is supposed to symbolize.

Locke made it clear that we are not born with innate ideas, as rationalists like Descartes claimed. We have no innate idea of justice, honor, and truth. This concept underlines the importance of the educative process. Our mind is a blank tablet at birth; it is the task of education to train the mind, so that we can live *virtuously*.

The goals of education of Locke are virtue, wisdom, breeding, and knowledge. Virtue implies conformity to moral laws, faith in righteousness, a recognition of the justice of God. Wisdom includes sound deliberation, the ability to evaluate and not to be tempted by the passions of the moment. Breeding implies excellent manners, courtesy, and dignity in our way of life. Character and knowledge, according to Locke, are closely identified. Learning, to Locke, is of less importance than virtue, for to Locke the scholar plays a secondary role in civilization. He admired the man of action rather than the theorist whose viewpoint is essentially impractical.

Benjamin Franklin

The same ideal of education and knowledge governed the work of Franklin. Like Locke, Franklin had little faith in formal schooling. Was not Franklin self-educated? Had he not read profoundly the book of the world? Was not science superior to theology? To Frank-

GOD AND EDUCATION

lin, as to Locke, one of the main goals of education was virtue. Moral ideals could never be neglected in our schools. Morality, to Franklin, was a practical matter; it increased our economic success and it made for greater business efficiency. Yet morality implied righteousness, not Machiavellian expediency.

Franklin stimulated the development of the academy movement in the United States. The academy was to produce a sound mind in a healthy body. Students were encouraged to take part in sports such as wrestling and swimming. They were to be taught useful subjects which would prepare them for professional life.

Franklin, like Locke, had no great love for the classical languages. This does not imply that he wanted to eliminate classical learning; on the contrary, he loved the ancient Greek and Roman authors. He was only opposed to an over-emphasis upon the classics. He wanted to expand the curriculum and so he urged the study of modern languages, especially French and German. Furthermore, he urged greater concentration upon mathematics and the natural and physical sciences. He was interested in the application of knowledge; thus he urged the schools to teach the elements of agriculture to the youngsters.

But it is a mistake to look upon Franklin as a mere utilitarian thinker. He had a great love of philosophy and helped to establish the Junto, one of the most remarkable discussion clubs in colonial America. He aided in the development of the public library; he was partially responsible for the founding of the American Philosophical Society; he was an inventor of note, whose experiments in electricity evoked the admiration of leading minds both in the United States and abroad. Franklin indeed symbolized the possibilities of a dynamic society, unburdened by traditionalism and a static class system. He was most remarkable in his tolerance, and in his willingness to change his mind. In 1787 he expressed his tolerant attitude in a speech on the constitution:

Mr. President,
   I confess, that I do not entirely approve of this Constitution at present; but, Sir, I am not sure I shall never approve it; for, having lived long, I

THE FOUNDATIONS

have experienced many instances of being obliged, by better information or fuller consideration, to change my opinions even on important subjects, which I once thought right, but found to be otherwise. It is therefore that, the older I grow, the more apt I am to doubt my own judgment of others. Most men, indeed, as well as most sects in religion, think themselves in possession of all truth, and that whatever others differ from them, it is so far error. Steele, a Protestant, in a dedication, tells the Pope that the only difference between our two churches in their opinions of the certainty of their doctrine, is the Romish Church is *infallible,* and the Church of England is *never in the wrong.* But, though many private persons think almost as highly of their own infallibility as of that of their sect, few express it so naturally as a certain French lady, who, in a little dispute with her sister, said, "But I meet with nobody but myself that is *always* in the right. *Je ne trouve que moi qui aie toujours raison.*"[1]

Franklin, like Locke, had a strong faith in God. He did not bother to define the essence of God, but he was certain that God would reward virtue and punish vice. He believed that man needs faith, still faith should be expressed in rational terms. He was certain of the existence of a future life, but he was unconcerned regarding the divinity of Jesus. In short, he looked upon religion as a moral concern and as a prelude to the *enlightenment* of mankind.

Thomas Paine

Deism, in Paine, was far more radical than in Franklin. Did not Paine deny providence? Did not Paine urge the study of nature rather than the study of the Bible? Paine's attitude was that of the radical, while Franklin, as a liberal, was more restrained and moderate in his opinions.

Education of Deism

The Deistic ideal of life contributed to a re-examination of classicism. We cannot understand colonial thinking without a grasp of its classical background, even in Franklin who urged more of a contemporary emphasis in education. The Deists were suspicious of Plato. Had not Plato been rather intolerant in his *Republic?* Had

---

[1] Franklin's Writings, Vol. IX, p. 607.

not Plato emphasized that reality could only be found in an immaterial world? Was not Plato opposed to the ideals of democracy? The Deistic thinkers instead turned to the moral ideals of Aristotle. They noted with satisfaction that Aristotle believed in the government of the Middle Class, that he advocated a life of reason, and that he regarded man as a social animal who could find fulfillment in the service of society.

Classical thinkers like Aristotle, Seneca, and Cicero gave to the Deists more than a formal philosophy, they supplied *a way of life*. With the classical thinkers, the Deists stressed life on earth, rather than in the Beyond. They tried to achieve a *balanced* view of man and society and they believed in the rule of moderation signified by the classical ideal: "Nothing to excess."

The weakness of the Deistic view was its overemphasis on reason. The basis of religion, as Schleiermacher indicates, is *emotion* rather than reason. If we neglect the wisdom of the heart, a sterile philosophy results. The most penetrating criticism of Deism was undertaken by David Hume, who maintained that feeling dominates man and that, rationally speaking, no philosophical evidence could justify faith in metaphysics or immortality.

Educational influence

In education, however, the influence of Deism was beneficial. *For education cannot progress without reason, faith in progress, and faith in humanity*. The Deists thus were the real liberators of the American mind.

The greatness of Deists like Franklin lies in their broad and universal grasp of culture. Thus Franklin believed in usefulness and discipline as ideals of learning; he had faith both in knowledge and in wisdom. In this way he avoided the pitfalls of practicalism. Too often the educator who stresses a practical view of culture has a rather narrow concept of the curriculum. He sees only the utilitarian subjects, he believes only in preparation for making a living; *he does not recognize the spiritual values of the past and the liberating influence of the liberal arts*.

THE FOUNDATIONS

The Society of Friends

Beliefs

The idealism of American civilization is perhaps best represented by the Society of Friends, which has produced great thinkers and educators from John Woolman to Rufus Jones. The Quakers believed in a simple philosophy of life symbolized by the concept of *love*. The light of God was in every man. Hence no individual could be regarded as a tool of society. War was an unmitigated evil; nonviolence was the only Christian solution to war.

The Quakers were opposed to formal organization. Their churches and schools were less concerned with dogma and knowledge than with the heart of the individual. Throughout their history, they have attempted to improve the lot of the underprivileged. They were the most insistent opponents of slavery, and they fought segregation in the public school.

The ideal of Quaker education is to produce an individual who is imbued by love of God and love of his fellow-man, who is never guided by expediency and selfishness, and who follows the spirit of Jesus. This does not imply a narrow concept of religion and education. The Quakers have been apostles of universalism, *for the light of God knows no boundaries of race, religion, and nationality.*

John Woolman

Woolman, the great Quaker of colonial times, had a far less extensive education than Jonathan Edwards. The two are interesting studies in contrast. Edwards believed that God's justice was invariable, while Woolman stressed God's mercy. Edwards emphasized original sin, while Woolman stressed man's goodness. Edwards neglected the social implications of Christianity, while Woolman indicated that religion is a way of life. Edwards made theology the center of education, while Woolman based education upon ethics. Edwards stressed authority and the group, whereas Woolman had faith in the sovereignty of the individual.

GOD AND EDUCATION

The *Journal* of Woolman reveals a mind of universal moral insight. He shows, for example, that hatred only creates more antagonism and that slavery and war can never be combined with a religious conscience. Unlike other thinkers of his time, he favored a just treatment of the Indians, who also were children of God.

Quaker education and faith

The schools and colleges which were established by the Quakers emphasized freedom of thought and freedom of expression. The students were taught to accept diversity with tolerance and humility, and to trust the dictates of love.

The ideal of love is beautifully expressed by George Herbert:

LOVE

Love bade me welcome; yet my soul drew back,
    Guilty of dust and sin.
But quick-ey'd Love, observing me grow slack
    From my first entrance in,
Drew nearer to me, sweetly questioning
    If I lack'd anything.

"A guest," I answer'd, "worthy to be here";
    Love said, "You shall be he."
"I, the unkind, ungrateful? Ah, my dear,
    I cannot look on thee!"
Love took my hand, and smiling did reply,
    "Who made the eyes but I?"

"Truth, Lord; but I have marr'd them; let my shame
    Go where it doth deserve."
"And know you not," says Love, "who bore the blame?"
    "My dear, then I will serve."
"You must sit down," says Love, "and taste my meat."
    So I did sit and eat.

The Quakers were imbued with faith in a simple way of life. To avoid ostentation and conspicuous consumption, material goods were subordinated to spiritual attainments. Success was measured in human, rather than economic terms. Authority was never regarded

THE FOUNDATIONS

with awe, for are not all equal? Are not all human beings the same in the sight of God? Do we not all have the same destiny?

The Friends Service Committee

In our time the American Friends Service Committee has established projects to appeal to the idealism of youth. Work camps give practical experience in constructive social action. The intellectual learns how to use his hands and how to share in cooperative activity. International student seminars attract students of all faiths with diverse backgrounds. No attempt is made to accept a one-sided viewpoint or to convert others; rather the emphasis is on understanding and mutual tolerance. Reconstruction work abroad has been stressed by the Quakers who believe that practical help is the essence of religion. Thousands of young American students have gone abroad, dedicated to the ideals of genuine humanitarianism.

Idealism in action

One of my colleagues recently returned from Vienna and he was asked what group of Americans had impressed most favorably the Austrians. He replied without hesitation: "Our students, especially those working for a humanitarian cause in Austria." Various religious groups, like Methodists, Unitarians, Congregationalists, Catholics, and Jews, have encouraged their young people to engage in constructive projects both in the United States and abroad.

American education from early colonial times to the present times has had an idealistic background. To be sure, idealism occasionally was expressed in narrow terms and tended to be coercive. This was especially true among the Puritans. But our great colonial leaders pointed out that education involves a vast *political and social responsibility*. Thus Franklin and Jefferson entered the political arena to spread enlightenment among mankind.

Questions and Topics for Discussion

1. How has Puritanism influenced American culture?
2. What were the main theological beliefs of Puritanism?

GOD AND EDUCATION

3. Evaluate the early New England textbooks. Compare them with 20th century texts.
4. How did the Puritans look upon the teacher?
5. Why were the early colleges established in the United States? Compare the status of Harvard in the seventeenth century with that of Harvard in our own time.
6. Why is intolerance such a threat in American education?
7. In what ways has American education been attacked since World War II?
8. What are the advantages of Puritanism? How would a Puritan judge twentieth century America?
9. Do you agree with Toynbee's philosophy of history? Explain.
10. What is the significance of deism? Compare and contrast deism with Puritanism.
11. What was Locke's philosophy of education? What are the advantages and limitations of his viewpoint?
12. Discuss Franklin's philosophy of education.
13. What is the basic philosophy of the Quakers? Do you think it is practical?
14. How did the Quakers contribute to American education?
15. Compare the Quakers and the Puritans.
16. What is the general relationship between religion and American education?
17. How, in your opinion, can moral and spiritual values best be taught in our school system?

Selected References

ANDERSON, P. R., and M. FISCH, *Philosophy in America from the Puritans to James*, 1939.
AARON, R. I., *John Locke*, 1937.
BOURNE, H. R. F., *The Life of John Locke*, 2 vols., 1876.
BRUCE, W. C., *Benjamin Franklin*, 2 vols., 1917.
CASSIRER, E., *The Philosophy of the Enlightenment*, 1955.
ELIOT, C. W., *Four American Leaders*, 1906.
FRANKLIN, B., *The Writings*, 10 vols., 1907.
———, *Representative Selections*, 1936.
LYND, R. S., and H. M. LYND, *Middletown in Transition*, 1937.
MAYER, F., *History of American Thought*, 1951.
———, *History of Modern Philosophy*, 1951.
———, *Education for Maturity*, 1956.
RUSSELL, P., *Benjamin Franklin, the First Civilized American*, 1926.
SOARES, T. G., *Fundamentals of Democratic Education*, 1928.

THE FOUNDATIONS

SPERRY, W. L., *Religion in America*, 1946.
THAYER, V. T., *Misinterpretation of Locke as a Formalist in Educational Philosophy*, 1921.
THORPE, F. N., *Franklin's Influence in American Education*, 1903.
ULICH, R., *History of Educational Thought*, 1945.
———, *Fundamentals of Democratic Education*, 1940.
VIETH, P. H., *Objectives of Religious Education*, 1930.
WOODY, T. (EDITOR), *Educational Views of Benjamin Franklin*, 1931.

IV. JEFFERSON AND THE IDEAL OF FREEDOM

Specialization and Universality

THE GOAL OF EDUCATION is to produce both specific skills and general knowledge. In certain periods of history specific competence has been emphasized. This happened in Alexandria when knowledge became compartmentalized and it is happening again in our own time when the specialist dominates education. In other periods, the ideal of education was to produce all-round excellence as in the times of Socrates, Erasmus, and Jefferson.

It can be said with a degree of truth that universality in knowledge is impossible in our complex civilization. Are not subjects becoming more technical all the time? Do we not advance in science by concentrating upon specific events? Does not general education often lead to vagueness and superficial generalization? Is not mastery of one subject better than a dilettante dabbling in all areas of inquiry?

Dangers of specialization

Yet the over-emphasis upon specialization is destroying the unity of our culture. Ortega y Gasset in *The Revolt of the Masses* notes that specialization produces the mass-man who is dominated by the gospel of vulgarity. Whitehead in his eloquent book *The Aims of*

THE FOUNDATIONS

Education indicates that the goal of education is not the knowledge of history, or geography, or algebra, or geometry, *but an understanding of life in all its complexities and dimensions.*

Specialization produces the type of scholar who sees only his own field, who does not appreciate the interrelationship of cultural institutions. In the modern world decisions have to be made which involve all of us, as human beings interested in the survival of mankind. Note, for example that atomic power has implications not only in physical science, but in medicine, biology, politics, economics, sociology, psychology, philosophy, and education. The great advances in physical science have often been accomplished by individuals from various fields co-operating in the solution of research problems. The same co-operative spirit, applied to the social sciences, may bring about a more solid foundation for the exploration of pressing social problems.

Schweitzer and universal culture

Universal culture in our time is not an impossibility, as the life and thoughts of Schweitzer indicate. Schweitzer gained note in medicine, theology, music, philosophy, history, and many other fields. All his interests were unified by his moral ideals and by his reverence for life. Universality in culture does not imply an encyclopedic spirit. We can know many facts about many different subjects, and still be extremely ignorant. Rather, universality implies expanding interests in various fields, and a central concern which gives meaning and coherence to our strivings. It is this central moral concern which contributes to the greatness of Schweitzer, who throughout his life has tried to overcome the dualism between the ideal and the actual.

Jefferson's Philosophy

Background

Jefferson, like Schweitzer, achieved a unique depth of knowledge.[1] Scientist, statesman, philosopher, supporter of the humanities,

[1] Cf. Vossler, *Die Amerikanischen Revolutionsideale in ihrem Verhältniss zu den Europäischen, untersucht an Thomas Jefferson.*

educator, Jefferson ranks in history as one of the great leaders of mankind. He read prolifically such authors as Cicero, Locke, Condorcet, Aristotle, Plato, and Epicurus. He was never self-satisfied; until the last days of his life he was interested in self-improvement, in the expansion of his intellectual horizon. Like Locke he believed in the application of knowledge. Thus he observed sharply, as his letters indicate, and he read above all the book of the world. Unlike most scholars of his time, Jefferson expressed himself in an elegant, clear style which could be easily understood. He was sensitive to the beauties of nature, for he thought man learned as much from the contemplation of beauty as from intellectual studies.

Religious views

The religion of Jefferson was extremely simple. He believed in one God and in a future life. The essence of religion was contained in the moral life of the individual; *his heart, not his profession of faith, mattered.*

Jefferson was certain that the vitality of Christianity had been undermined by theology. He was especially opposed to Calvinism. The doctrine of the Trinity appeared to him absurd, the over-emphasis upon faith would lead to superstition; the doctrine of predestination was a form of moral callousness, according to the philosophy of Jefferson. Would not the doctrine of predestination create a fatalistic viewpoint? What was the evidence for such a faith? How could it be supported by scientific research?

Jefferson believed instead in good works and in doing *justice* to one's neighbor. Salvation depended on our motives and actions, not on a statement of dogmas. He believed in Jesus as a model for man, who had rescued morality, religion, and education from formalism.

Jefferson and Platonism

Besides Calvinism, Jefferson was bitterly opposed to Platonism. Had not Plato based his philosophy upon mythology? Was not Plato an objector to freedom and individualism? Was not Plato an apologist for the militarism of Sparta? Plato and Jefferson represent different poles in philosophy. Plato was interested in universals, while

Jefferson stressed the *specific* aspects of life. Plato believed in authoritarianism, while Jefferson was the foe of every form of coercion, and he was always *optimistic* regarding the nature and destiny of man.

Yet both believed in the philosopher-king. Only the philosopher-king of Plato was a man who loved contemplation, who supported a dualistic standard of morals, and who accepted the authority of the state, whereas the philosopher-king in Jefferson was kindly and humane and interested in the improvement of society. As a genuine aristocrat, Jefferson believed that wealth demanded a sense of responsibility and a social conscience.

The good life

The ideal life to Jefferson was an existence dedicated to reason. How could it be achieved? We should cultivate, Jefferson asserted, a sense of serenity and calmness. We are to treasure those things in life which we can control. Education ought to convince us that fame, power, and material riches are transitory pleasures and that lasting happiness cannot be found through an escape to the idols of society.

As an optimist, Jefferson believed that we are naturally good and that we gain most by cooperation. The distinction between right and wrong is not artificial. No society can exist permanently, which is governed by dualistic moral standards. The same laws that govern individual behavior are to govern social behavior.

Educational implications

All these views have important educational implications. Jefferson felt that knowledge would create a rational faith for the individual, so that he would look forward, rather than backward. Those who find perfection in the past only lead us to the darkness of the past. Are not most bigots guided by traditionalism? Is not excessive conservatism a sign of stagnation? Is not the present more significant than ancient times?

The teacher thus should be concerned with the improvement of his own generation. Before this could be accomplished certain idols had to be destroyed. The foremost idol was the belief in infallibility in religion. A state religion meant to Jefferson a form of spiritual tyranny. Were not religious beliefs relative rather than absolute? Was not religion a matter of subjective faith, rather than of social conformity? Separation of state and church thus was the basis of Jefferson's educational philosophy.

Another idol which he attacked sharply was the over-emphasis upon mere intellectual knowledge. While he had respect for intellectual powers, he made it clear that the mind depended on the body. He advocated that all individuals should exercise at least two hours a day. Physical education was to be stressed in the school, otherwise the health of the nation would be undermined.

He felt that when education appeals only to the few, it has a narrow and unstable basis. Democracy is to provide a genuine system of mass education. His suggestion for a new system of education included primary schools for each locality, and secondary schools, which both poor and rich could attend. Enough scholarships should be given to the poor so that talented students would receive the benefit of further education, and the creation of universities would promote research and teaching in the humanities and sciences.

Jefferson had a broad concept of education. It should include not just classical but also vocational subjects. While he had great admiration for Latin and Greek, he did not regard these languages as ends in themselves, but rather as preludes to a universal, liberal culture. The *study of science he recommended for its capacity to discipline the mind and to control nature.*

As a vigorous critic of the education of his time, Jefferson made it clear that narrow knowledge was an obstacle to wisdom. He described how teachers in the academies possessed only a smattering of Greek and Latin, only a superficial knowledge of mathematics and astronomy and yet felt arrogant about their learning. Too often, education, according to Jefferson, alienated the student from an active life and gave him the conceit of knowledge when, in reality, his imagination was feeble and his judgment undeveloped.

Much of Jefferson's time was spent in planning the curriculum of the University of Virginia. It was to be a secular institution with complete freedom of inquiry. It was to stress the elective system, rather than a stereotyped curriculum. So suspicious was Jefferson of sectarianism, that no chair for theology was provided at the University of Virginia.

The need for skepticism

The beginning of Jefferson's educational philosophy was skepticism. In a letter to Peter Carr he advised the latter to doubt everything, even the existence of God. For how could we achieve maturity without intellectual honesty? But doubt was never to be ultimate; it was to be a prelude to moral affirmation. The moral power of mankind was the source of its advancement; teaching about morality was less adequate than living in a righteous way. The professor, compared with the common man, often had a poorer moral judgment because he was led astray by rules and ethical conventions.

As a careful student of history, Jefferson felt that the past offered no consolation for education. The story of mankind so far had been one of darkness, illuminated occasionally by the light of reason. *The American experiment in education was to produce a self-reliant society, without absolutes and without dogmatism.*

Aims of education

Education to Jefferson was the *bastion* of democratic liberties. Public education had the following objectives:

1. To give every citizen the information he needs to transact his own business.
2. To enable him to calculate for himself and to express and preserve his ideas, contracts, and accounts in writing.
3. To improve, by reading, his faculties and morals.
4. To understand his duties to his neighbors and his country, and to discharge with competence the function confided to him by either.
5. To know his rights; to exercise with order and justice those he retains; to choose with discretion the fiduciary of those he delegates.
6. And, in general, to observe with intelligence and faithfulness all the social relations under which he shall be placed.[2]

[2] Jefferson, *On the Objects of Primary Education.*

Democratic ideals

The educational philosophy of Jefferson rested upon his vigorous faith in equality. This did not imply that all men had the same capacities and the same talents, but all had *equal rights*. The only aristocracy was that of virtue and talents; the aristocracy of birth was a false one.

Democracy, in Jefferson's philosophy, rested upon the will of the majority. Without an adequate system of education the majority would often be irrational and overcome by hysteria. Writing to James Madison, Jefferson remarked:

> *Above all things, I hope the education of the common people will be attended to; convinced that on their good sense we may rely with the most security for the preservation of a due degree of freedom.*[3]

Jefferson believed in the rights of the individual states. Centralization of power created an intrenched bureaucracy and a threat to freedom. Local control would make for a more plastic government and would create more initiative on the part of the individual. Laws were to be *progressive*; they were to be changed when conditions altered. The human mind was more important than legal conventions. He advocated even an occasional rebellion so that freedom would be more than a pretense.

As the proponent of decentralization, Jefferson favored only minimum functions for the central government. Its activities should be carried on in as frugal a manner as possible. It should be under *civilian control*; it should protect fundamental freedoms, especially freedom of religion, freedom of the press, and freedom of inquiry. It should seek friendship with other nations, rather than entangling alliances. In short, its effectiveness could be measured by its contribution to human welfare.

Jefferson hoped that the future would witness an expansion of agriculture in the United States. He had a distrust for city life with its shifting population. The prophecy of Hamilton in this respect has been more accurate, for the United States has moved away from a

---

[3] Letter to James Madison, December 20, 1787 (italics mine).

rural basis and has moved more and more in the direction of centralization. Yet the warnings of Jefferson are still valid today. Too much concentration of power almost inevitably creates a threat to freedom.

The Problem of Freedom

Freedom in the twentieth century

The problem of freedom is of central importance to our own time. We have witnessed in this century a steady assault upon liberty. Dictators, like Hitler, Mussolini, and Stalin, have attacked the belief in parliamentary government and have resurrected the Hegelian view of freedom: that man can find himself only in service to the state. The modern state represents a terrifying concentration of power. In times of war, it regiments the life of the individual and controls not only his actions, but even his thoughts. The new barbarian emerges, whose ideals, thoughts, and actions are conditioned by the state. He finds fulfillment not in self-realization, but in subordination to superior authority. He believes implicitly in the leadership principle. This way, as Erich Fromm points out, he escapes from individuality.

Education and authority

Contemporary education often contributes to the cult of authority. *It creates literacy, but not independent thinking; it develops sameness, but not individuality; it stresses vocational efficiency, but not self-examination; it exalts the average, but not the natural aristocracy of talents.* This charge should not be made indiscriminately nor be applied to all forms of education, for in American education far greater progress has been made in the establishment of freedom than in many other forms of education.

Meaning of freedom

Now freedom does not imply anarchy. A laissez-faire attitude creates irresponsibility. The teacher who encourages every whim of the student, who abdicates his teaching function is not aiding the cause of freedom, but that of chaos. Margaret Mead in a revealing study of the natives of New Guinea indicates how too much freedom among the Manus children creates a materialistic, utterly unimaginative view of life. Even the art of the Manus children lacks depth and individuality. *Freedom is never a goal in itself, it must have direction and substance.*

Freedom in education implies, above all, a respect for the personal integrity of the teacher and the student. When we look upon students as mere numbers in the grade book of the teacher, when we rank them merely by percentages—for example, 5 percent A's, 20 percent B's, 50 percent C's, 20 percent D's and 5 percent F's—we are weakening the vitality of the educative process.

To respect the personality of the individual implies that we consider no case hopeless. We are making progress in the education of handicapped children and undoubtedly this advance will continue. One of the wisest statements regarding this problem was made by one of my students, who deals with handicapped children. He remarked: *"Just because they don't have our intelligence, do not imagine that they lack human feelings. On the contrary, they desperately yearn for love and affection!"*

Academic freedom implies the right of the teacher to state his own opinions. However, he should remember that his function is *not* to indoctrinate, but to state different points of view of a subject. He should encourage his students to oppose his opinions and to form their own judgments.

The scientific method and freedom

The use of the scientific method provides the best support of freedom. To Jefferson, as to Dewey, science implies activity, not merely static contemplation. We start with a problem and we explore various possibilities, we form theories and hypotheses, we experiment widely and finally develop a tentative solution which we try to verify. Very often, especially in politics, economics, and education, complete verification is impossible. Thus we accept the solution which leads to social utility and which adds to the enlightenment of mankind.

So far, the scientific method has been more successful in dealing with the objective world than in exploring the possibilities of man. Objects are more easily manipulated; they can be reduced to mathematical laws, whereas human beings are conditioned by subjectivity and by the idols of their environment. Furthermore, human beings are not only quantitatively, but also qualitatively different.

Two views of freedom

In our own time two extreme views of freedom compete in philosophy. One is the view of existentialism, that man is unconditioned and makes his own choices. The other view is that of Marxism, that man is part of the economic structure and thus of necessity expresses class consciousness.

Existential thinkers like Sartre, Heidegger, and Jaspers, express the belief that no institution can coerce man. Science, according to these thinkers, expresses only a superficial reality. It reduces life to a causal relationship, but man is a qualitative fact and not determined by the casual matrix. In its atheistic form, existentialism recognizes no dogma, no revelation, no infallible book, and no God. Man is isolated in the universe. This may give him at first a sense of anguish and dread, but in the end it will be the source of his deliverance. Does it not imply that he is autonomous? Does it not mean that he must make his own decisions and create his own values?

In Marxism, as practiced in Soviet Russia, freedom is regarded as a doubtful good. Independence in theology, political allegiance, economic practice, and educational policy is ruthlessly eliminated. The Party thus is like the *Koran* for the ordinary Mohammedan. But the party line may change frequently. To-day it may proclaim nationalism, tomorrow internationalism; to-day it may proclaim hostility for the West, next day it may be semi-hostility, or the philosophy of live and let live. The party member has to adjust to these changes or else he is purged, which may mean poverty, Siberia, or death. While the party line changes, the infallibility of its leadership is to be recognized.

The task of the teacher in the Soviet Union is to create tools of the state. The student is taught the virtue of discipline and obedience. No wonder that progressive education is outlawed by contemporary Russian educators, for it would encourage the individual to be self-reliant and to question the decisions of the party and of the state.

Jeffersonian view of freedom

As against this deterministic concept of life, which leads to the wasteland of 1984 as described by Orwell,[4] we have the Jeffersonian view of freedom. To Jefferson freedom did not imply either irresponsibility or state control, but rather development of individual creativity. In education and politics we should never forget that our ultimate concern lies not with standards or external authority, but with the living individual.

Questions and Topics for Discussion

1. What are the advantages of specialization?
2. How does specialization destroy the unity of culture?
3. What were Jefferson's religious views?
4. Why did Jefferson oppose Platonism?
5. What were Jefferson's moral views?
6. Why did Jefferson attack an overemphasis upon intellectual knowledge?
7. What are the values of scientific study, according to Jefferson? How in your opinion can the teaching of science be made more fascinating to the non-scientific major?
8. Why did Jefferson reject absolutism? How would Jefferson regard twentieth century America?
9. Why was Jefferson so optimistic about mankind? What is your viewpoint?
10. Why did Jefferson stress the importance of public education?
11. Why is the problem of freedom so important today?
12. Compare the American attitude toward freedom with that of Soviet Russia.
13. How does contemporary education contribute to the cult of authority?

[4] George Orwell, *Nineteen eighty-four.*

THE FOUNDATIONS

14. What are the dangers of a laissez-faire attitude in education?
15. Should controversial subjects be taught in the classroom? Justify your answer.
16. Discuss the statement, "Freedom is never a goal in itself, it must have direction and substance."
17. What is the meaning of academic freedom?
18. Should the teacher be neutral regarding political issues? Explain your answer.

Selected References

ADAMS, H. B., *Thomas Jefferson and the University of Virginia*, 1888.
ADAMS, J. T., *The Living Jefferson*, 1936.
ARROWHEAD, C. F. (EDITOR), *Thomas Jefferson and Education in a Republic*, 1930.
CHINARD, G., *Thomas Jefferson, the Apostle of Americanism*, 1939.
HENDERSON, J. C., *Thomas Jefferson's Views on Public Education*, 1890.
HIRST, F. W., *Life and Letters of Thomas Jefferson*, 1926.
HONEYWELL, R. J., *The Educational Work of Thomas Jefferson*, 1931.
JEFFERSON, T., *The Writings of Thomas Jefferson*, edited by A. F. Bergh, 10 vols., 1907.
———, *Democracy*, with an Introduction by S. K. Padover, 1940.
KOCH, A., *The Philosophy of Thomas Jefferson*, 1942-1943.
MAYER, F., *Patterns of a New Philosophy*, 1955.
MORSE, J. T., *Thomas Jefferson*, 1923.
ORTEGA y GASSET, J., *The Revolt of the Masses*, 1932.
ORWELL, G., *1984*, 1949.
PADOVER, S. K., *Jefferson*, 1942.
SCHWEITZER, A., *Out of My Life and Thought*, 1933.
THOMAS, E. D., *Thomas Jefferson: World Citizen*, 1942.
ULICH, R., *History of Educational Thought*, 1945.
WILD, J. D., *The Challenge of Existentialism*, 1955.

V. EMERSON AND THE QUEST FOR SPIRITUALITY

The Age of Emerson

A period of transition

THE PERIOD OF EMERSON (1803-1882) was an era of turmoil in American history. The American revolution had not resulted in the establishment of complete freedom. The Federalists believed in government by the few and they were afraid of the radical ideals of the French revolution. At first, liberal thinkers like Jefferson welcomed the French revolution with its ideals of liberty, equality, and fraternity but later many became disillusioned as they witnessed the establishment of an absolute dictatorship under Napoleon. In the United States a more solid basis to democracy was given by Jackson, but he used the spoils system and many intellectuals regarded him as a demagogue. Before the Civil War the slavery issue appeared to be most significant. Emerson, Thoreau, and Alcott were fervent abolitionists and they aided the cause of anti-slavery. The war produced the inspiring leadership of Lincoln, but afterwards came a materialistic age, perhaps best described by Whitman in his *Democratic Vistas*.

THE FOUNDATIONS

Educational advances in the nineteenth century

In education the nineteenth century witnessed a steady agitation for the democratization of the school system. At the beginning of the century the schools were largely supported by tuition fees, the wealthy families usually employed tutors, and the teachers were generally under-paid. Educational leaders like De Witt Clinton in New York, who promoted the New York Free School Society, attempted to expand public education. Perhaps most notable were Horace Mann in Massachusetts and Henry Barnard in Connecticut. Horace Mann became secretary of the Massachusetts State Board of Education and in that capacity he issued several reports, of which the seventh has become especially famous. He attempted to provide for complete separation of state and church and indefatigably worked for the improvement of teachers, administrators, and curricular methods, and for more adequate school buildings. Henry Barnard, after serving as a member of the state board of education in Connecticut, and later in Rhode Island, became the first United State Commissioner of Education. He edited the *American Journal of Education,* which tried to give a more cosmopolitan and scientific basis to the study of educational problems.

Free school systems were established by Massachusetts in 1827, and by Pennsylvania in 1834. The Kalamazoo case (1872) resulted in the universal use of tax money for the support of the public high school. By the time Emerson died, the American system of education had fully emerged with eight years of elementary school and four years of high school.

Influence of European education

The influence of European patterns of education was strong in the development of the American public school system. Thus Victor Cousin published *Report on the State of Public Education in Prussia.* William C. Woodbridge, Calvin E. Stowe, Horace Mann, and Henry Barnard all were influenced by European, especially German, educational ideals. Pestalozzi gained many followers in this nation, particularly in Edward A. Sheldon, who became superintendent of education at Oswego, New York. Emerson and Alcott had great admiration for Pestalozzi, and Emerson quoted Pestalozzi in *The American Scholar*. In higher education the German university ideal influenced the elective system, which was instituted at Harvard and contributed to the spread of graduate instruction, especially at Johns Hopkins and at Clark University. To many scholars, German education, German factual knowledge, and German philosophy were the models for American education.

Emerson's Philosophy

Influences

Emerson, like most of his contemporaries, had great admiration for the German ideal of scholarship. He had immense respect for Goethe and he looked upon Germany as the most civilized nation of Europe. His thoughts also owe much to English romanticism, especially to Wordsworth, Coleridge, and Carlyle. Had they not indicated the inadequacy of science? Had they not emphasized the need for intuition? Had they not stressed the unity of man and nature? Had they not shown that the great man molds civilization? In classical philosophy Plato, Plotinus, Bruno, Leibnitz, and Kant stirred his thinking. He looked up to Plato with a sense of awe and almost equated philosophic insight with Platonism. What attracted him to Plato was not so much the Platonic social philosophy as the symbolism and poetry in Plato. Oriental thinking also evoked his admiration, particularly the *Upanishads*. Was not matter a form of unreality? Was not man part of an absolute creation? Was not the goal of knowledge to see the relationship between man and nature, the subjective and objective poles of knowledge?

Transcendentalism

As a Transcendentalist, Emerson believed in the importance of intuition, in the spiritual nature of man, and in the basic unity of life. To him all forms of relativism were inadequate; skepticism was an inferior mode of knowledge, for behind experience was the Over-

Soul, the principle of reality. Basically, thinkers could be divided into two categories: those who, like Coleridge and Kant, saw that experience pointed to another world, and those thinkers who, like Locke and Stewart, made experience the center of philosophy. Mere experience, to Emerson, was only a prelude to the richness of an absolutistic structure.

The Over-Soul

But the world of the Over-Soul, Emerson held, existed within our heart. Had not Jesus already pointed out that the kingdom of God is within man? Had not the great mystics of all time shown that what matters is the *soul* of man, not so much his activity. Hence Emerson's philosophy is a call for inwardness.

Educational consequences

All these views have important educational implications. For Emerson was concerned with the spiritual perspective of the teacher. Education thus is not so much the communication of knowledge, as the communication of a *spiritual attitude,* a way of looking at life, an intense form of inwardness. Facts are subordinated to values; the teacher becomes a preacher who reminds his audience of the noble destiny of mankind.

Political ideas

Unlike Jefferson, Emerson was rather disenchanted regarding the possibilities of political improvement. To be sure, his heart was with progressive measures and he advocated liberal reforms, but he was conscious of the negativism of the American radical. He believed that the radical was driven by hatred rather than by love, by opposition rather than by constructive purposes. The conservatives, on the other hand, merely wanted to perpetuate the past, they lacked generosity and vision; they had no real friendliness for the poor and the oppressed. Yet they usually attracted the most cultivated leaders. Emerson could join neither party, for he felt that the wise man creates his own cause and can get along without governmental supervision.

Individualism

As the preacher of self-reliance, Emerson pointed out how institutions reflect the influence of great men; for example, how the Reformation reflected the impact of Luther, the development of Methodism the impact of Wesley, and Quakerism the inspiration of Fox. He called upon individuals to be *non-conformists*. Was not society engaged in a conspiracy against individual creativity? Was not society an artificial structure? To Emerson, as to Jefferson, the individual, not society, is the center of life.

Causality and creativity

Emerson believed that the specialist was less important than the man who understood basic relationships. Science may disclose a deterministic structure of the universe, but this is only a beginning. *Beyond causality is creativity, beyond determinism is freedom, beyond uniformity is the personality of man.* The scientist usually is overwhelmed by specific functions, he sees only quantitative laws. But as we contemplate the whole, we realize that analysis is inadequate, and that intuition of the pattern and the whole is needed. The laws of science thus are only preludes to the laws of the spirit. As Emerson wrote in "Brahma":

> If the red slayer think he slays,
>   Or if the slain think he is slain,
> They know not well the subtle ways
>   I keep, and pass, and turn again.
>
> Far or forgot to me is near;
>   Shadow and sunlight are the same;
> The vanished gods to me appear;
>   And one to me are shame and fame.
>
> They reckon ill who leave me out;
>   When me they fly, I am the wings;
> I am the doubter and the doubt,
>   And I the hymn the Brahmin sings.
>
> The strong gods pine for my abode,
>   And pine in vain the sacred Seven;
> But thou, meek lover of the good!
>   Find me, and turn thy back on heaven.

THE FOUNDATIONS

Meaning of culture

Culture, to Emerson, rested upon a basic insight. Culture was not escape into an absolute past, nor was it a form of parasitical existence whereby the few create and the many slave. Rather culture was a quest for moral perfection; it involved the total man, his mind and his reason, his heart and his intellect.

The function of the teacher

His ideal of education was not that of the professional teacher. The school-room is only an insignificant aspect of education. Are we not taught more by nature? Is not education a subjective process? Emerson was disturbed by the fact that treatises on education were so dull. That subject ought to be "as broad as man" and as inspiring as religion, and yet usually it gave only sterile rules and pedestrian ideas.

For Emerson, life was an allegory; beyond facts, we find a basic unity; beyond history, we find living greatness. The teacher ought to discover the sources of learning, he ought to appeal to man's poetic insight. Yet we teach usually in a shallow manner. *We are uninspired and our lethargic attitude is communicated to our students. We have lost the sense of adventure, and so we stifle curiosity in children.*

The great teacher, according to Emerson, has the openness of the child. He sees every day with a *new* perspective; he asks a thousand questions; he is overcome by a sense of reverence and wonder; he feels the closeness of God and he looks upon life with trusting eyes. One of the great crimes of education, Emerson believed, is that it does not realize the greatness of children. Do we not try to mold them into a pattern of sameness? Do we not instruct them as if they were objects? Do we not kill their curiosity prematurely? Do we not discourage their vivid imagination? Emerson was never too busy to take time out with children. In them he found renewed faith and a deeper appreciation of the spirituality of man.

Should the teacher conform to society? Should the teacher be a traditionalist? Should the teacher be completely objective? Emerson answered in the negative. We should realize that no society can coerce us, that we must make our own choices and develop our own judgments. Non-conformity thus is a duty on the part of the teacher: only in this way does he achieve individuality; only in this way does he understand his spiritual potentialities; only in this way can he be a creative influence in the life of his students.

Moral ideals

Emerson stressed the goodness of man. Evil to him was ultimately unreal; its function was to exercise our moral capacities. Like Socrates he held that knowledge is virtue, that the truly wise man is the good man. Morality does not depend on rules or regulations, but on insight. We all have a capacity for self-sacrifice and loyalty, we all have a capacity for love. It is the task of education to stimulate these traits so that our character emerges in a noble form. Once we have defined ourselves, once we have recognized the essential self, once we have understood the structure of the universe, we have become truly emancipated and enlightened. Education, according to Emerson, ought to teach us that our destiny does not lie in the material world, but in the spiritual realm, that fame and power are transitory goods, that we must be self-reliant rather than escape to the certainty of dogmatism.

Genius and drill

To be educated we need not merely inspiration, but also correct habits. Just as nature is composed of matter and form, so the educative process demands *Genius and Drill*. Genius is the main aim of education; drill, Emerson held, gives shape to educative growth. Like William James, Emerson did not believe in an over-emphasis on formal discipline. After all, school life is not like military existence. The child is to be taught correct habits, so that they become part of him and so that he develops the foundations for *genuine freedom*.

The power of education

Emerson believed in the power of education. Did not France feel the trenchant wit of Voltaire? Did not Germany go to school with

THE FOUNDATIONS

Goethe? Emerson realized at the same time that modern education had to appeal to many who lacked enthusiasm and who objected to education. No wonder the teacher would be like a policeman and would emphasize the routine aspects of education. No wonder education would be dominated by the mediocre. Emerson felt that when our schools appealed mainly to the average student, they would disintegrate; the vision of education would be lost and they would become like factories in which students would live a depersonalized existence. The teacher, thus, should not try to reach all, nor should he adjust his instruction to the lowest denominator in the class. Rather he should uphold an ideal of education which would motivate and inspire by its very transcendence.

Education to Emerson was a form of spiritual dedication:

Our culture has truckled to the times—to the senses. It is not manworthy. If the vast and the spiritual are omitted, so are the practical and the moral. It does not make us brave or free. We teach boys to be such men as we are. We do not teach them to aspire to be all they can. We do not give them a training as if we believed in their noble nature. We scarce educate their bodies. We do not train the eye and the hand. We exercise their understandings to the apprehension and comparison of some facts, to a skill in numbers; in words; we aim to make accountants, attorneys, engineers, but not to make able, earnest, great-hearted men. *The great object of education should be commensurate with the object of Life.* It should be a moral one; to teach self-trust; to inspire the youthful man with an interest in himself; with a curiosity touching his own nature; to acquaint him with the resources of his mind, and to teach him that there is all his strength, and to inflame him with a piety towards the Grand Mind in which he lives. Thus would education conspire with the Divine Providence.[1]

The American scholar

In his Phi Beta Kappa speech at Harvard, Emerson outlined a new ideal for the American scholar. The scholar was to realize that not all wisdom could be found in books, he was to learn from action and from nature as well as from intellectual studies. He was to see the unity of nature and God so that knowing oneself and studying nature would become the same.

---

[1] Emerson, *Education.*

Unlike the modern existentialists, Emerson believed in the moral purpose of nature. Was not nature a form of discipline? Did not nature display the greatness of God? Did not nature indicate the existence of moral ideals? Existentialists like Sartre would look upon nature as a conspiracy against man, who would feel a sense of alienation and aloneness in his relationship with the external environment. But Emerson was more optimistic than Sartre, for he was guided by a faith in the equivalence of moral and spiritual ideals, and that purposes exist both subjectively and objectively.

The scholar in Emerson's philosophy is the guide of mankind. He is to live the examined way of life, and rebel constantly against the obsolescence of the past. He is not to confine his teachings to the few; he is not to fight the war of the footnotes; his researches are never to be ends in themselves, rather they are to be guides to a more meaningful present and a more constructive future. Emerson, like Jefferson and Dewey, believed in the application of knowledge. Merely to be conscious of one's intellectual brilliance led to a wasteful existence; merely to know life was inferior to the mastery of life. The ideals and ideas of the scholar thus had to *radiate* if they were to be completely effective.

Emerson called for an intellectual declaration of independence. This did not imply intellectual provincialism or isolationism. Nor did it mean nationalistic conceit. Rather, Emerson felt that the American scholar would contribute most to world civilization if he developed the potentialities of his own culture instead of imitating the traditions of Europe and Asia. He had to learn how to rely on his own powers and his own talents, and how to live in his time instead of escaping to the comforts of another age.

Education and spirituality

The spiritual nature of education was outlined by Emerson in his Divinity School Address. Did not both religion and education depend on inspiration? Did they not both involve an intensely personal awareness? Did they not both lead to a new birth and a new perspective? The laws of morality, according to Emerson, were those of the soul. They were beyond space, time, and circumstance. The real drama of life thus was subjective. The man who fought a noble cause was ennobled; the man who withstood temptation was purified; while the man who was villainous and who deceived others only deceived himself. Religion like education demanded action, not theory. How could man live a meaningful life if he did not see eternity? How could he find himself without understanding the everlasting vitality of the spirit? How could he act without a vital faith?

Yet Emerson throughout his life fought orthodox religion just as he opposed orthodoxy in education. *Orthodox religion had substituted the past for the present, dogma for insight, and beliefs about religion for living religion.* It had upheld fear and coercion; it had pointed to the Beyond, instead of the present; it had spoken of sin instead of goodness, of damnation instead of self-realization. It had shown a transcendent savior, instead of the human qualities of the saint, who has compassion for all mankind.

Religion, like education, depended not on institutions, but on *man*. The miracle was the creativity of man, not the infallibility of the Bible. "When a man comes, all books are legible, all things transparent, all religions are forms." Theology had made religion stale and had deprived faith of its moral fervor. It was up to man to see the living reality of religion, to realize the infinite potentialities of life, and to recognize that *"God is, not was."*

The teacher and the preacher thus would combine to awaken mankind from the dogmatic slumber and create a new culture. Truth, beauty, justice, and spirituality were to be unified. All would point to the perfectibility of man and the unity of culture.

The Quest for Significance

Life is a struggle for meaning and significance. Writers, like Cassirer in his *Essay on Man,* Langer in *Philosophy in a New Key,* Whitehead in *Science and the Modern World,* have shown the importance of symbolism in individual and collective existence. The symbolism of art, religion, music, literature, and education thus often is more significant than the facts of these inquiries.

Biological activities

We find meaning at first in biological activities; we enjoy the infinite variety of the sensate realm. Even in our highest moments of intellectual depth and creativity, we are dependent on biological factors. For man is not a creature of mere reason or immaterial knowledge; he is dependent on his body for vitality and sustenance. Education, as Whitehead wrote, fails when it does not recognize that students have bodies and natural desires.

Social activities

We find meaning, furthermore, in social activities. For the self is fragmentary and partial, and needs the stimulation and motivation of others. The life of isolation, as Aristotle indicated, is for brutes and Gods. Society enters into our beliefs, for are we not all governed by certain assumptions which are derived from our cultural background?

The intellectual life

The intellectual life combines selfhood and society. We realize as we become more mature that biological activities are limited, that too much physical pleasure leads to boredom or pain, and that society is not the ultimate standard of perfection. We are interested in our own fulfillment, in gaining perspective, and in entering a wider society of thinkers, artists, and scientists, who are not limited by time, space or circumstance. *The province of the scholar thus is the universe, not his own time or his own nation.*

Yet all the time we feel a sense of limitation. We realize that our views are fallible, that our studies are incomplete, and that our knowledge is imperfect. We know that time is a stern master, and that death is inevitable. The fear of death is a steady companion. It can be overlooked when we are successful; it can be ignored in times of joy; but sooner or later it emerges and makes us conscious of the irony and uncertainty of human existence. When it fills our being it can give us either a sense of dread, a profound anxiety, or it can give us a deeper purpose and more lasting dedication.

THE FOUNDATIONS

The spiritual life

The significance of the spiritual life lies in its realization of dilemmas. *We are mortal, yet culture contains an element of immortality; we die, and yet the spark of creativity does not disappear; we are part of nature, and yet we transcend nature; we are mastered by time, and yet time and death never completely obliterate us.* As John Donne wrote:

DEATH

Death, be not proud, though some have called thee
Mighty and dreadful, for thou art not so;
For those whom thou think'st thou dost overthrow
Die not, poor Death; nor yet canst thou kill me.
From Rest and Sleep, which but thy picture be,
Much pleasure; then from thee much more must flow;
And soonest our best men with thee do go—
Rest of their bones and souls' delivery!
Thou'rt slave to Fate, chance, kings, and desperate men,
And dost with poison, war, and sickness dwell;
And poppy or charms can make us sleep as well
And better than thy stroke. Why swell'st thou then?
One short sleep past, we wake eternally,
And Death shall be no more; Death, thou shalt die!

Our reason tells us that man's destiny is like that of the animal world, yet our faith desires a more noble destiny. These paradoxes are never completely solved either in religion or in education. Yet basic contradictions need not paralyze us, as the faith of Emerson indicates. Did not Emerson say that "the man who renounces himself, comes to himself?" As we realize that we are part of a greater cause and a greater pilgrimage we receive a measure of serenity and tranquillity.

The faith of the teacher

The great teacher is not concerned with immediate results, he is not primarily interested in popularity or social approval, he does not bow to the idols of his time, rather he appeals to long-range goals and to long-range ideals. He is dedicated to education, because it is more than a form of learning, it is an intimation of man's greatness, of man's long march away from bestiality and brutality. He realizes that education is never complete and that our society is constantly threatened by the idols which we have left behind. Especially in times of crisis, man turns backward and seeks a haven in the past. Especially in times of crisis, the tribal drums beat insistently.

The return to absolutism

Not so long ago a young theologian rejoiced that his generation had rediscovered the meaning of sin and had abandoned belief in progress and humanity. He was certain that man was evil and would not find salvation except through the mysterious designs of God. This viewpoint illustrates the inadequacy of education. Does not such a concept of faith imply a rebellion against reason and a return to the harshness of Calvinism? The rebellion would be less disconcerting had it not attracted some of the ablest minds of our time, like Niebuhr, Barth, and Brunner.

The teacher as a spiritual guide

Spirituality in education does not imply a return to categorical standards, the resurrection of Calvin or St. Augustine in a modern disguise. It does imply, however, a sense of *limitation*; we are not the climax of history; our knowledge is not the acme of perfection. But our little knowledge is precious, for it is a symbol of a perennial quest and a perennial pilgrimage.

It may be objected that this ideal of education is too high. Are not most of our students interested in vocational subjects? Is not the average intelligence in our schools fairly low? Are not the great writers beyond the comprehension of the mediocre student? We must not make the mistake of condemning our students to a premature *hell of mediocrity*. Students are lethargic in most cases because their teachers are uninspired. *Only a fully awakened teacher can create a great culture; only a dedicated teacher can create a great society; only a spiritual teacher can point the way to survival.*

THE FOUNDATIONS

Questions and Topics for Discussion

1. Discuss the social environment of Ralph Waldo Emerson.
2. What were some of the educational advances of the nineteenth century?
3. How did German education influence the development of American schools?
4. What are the advantages and limitations of the German concept of scholarship?
5. Why did Emerson stress the role of intuition?
6. Compare and contrast Emerson's philosophy with that of Jefferson.
7. Why was Emerson such a great individualist? Would his individualism be practical today?
8. What was the Emersonian concept of culture?
9. What are the attributes of the great teacher, according to Emerson? Who were the great teachers in your own life? What were they like?
10. Why did Emerson stress the power of education? Can education change civilization?
11. Why did Emerson believe in the moral purpose of nature?
12. What did Emerson mean by an intellectual declaration of independence?
13. Do you believe that education is a spiritual process? Explain.
14. What are the basic similarities between education and religion?
15. Discuss the statement, "life is a struggle for significance."
16. Evaluate your own quest for significance.
17. Compare and contrast Emerson's educational philosophy with that of Jefferson.
18. Discuss the statement of Emerson, "The secret of education lies in respecting the pupil."

Selected References

BROOKS, VAN WYCK, *Life of Emerson*, 1932.
BUTTS, R. F. and CREMIN, L. A., *History of Education in American Culture*, 1954.
CASSIRER, E., *Essay on Man*, 1944.
DANA, W. F., *The Optimism of Ralph Waldo Emerson*, 1903.
DILLAWAY, N., *Prophet of America*, 1936.
EMERSON, R. W., *Complete Works*, 12 vols., 1903-1904.
———, *Essays and English Traits*, 1909.
———, *The Heart of Emerson's Journals*, edited by Bliss Perry, 1926.
———, *Representative Selections*, 1934.

EMERSON · QUEST FOR SPIRITUALITY

FIRKINS, O., *Ralph Waldo Emerson*, 1915.
HOLMES, O. W., *Ralph Waldo Emerson*, 1905.
LANGER, S. K., *Philosophy in a New Key*, 1942.
MOSIER, R. D., *Making the American Mind*, 1947.
PALMER, G. H., *Ethical and Moral Instruction in the Schools*, 1909.
PERRY, B., *Emerson Today*, 1931.
RUSSELL, P., *Emerson, the Wisest American*, 1929.
SANBORN, I. B., *The Personality of Emerson*, 1903.
WHITEHEAD, A. N., *Science and the Modern World*, 1925.
WOODBERRY, G. E., *Ralph Waldo Emerson*, 1926.

VI. DEWEY AND THE IDEAL OF UNCERTAINTY

Foundations of Dewey's Philosophy

Influence of Dewey

THE INFLUENCE of Dewey upon contemporary civilization cannot be overestimated. His educational ideals have spread as far as Turkey and Japan. His books have been widely translated and when he died in 1952, at the age of ninety-three, he was generally recognized as America's foremost thinker. His influence was less due to his style, which was severely technical, or to his manner of teaching, which tended to be somewhat dry, than to his ideals which reflected the new democratic faith and the expansion of American society.

Spokesman for democracy

In Dewey, democracy found its most eloquent spokesman. He stressed the ideal of co-operation. He held that philosophy should come down to earth and aid the average man in clarifying social, political, religious, and educational ideals. As an apostle of action, he advocated a genuine reconstruction of culture. The same faith that motivated American industrial society dominated Dewey. It was faith in novelty, love of adventure, and the quest for hypothetical solutions. Some thinkers like Russell charge that Dewey lacked a sense of cosmic piety and that Dewey did not recognize the limitations of man and nature. However, this charge is essentially incorrect, for Dewey realized that although man is not omnipotent, he can establish a new society based upon scientific experimentation and scientific control.

Works

His intellectual productivity was immense. He wrote *Experience and Nature, The Quest for Certainty, Logic, Essays in Experimental Logic, Reconstruction in Philosophy, Human Nature and Conduct, A Common Faith, Freedom and Culture, The Public and Its Problems,* and *Art as Experience*. He collaborated with Tufts in *Ethics* and with Bentley in *The Knower and the Known*. In education his most influential books are *How We Think, Democracy and Education, The School and Society, My Pedagogic Creed,* and *Experience and Education*. What impresses the reader is his range of knowledge and his ability to stimulate thinkers in various fields of inquiry. With Bacon and Leonardo, Dewey ranks as one of the truly universal minds of history.

Influences

He was influenced both by modern and classical thinkers. Among the Greek thinkers, he owed a great debt to Plato, although he could not agree with Plato's concept of Ideas and Plato's hierarchical society. He liked better the early works of Plato than the later writings of the great Greek thinker, for when Plato became older he turned reactionary, as his *Laws* indicate.

Bacon and Dewey

Bacon was a life-long influence upon Dewey. Bacon indicated that knowledge should be used concretely and he rebelled against medieval philosophy. In regarding abstraction for the sake of abstraction as useless, he anticipated modern pragmatism. Hegel also played a role in the development of Dewey, who at first was a confirmed Hegelian. W. T. Harris for a while thought that Dewey might be-

THE FOUNDATIONS

come the outstanding Hegelian in the United States, but later Dewey rebelled against Hegel's metaphysical logic and anti-democratic spirit.

Darwin and Dewey

Darwin, throughout Dewey's career had an enormous impact upon the great American thinker. Darwin indicated that change dominates biology, he recognized the naturalistic matrix of man's life and he stressed the importance of adaptation. The same revolution that Darwin had accomplished in the biological realm was to be undertaken in the field of philosophy. Away with abstractions! Away with preconceived theories of man and the universe! Away with eternal essences! Dewey, like James, believed in concreteness and the rule of experience.

The impact of James

James, of course, was the most direct influence upon Dewey. Like James, Dewey valued the evolutionary features of life, and believed in the close connection between psychology and philosophy. Like James, Dewey was the enemy of all forms of absolutism; he accepted the importance of methodology; and he thought that the main task of philosothy is not that of description, but of reconstruction of values. But we must not overlook certain differences between the two thinkers. Basically, James was more religious than Dewey and stressed the *will to believe*. Dewey's interests were more along biological lines, and he was less friendly to the views of supernaturalism than James. Dewey, furthermore, was less of a romanticist than James, who believed in the wisdom of the heart and who stressed emotions rather than intellect. James was concerned with the problem of mysticism as his *Varieties of Religious Experience* indicates, whereas Dewey felt rather negative about any type of mysticism.

The pragmatic revolt

The pragmatic revolt which began with Peirce, and which was climaxed by James, Dewey, and Kilpatrick, had an enormous effect upon American education. Within less than a hundred years American education changed profoundly, partially because of the influence of these thinkers who believed that education, like science, ought to be emancipated from traditionalism and ought to be based upon scientific methodology and scientific assumptions.

Basic Ideas

Social nature of knowledge

As an excellent student of history, Dewey emphasized the social nature of knowledge. Our ideas do not come to us in an immaculate form; rather they are usually derived from the social environment. Philosophy is not the means whereby ultimate reality can be known; rather it is a tool for dealing with controversial social issues and bringing about a sense of unity in civilization.

Dewey contrasted the medieval view of life with our modern *Weltanschauung* (world view). In the middle ages, hierarchy dominated the thinking of man; science was subordinated to theology; and man's problems were neglected in the quest for God and salvation. In modern science, however, interest is transferred from the eternal to the problem of change; the universal aspects of experience are less significant than the specific aspects of life; authority is criticized; nature is being investigated, rather than being regarded as a religious symbolism.

Logic and intelligence

Logic thus, in Dewey, would deal with inquiry; absolute categories are abandoned; the scientific method is to govern both the natural and the social sciences. Instead of absolute conviction, *tentativeness* is stressed; instead of dogmatism, the open mind is emphasized; instead of preconceived ideas, experience becomes the guide to knowledge. The instrumentalistic changing nature of knowledge is emphasized by Dewey. Truth ceases to be capitalized, and now depends on verification. Thinking ceases to be an isolated activity and depends on its connection with our adjustment to life.

Intelligence in Dewey is not an entity, but a capacity. Like G. Stanley Hall, Dewey felt that our mind evolved and that it should be studied biologically. Are not the generalizations about the mind aspects of pre-scientific thinking? The mind's functions, rather than its innate traits, were stressed in Dewey's psychology.

Educational implications

Dewey's views have significant educational implications. Since change prevails in the universe, fixed subject-matter is outmoded and the concept of growth should dominate the schools. Thinkers and educators should abandon the Aristotelian syllogism. Instead they should turn to the problem-solving method which involves a felt need, analysis of the problem, experimentation with various solutions, tentative theories, verification, and the forming of a conclusion which can be applied concretely. Like the scientist, the educator should be hypothetical in his approach to life, and he should be more concerned with methodology than with ultimate standards.

Moral ideals

The moral impact of Dewey's philosophy is vast. Those who blame man's weaknesses upon an innate human nature are severely castigated. The moral man is never self-righteous or arrogant; he never rests upon his laurels; rather he is constantly interested in self-improvement and growth. The immoral man is one who stands still and who inhibits further avenues of development.

Rejecting both pessimism and optimism, Dewey accepted the concept of *meliorism,* which implies that the world is neither good nor bad, but can be changed. Pessimism, Dewey asserted, leads to moral paralysis and cynicism, while optimism leads to a foolish faith that this is the best of all possible worlds. What matters is *how* man is to be changed. This implies interest in the *specific* conditions of human existence, not in eternal values.

Education and social change

Dewey looked upon education as the most adequate method of social change. Education involves not merely the acquisition of knowledge, rather, it should stress the "reconstruction of experience." To Dewey education is a life-long process. Had not the traditional school regarded education as a preparation for life rather than as a mirror of life? Had not the traditional school created a gulf between education and society, the teacher and the learner? Had not the traditional school emphasized effort rather than interest?

Vocational education

Dewey was a strong proponent of vocational education. Traditional liberal education had created a snobbish spirit; it had led to a worship of the classics, and had created a disdain for manual activity. Vocational education would bridge the gulf between knowledge and action, and would develop a more co-operative spirit. Do we not learn by doing?

Background of Dewey's educational thought

A variety of thinkers contributed to the educational outlook of Dewey. From Rousseau he inherited a dislike of formal discipline; from Herbart he accepted the importance of interest; Froebel gave him his faith in the creative possibilities of activity and in the importance of play; Hall imbued him with the need for a scientific study of childhood. Dewey, however, did not merely synthesize, he created a *new* educational philosophy. For example, in his discussion of the problem of interest *vs.* effort, he showed how a false dualism had been established by Harris, who had over-emphasized effort, while Herbart had made too much of interest. Actually, interest and effort were correlated; interest was the inward aspect of educative growth, while effort was its outward manifestation.

The progressive schools

The progressive schools, mainly through the influence of Dewey, stressed the fact that education should be concerned with the needs of the child, not with the dogmas of the adult world. The child was to give up passivity, was to cease to be a spectator, and instead was to develop patterns of participation.

The new education shunned drill and memorization, for they

THE FOUNDATIONS

would only lead to imitation and would inhibit genuine growth. The *living* aspects of education were stressed. Activity rather than formal learning governed the class-room. Progressive educators emphasized that we forget quickly those facts which have no relationship to our life and that we lose interest when one abstraction is piled upon another. They pointed out that learning is intensified when our sense of adventure is stirred.

Social studies occupied a prominent place in the new school. Children were encouraged to obtain first-hand experiences of the community in which they lived. When they studied civics, for example, they would visit the city hall, talk to the mayor, and perhaps attend a council session. Education thus became more vivid and more dramatic and lost part of its cloistered atmosphere.

The old curriculum had depended on the logic of the subject matter. In the new curriculum the subject matter plays a secondary role. Searching questions are being asked by the progressive educator; for example, how do the subjects contribute to the growth of the individual? How do they develop democratic living? How do they improve the student's adjustment? The motivation of the child is stressed. Fixed subjects are avoided, while flexible planning is encouraged. The teacher ceases to be a lecturer and instead becomes a discussion leader.

Play and work-experiences are co-ordinated in the new school. Conservative educators felt that a separation of play and work was essential, but Dewey pointed out that play often is more creative than work. Were not many books written in times of leisure? Is not the esthetic experience the result of leisure-time activities? Does not play give the child a good balance for his work experiences?

Artificial incentives such as grades are held to a minimum by the new school. Dewey felt that education should not rely upon coercive measures. Flunking a student would only make him feel resentful of the school. Discipline was a matter of inward attitude; lack of discipline usually indicated lack of interest.

In the progressive school the "3 R's" lost their place of eminence. Reading, writing, and arithmetic were only preludes to social understanding and social effectiveness. Teachers were told that it is a mistake to apply one standard to the entire class, rather each individual was to be measured by his growth and by his changing behavioral patterns. The concomitant learnings were stressed. This meant that the significance of a child's education could be evaluated not so much by his formal knowledge as by the values, ideals, and aspirations which resulted from learning.

School and society

The school was to be a genuine democratic society. In the school the student would learn respect for diversity, the need for freedom, and the significance of co-operative activity. In the school no class hierarchy was to be tolerated; minorities were to be respected; religious differences were to be overlooked. The student-body was to establish its own government and frame its own regulations.

Dewey's ideal was a pluralistic society, as he stated in *The Public and Its Problems*. This meant a respect for individuality rather than trust in central authority. This ideal was applied to school organization, which now accepted a pluralistic rather than a monistic structure.

The new art education

Dewey contributed to the esthetic enrichment of the curriculum. The distinction between the fine arts and the industrial arts was to be minimized as much as possible. Talk about art was regarded as being inferior to *experience* in art. The adult was not to use his own standards in evaluating the art of children, rather he was to appreciate the integrity of the child's esthetic interests.

Absolute and Relative Values

Dewey as a relativist

The educational philosophy of Dewey raises the problem of absolutism vs. relativism. Is the concept of growth a valid guide for modern man? Can man live by relative standards or does he need absolute certainty?

Dewey, as a relativist, rejected the idea of absolute faith or absolute knowledge. In religion he stressed the ethical meaning of faith and the practical power of ideals. In religion, ideal and actuality met; the force of ideals should never be underestimated. God stood for the unification of life; how He was to be interpreted was an individual matter. What was important was that religious ideals should transform actual existence.

Ideal values, according to Dewey, were not confined to the religious person. The scientist in his laboratory, the teacher in the class-room, the statesman in Congress, the doctor in the operating room, all exemplified the power of aspiration in guiding our lives. Mankind, according to Dewey, has the choice of two alternatives: Either we could be guided by supernaturalism, in which case we would be escapists and look upon unbelievers with distrust; or we could accept the naturalistic function of religion, which would mean that we concentrate our energies upon the improvement of this life. Dewey naturally favored the second course. Religion, like education, was not the guide to certainty but to *uncertainty*.

Absolutism

The absolutist, like Niebuhr or Maritain, would say that man cannot progress without complete dependence on God. Does not the relativity of life point to an absolute principle of perfection? Does not the testimony of the past indicate a supreme purpose in the world? Does not the moral weakness of modern man indicate the need for absolutism?

When we ask how absolutism is to be found, the answer usually is: through a particular ecclesiastical organization. Outside of that organization no salvation can be obtained. What then happens to the unbeliever? The answer often is that he has to pay the price for his faithlessness. To the orthodox, one of the worst sins is pride. No wonder that pragmatism is castigated as a heresy, which would substitute the authority of man for the authority of supernatural ideas.

In education, the absolutist, like Mortimer Adler, usually claims that knowledge involves belief in eternal truth, and that the subject-matter is more important than the desires of the individual. What is needed then is discipline, rather than self-expression; the study of the past, rather than the exploration of the present; the reading of the great books, rather than scientific experimentation. Still when we read the great books we find that they are not absolute guides to wisdom or to the improvement of the understanding.

Towards synthesis

Education, like religion, is involved in a constant flux. We can understand only a few manifestations of the creative life, and those manifestations depend on personal as well as social factors. Pure relativism and pure absolutism both are inadequate viewpoints. Pure relativism may lead to the Machiavellian perspective, whereby the end justifies the means; it may glorify power; it may regard all experiences as being on the same level; while pure absolutism may create stagnation, dogmatism, and arrogance.

The essential problem is not the conflict between relativism and absolutism but between particularism and universalism. Since our experiences are partial, since our understanding is incomplete, since our insights are temporary, since we are part of the process of evolution, we can have no absolute knowledge. At the same time, some of our insights are more universal than others. Experience has taught us that we move from interest in the self to interest in a universal society; from the narrow self to the wider self; from expediency to genuine idealism. The educated individual thus tries to universalize his knowledge, for he realizes that absolute boundaries do not exist. As Spinoza said, he becomes the spectator of all existence. Living for a universal cause gives him depth and a more *fervent* hope.

Education and mysticism

The process of educative enlightenment can be compared with the stages of mysticism in religion. Like the mystic in his search for God, we start with a solid determination. We are not interested in externals, we desire not just to know facts, but to gain an understanding of relationships, to see the *unity* of man and nature, and man and the universe.

Like the mystic, we feel that real education involves spiritual turmoil. A genuine intellectual experience appeals not merely to our minds, but also to our emotions. A great teacher can change the course of our existence. Was this not the influence of Socrates upon Plato, of Albertus Magnus upon Aquinas and of Dewey upon Kilpatrick? A new idea, a new concept of life, can create a transvaluation in our philosophy. Before, the world appeared to be well organized, we felt we had a grasp of truth; now we challenge our previous assumptions. Yet ultimately, just as with mysticism, a feeling of unity results. We have gained a basic insight. However, this insight is never complete and is constantly expanded by the "experiential continuum."

Questions and Topics for Discussion

1. Why was Dewey so influential as a thinker?
2. What are his main works and why are they important?
3. Who were the thinkers that shaped Dewey's philosophy?
4. To Dewey philosophy was primarily methodology. Do you agree?
5. What is Dewey's concept of intelligence? What is your own view?
6. What does Dewey mean by "meliorism"?
7. Why did Dewey reject traditional liberal education?
8. Do you favor an emphasis upon liberal or vocational education? Defend your viewpoint.
9. What are the main tenets of progressive education? How does it differ from traditional education?
10. Why has progressive education been attacked so sharply in our time? How do you feel about progressive education?
11. How did Dewey try to change the curriculum?
12. What are the issues involved in the controversy between absolutism and relativism?
13. Do you believe in eternal truths? If so, why?
14. Is education ultimately a mystical process?
15. Evaluate the weaknesses and strengths of Dewey's philosophy.
16. Discuss the statement of John Dewey: "Theory is in the end . . . the most practical of all things."

Selected References

BRAMELD, T., *Toward a Reconstructed Philosophy of Education*, 1956.
CHILDS, J. L., *Education and the Philosophy of Experimentalism*, 1931.

DEWEY, J., *Art as Experience,* 1934.
———, *A Common Faith,* 1934.
———, *Democracy and Education,* 1916.
———, *Experience and Education,* 1938.
———, *How We Think,* 1933.
———, *Human Nature and Conduct,* 1922.
———, *My Pedagogic Creed,* 1910.
———, *Reconstruction in Philosophy,* 1920.
———, *The School and Society,* 1915.
HOOK, S., *John Dewey,* 1939.
KILPATRICK, W. H., *Foundations of Method,* 1925.
SCHILPP, P. A., (EDITOR),*The Philosophy of John Dewey,* 1939.
SCHOENCHEN, G., *The Activity School,* 1940.
WAHLQUIST, J. T., *Philosophy of American Education,* 1942.

VII. THE DILEMMAS OF AMERICAN EDUCATION

Education and Materialism

THE BASIC INADEQUACIES of American education are in part due to our faith in strength and bigness. In the realm of politics bigness and strength may be a sign of power; in the field of technology gigantic machines may aid progress; but in the field of education bigness alone is a doubtful good. Perhaps one of the best systems of education developed in Athens, a relatively small community, when measured by the standards of the large American cities. This does not imply that bigness necessarily is incompatible with a great system of education, rather it means that other factors may be more important in the development of education.

The nature of power

Real power, as Toynbee indicates in his *Study of History*, is not quantitative, but qualitative. The most successful nations have realized that the greatest challenge is not along material, but along spiritual lines. Real power involves a knowledge of limitations and a stress upon the things that matter most, instead of an idolization of the transitory and ephemeral aspects of life.

DILEMMAS OF AMERICAN EDUCATION

Technology and education

We should not underrate the importance of technology and the significance of a sound material foundation for education. In countries like Egypt, Iran, and Spain, where poverty prevails, education has made relatively little progress. The common people are so occupied with just existing and making a livelihood, that the life of reason is left to the few, who usually develop parasitical tendencies. Because of our technological proficiency we have developed scientific institutes like the California Institute of Technology and the Massachusetts Institute of Technology, which rank among the best in the world. Our buildings and our equipment, particularly in science, evoke the respect and often the envy of educators in other nations. But buildings are not the substance of education. We tend to forget that the *person* is the creator of education and that material goods and techniques are secondary. The temptations of education are the same as those of religion. In both fields the vitality of the spirit is often overlooked and instead the institution and the material surroundings are extolled; education, like religion, depends on a living inspiration, on an ever-deepening vision of the possibilities of man.

Abuses

Administrators, frequently, are too much concerned with buildings. In times of depression too many buildings may become a burden, and may result in even lower wages for the teacher. Football coaches in some universities receive more money than full professors. Certainly football has its place in the educative scheme, but it must never become the central concern of education. On the primary and secondary levels, classes frequently are still too large and the teacher has to instruct too many hours. The result is that his teaching will often be mediocre and utterly pedestrian.

Status of the teacher

A symptom of our materialistic philosophy is the tendency to underrate the importance of the teacher. In many communities the teacher occupies an inferior place. He ranks far lower than the banker, the physician, the lawyer, the corporation counsel, or even the motion picture star. Too many communities evaluate individuals by their possessions, by material success instead of their social and intellectual contributions.

Dangers of activism

Yet when we stress activity for the sake of activity, success for the sake of success, we succumb to unstable idols. We become mechanized human beings who have lost the joy of living and who lack genuine individuality. We succumb to slogans and are guided by social approval. We are afraid to develop uniqueness, for fear that our neighbor may disapprove. In a famous essay Emerson stated that

> society everywhere is in conspiracy against the manhood of every one of its members. Society is a joint-stock company, in which the members agree, for the better securing of his bread to each shareholder, to surrender the liberty and culture of the eater. The virtue most in request is conformity....[1]

The dilemmas of Babbitt

The tragedy of Babbitt, as Sinclair Lewis pointed out, is that he is a stereotyped human being. To him Zenith is the center of the world, the real-estate profession the greatest profession, his party the only party, and his religion the only genuine form of spirituality. He respects others when they are successful and despises them when they fail. This attitude creates a lonely human being, who is governed by his fears and suspicions rather than by positive drives.

Arrowsmith as an example

In adult life we all have to make decisions which may cost us our comfort, but save our *integrity*. Take the dilemma of Martin Arrowsmith in Lewis's great novel. Before the book ended, Martin had married a woman who had all the material advantages. Her ambition was to make a socialite out of Arrowsmith. But Arrow-

[1] Emerson, *Self-Reliance*.

smith was a scientist with a passion for research, and he cared little for social climbing and for small talk. She did not mind his scientific success and, in fact, was rather proud of him as long as he paid attention to her and her friends. When he spent more and more time in the laboratory she felt abused. Had she not provided Martin with material comfort? Had she not even built a laboratory for him? But Arrowsmith felt that he could not combine scientific investigation with an active social life, that his existence of ease was undermining his integrity; so he left her and started a new laboratory with another brilliant young scientist.

Very often in life we have to make a choice between material success and creativity. Martin Arrowsmith chose wisely, for he realized that he would have been dissatisfied the rest of his life, and would have been untrue to himself had he accepted an existence of luxury and comfort.

Weaknesses in Education

Trivial activities

In our educational institutions we often emphasize trivial activities. Occasionally, the school becomes merely a social center. Serious studies are neglected; intellectual depth is not required; co-eds are interested only in getting a man; the boys are interested mainly in joining social organizations. This does not imply that social adjustment should be neglected in education; on the contrary, it should be one of the central concerns of our schools. But when it becomes an end in itself and when it prepares the girl only for the life of a superficial socialite and when it makes a Babbitt out of the man, then education certainly has failed.

In education our most serious failings do not lie in our errors, but in the possibilities we do not explore, and in the potentialities we do not exhaust. Recently, an elderly lady came back to college. She said that she was not interested in a degree, she wantd to take "unessential" subjects like philosophy, literature, and anthropology. She had gone to college fifty years ago, but then she had taken snap courses, and she had regarded her professors as fossils who had no understanding of modern youth. At that time she had not let her courses interfere with her social life. She had read few of her textbooks and had done no outside reading. Later, she found out how much she had missed and how abysmally ignorant she was. Now, at last, she could go back to college and really receive an education. Her case illustrates what a mistake we make when we concentrate on immediacy and when we do not explore the full possibilities of education.

Athleticism

Athleticism often is a road-block to education. This does not mean that football should be eliminated from the curriculum or that "Bowl" games should be abandoned. Football, after all, lends color to American education. However, it should not become a Leviathan. When coaches tell their players that their studies are insignificant, and that their main task in college is to make the team and to win games, then education is being undermined. When schools apply different scholastic standards to athletes than to non-athletes, educators have the right to be indignant. When the desire to win becomes fanatical and fair play is neglected, football ceases to have a creative function in education. We should use athletics to imbue our students with a sense of honor, to develop a genuine team spirit and respect for our opponents. Some of the best teaching today is being done by coaches who are close to their players and who see the moral values of athletics.

Need for inspired teachers

The central function of our educational institutions is to develop brilliant teachers, but in many institutions teaching occupies a secondary place; instead, research is emphasized. Graduate schools turn out scholars who have qualifications for everything but teaching, and who regard the classroom as a secondary field of activity. The routine and the traditionalism of the academic profession lead to mediocre teaching. It is not uncommon for college instructors to use the same notes for ten years, and to tell the same jokes to every entering class. On the primary and secondary levels, less repetition prevails, but here not enough serious intellectual work is being done, and the teacher, often, does not keep up with his own field, or with the developments in general culture.

Need for integration

Education can become meaningful only when it transcends departmental lines, yet our theses and dissertations often deal with insignificant points of scholarship. In the liberal arts, specialization creates the archeologist of knowledge, who all his life studies the syntax of Chaucer; in the field of education, it creates a concern regarding blackboard administration, or how to teach the playing of handball.

Controversy about professional education

Liberal arts professors lately have specialized in attacking the schools of education. Certainly, education courses could have more content, and could be taught in a more imaginative manner; but the same attacks can be made against the liberal arts, which often stress the obsolete and the obsolescent and which frequently are dominated by grammarians. It should also be remembered that the science of education is of recent origin and hence tends toward extremes. But already the field of education, especially in the development of the new primary schools, has made a *major* contribution to American civilization.

At the University of London, the graduate school of education emphasizes history, sociology, and philosophy of education rather than methods courses. In the United States we often over-emphasize methodology and neglect philosophy. A better balance between the two fields is desirable, and a wider cultural background should be given to the future teacher. The more we develop an inter-departmental approach, the more education will prosper.

The Greek ideal

In Greece, the ideal of education was preparation for a leisure-time existence. Both Plato and Aristotle valued the life of contemplation and they had disdain for manual activity. To apply theories concretely would only disturb the sublime atmosphere of reason. Scientific experimentation thus was less important than understanding the principles of science. To know meant to be interested in ultimate purposes rather than in the control of nature. This attitude had both advantages and disadvantages. The advantage was that man's curiosity was stirred and his natural philosophic impulses were stimulated; the life of reason was treasured as never before in civilization. The disadvantage was that empirical science was neglected, and that mechanical inventions were overlooked.

American extremes

In the United States we have gone to the other extreme. We have added so many subjects to our educative process that often the liberal arts are lost, and facts rather than values are cultivated. The result is that a B.A. may mean anything; it may have been gained studying physical education or philosophy, home-economics or French. In the graduate school, we find serious gaps in the sciences, in philosophy, and above all, in general education.

The cash values of education are over-emphasized. Certainly, vocational efficiency is one of the main aims of education. But when the student is interested only in the shortest road to success, in getting through high school and college with minimum effort, when he neglects his esthetic interests—then he becomes a *specialized barbarian* who will be mainly concerned with the accumulation of material goods. The painter Kokoschka said to his students that he would not teach them how to paint, but how "to see again—a capacity which modern man has lost." Is it not our function, as teachers, to encourage a profound vision so that the student will become aware of his own possibilities and the potentialities of life around him?

Without sensitivity, without the power to experience deeply, we shall be slaves to convention. We shall all read the same best-sellers and applaud the same composers and listen to the same famous lecturers. Fashion will govern our existence, we will imitate our neighbor without becoming conscious of our own individuality.

Too often we leave the class-room utterly uninspired; we are bored by the lectures, bored by the discussions, and indignant about the tests. We read the text superficially and monotonously. Objective tests exaggerate the importance of specific knowledge. For example, in literature courses we are asked about Beowulf's relatives, or the behavior of the clerk of Oxford in *The Canterbury Tales*. Objective tests become ridiculous when they are in the true and false form. This way, empty memorization is encouraged and we usually forget the material after the final examination.

Facts and values

This does not imply that factual knowledge can be overlooked. Due regard for facts is imperative, if the sciences are to progress. But as Whitehead pointed out in *Science and the Modern World*, facts cannot be isolated from values; facts are related with each other and they form a continuum. What matters then ultimately in education are not facts, but relationships. When facts are illuminated by values, they become alive and concrete, and they tend to transform human existence.

Empiricism should not create an unpoetic philosophy. As Emerson said:

> Empirical science is apt to cloud the sight, and by the very knowledge of functions and processes to bereave the student of the manly contemplation of the whole. The savant becomes unpoetic. But the best read naturalist who lends an entire devout attention to truth, will see that there remains much to learn of his relation to the world; and that it is not to be learned by an addition or subtraction or other comparison of known quantities, but is arrived at by untaught sallies of the spirit, by a continued self-recovery, and by entire humility.[2]

The great teacher

The great teacher translates the ideal into the actual. Thus when he tells us about Spanish civilization we actually feel the presence of Don Quixote and Unamuno, and we actually see the paintings of El Greco. In studying French civilization we become skeptics with Montaigne, mystics with Pascal, satirists with Voltaire, lovers of

[2] Emerson, *Nature*.

nature with Chateaubriand, romantics with Rousseau, and existentialists with Jean Paul Sartre. In becoming acquainted with German civilization we become rationalists with Leibnitz, part of the enlightenment with Lessing, part of universal culture with Goethe, pietists with Francke, melancholy romantics with Heine, and humanists with Thomas Mann. Culture and education fail when they only appeal theoretically; they must fill every fibre of our being.

Mediocre results

Yet how many college graduates develop this type of emotional intensity? How many have a deep interest in culture? As *Middletown* and *Middletown in Transition* indicate, the businessman is too busy making money and getting ahead, while his wife takes only a dilettante interest in cultural affairs. She may listen to a lecture on Chinese Art, or French philosophy, or contemporary England; she may read the best sellers; but in most cases she is more interested in impressing her friends than in developing a genuine interest in the arts and sciences.

Decline of philosophy

Part of the weaknesses of contemporary education can be traced to the decline of philosophy. As we have become more and more specialized, philosophy has lost its place of eminence in the college curriculum. In the high schools the student is not even on speaking terms with philosophy. Often he graduates without developing a constructive view of life, and without being conscious of the values fundamental in civilization.

The philosopher bears part of the blame. Too often he merely imitates the scientists and regards his field as another form of specialization. Too often the student is merely introduced to the history of philosophy; too frequently philosophy becomes merely an exercise in classification so that the student knows that James was a pragmatist, Russell a realist, and Berkeley an idealist. In many cases, abstraction rather than concreteness is prized by the professional philosopher, who feels that incomprehensibility is a sign of intellectual stature.

DILEMMAS OF AMERICAN EDUCATION

The real mission of philosophy

The paramount need in philosophy is to develop individual rationality. It should be the most dramatic study of the curriculum, yet frequently it is the most boring, and completely unrelated to the life and interests of the student; it ought to explore the possibilities of the present, rather than the glories of a faded past; it ought to make ethical and educational problems central, rather than technical problems dealing with the theory of knowledge and the search for reality or unreality. Above all, philosophy ought to develop an affirmative view of life and society on the part of the student, so that he becomes an enlightened human being.

Questions and Topics for Discussion

1. How does technology aid the advancement of education?
2. What are the dangers of an activistic philosophy?
3. How did Emerson regard society? What is your own viewpoint?
4. What is the significance of Sinclair Lewis' *Arrowsmith*?
5. What are the most important choices we have to make in life? How can we make them more rationally?
6. What are the educational values of athletics?
7. Is education a science or an art?
8. Discuss the Greek ideal of education.
9. Evaluate the statement, "The cash values of education are overemphasized."
10. What is the relationship between facts and values?
11. How does the great teacher translate ideals into actuality?
12. Why is philosophy often such an anemic study?
13. Do you agree with Plato that there ought to be philosopher-kings?
14. How can the weaknesses of American education be overcome?
15. Compare and contrast American education with that of ancient Greece.
16. How are the inadequacies of American education related to the lags of American culture?
17. What is your own concept of power?
18. Illustrate the power of ideas in civilization.

THE FOUNDATIONS

Selected References

BAGLEY, W. C., *Educational Values*, 1911.
BESTOR, A., *The Restoration of Learning*, 1955.
BRAMELD, T. (EDITOR), *The Battle for Free Schools*, 1951.
CUNNINGHAM, W. F., *Pivotal Problems of Education*.
DAVIS, A., *Social-Class Influences upon Education*, 1948.
FLAUM, L. S., *The Activity High School*, 1953.
FRANK, J., *Fate and Freedom*, 1953.
FROMM, E., *The Sane Society*, 1955.
HUTCHINS, R. M., *The Conflict of Education in a Democratic Society*, 1953.
———, *The Higher Learning in America*, 1936.
LYND, R. S., *Knowledge for What?* 1939.
MacIVER, R. M., *Academic Freedom in Our Time*, 1955.
MAYER, F. and F. Ross, *Ethics and the Modern World*, 1952.
OTTO, M. C., *Things and Ideals*, 1924.
THAYER, V. T., *Public Education and its Crisis*, 1954.
TOYNBEE, A., *A Study of History*, (Abridgment by D. C. Somervell), 1947.
YAUCH, W. A., *Improving Human Relations in School Administration*, 1949.

PART TWO

Philosophy in Action

VIII. ASPIRATIONS AND CONDUCT

Idealism and Materialism

The importance of premises

THE STARTING POINT of an educational philosophy is all-important. Our premises often determine our conclusions, and our assumptions are the foundations upon which our theories rest. Once we accept certain premises we are committed to a course of action. It is foolish to argue with our opponents about their conclusions; it is much more profitable to clarify the postulates upon which their conclusions are constructed.

Two theories

The two main theories which govern philosophical thinking are idealism and materialism. Both have an ancient lineage. Idealism has been championed eloquently by great minds like Plato, Plotinus, Berkeley, Hegel, Emerson, Croce, and Radhakrishnan. Materialism included among its supporters thinkers like Hobbes, Holbach, Priestley, Cooper, Feuerbach, Marx, and Büchner.

Naturally, idealism and materialism have different forms. Thus we distinguish between the subjective idealism of Berkeley who believed that to be is to be perceived, and the absolute idealism of Hegel who felt that the real is rational and the rational real. Likewise we distinguish between mechanistic materialism as represented by Hobbes who reduced the world to matter and motion, and the dialectical materialism of Karl Marx who developed the theory of economic determinism and who believed that ultimately a classless society will emerge. Our interest, however, is not in the academic implications of idealism and materialism, but rather in their concrete meaning.

The view of idealism

"The World is My Idea" this is how Schopenhauer starts his great work: *Die Welt als Wille und Vorstellung*. This concept of the unreality of matter is the keynote to idealism. The idealist feels that reality has levels—the lowest is the material level; then comes the level of human experience; the highest level, however, is the mind. Subconsciously, the idealist is usually a Platonist. Did not Plato indicate that love moves from the physical body to the real, while the world of experience and nature are aspects of illusion?

The idealist suffers from metaphysical homesickness. The sensate level of existence only reminds him of the perfection of reality. Nature is a prelude to the mind; science is an overture to metaphysics. Man's body becomes a tenuous cover for man's soul. The imperfection of man points to the perfection of the Absolute—God. Thus the idealist frequently seeks for a Lost Horizon in Absolutism. He maintains that the very relatively of existence points to an eternal principle, which is exempt from change.

The idealistic concept of philosophy is eloquently represented by Shelley in "Mont Blanc":

> The everlasting universe of Things
> Flows through the Mind, and rolls its rapid waves,
> Now dark—now glittering—now reflecting gloom—
> Now lending splendour, where from secret springs
> The source of human thought its tribute brings
> Of waters,—with a sound but half its own,
> Such as a feeble brook will oft assume
> In the wild woods, among the mountains lone,
> Where waterfalls around it leap forever,
> Where woods and winds contend, and a vast river
> Over its rocks ceaselessly bursts and raves.

Educational implications

In education idealism leads to an emphasis upon formal instruction. This may have both negative and positive consequences. In Froebel, the founder of the modern kindergarten, idealism meant faith in the infinite possibilities of the individual, for are not God and man one? In Hegel, on the other hand, the individual student is subordinated to the authority of the teacher; freedom plays a secondary role compared with authority. This type of idealism leads to totalitarianism and thus plays a negative role in the history of education.

The idealist usually believes that education ought to be standard-centered. This is justified often by an appeal to the Socratic method. Did not Socrates maintain that truth is absolute, not relative? Do we not grow in proportion as we identify ourselves with an eternal principle of perfection? No real standards, according to idealists like Eucken and Harris, can be achieved without effort and discipline. Consequently, idealists feel that progressive educators have too sentimental a view of human nature and over-emphasize the importance of interest and individuality.

The philosophy of materialism

While the idealist usually is tender-minded, to use James's famous term, the materialist is tough-minded. To the materialist the objective universe has a reality of its own. He reduces the world to measurable quantities; he is interested not in abstract ideals, but in concrete reality. He asks the idealist: What evidence do you have that God exists? How do you know there is a soul? What justification can there be for faith in the spiritual nature of man?

The materialist sees man in his evolutionary setting, as part and parcel of nature. To understand man we should exclude sentimentality and vague aspirations and instead concentrate upon man's physiological nature. The faith of the materialist is ably represented by Pavlov, who contributed to physiological psychology by his studies of the saliva of the dog. In fact, behaviorism is a psychological version of philosophical materialism.

Notice how different the approach of materialism is from that of idealism. Materialism treasures objectivity, while idealism values subjectivity. Materialism denies existence of ultimate purposes, while idealism sees the world as a purposeful structure. Materialism uses physical science as the model for behavioral studies, while idealism uses religion as the ultimate model for the investigation of man, society, and nature.

Materialism and education

In education materialism fights a constant warfare with theology. The student is taught that this world is the only existence, that faith in religion represents a prescientific way of thinking, and that man can solve his problems only by excluding his wishes and desires from the universe. The materialist thus is interested in a reconstruction of education, for he feels that man cannot advance unless he abandons old superstitions and old beliefs, and unless he is guided by the quantitative method of science.

Towards synthesis

Some might say that perhaps a mixture of materialism and idealism may prove to be the best type of philosophy. Did not Descartes indicate that there are two realms: The realm of matter and that of mind? Do we not all feel the conflict between material and spiritual ideals?

Descartes' dualism is representative of the dilemmas of modern science. To Descartes the world of matter was subject to blind causality; it included our bodies and the entire sensate realm. The world of mind, on the other hand, was guided by purposes and ideals.

This separation of matter and mind had important consequences in education. The early modern educators like Sturm often thought that the body had to be disciplined if the kingdom of the mind were to be achieved. Classical languages were especially favored in the seventeenth and eighteenth centuries, for they were unrelated to modern times and their purity contrasted with the imperfection of science. The sharp division between the humanities and the sciences represents a modern version of Cartesianism. Often the humanities are studied as part of a teleological system of values leading to the worship of the past, while the sciences are viewed as part of a mechanistic world view. A genuine historical view of the humanities and the sciences would lead to a more unitary concept of knowledge, for both are subject to change and reconstruction and both are dependent upon the social environment in which they develop.

As Sarton points out, a scientific view of the humanities would recognize their basic methodological assumptions, while science studied in a historical context becomes not merely a quest for facts, but also a yearning for values which transcend immediacy.

The conclusion is that both materialism and idealism are one-sided world views. Materialism over-emphasizes the quantitative aspects of nature, while idealism stresses too much the purposeful structure of the universe. The basic question actually is not: What is the essence of the universe, rather what is the meaning of existence? Life thus is an existential, rather than an ontological, problem.

Objectivity and Subjectivity

Objectivity

Can philosophy be completely objective? Is the main function of philosophy descriptive? Can philosophy be completely scientific? These are fundamental questions with significant implications in education. For if objectivity and the scientific method are completely reliable guides in philosophy, they can likewise be applied to education.

Most philosophers claim that they are entirely objective, but as we study them historically we see their biases—subjective and social—and we realize how their systems represented their cultural environment. The sociology of knowledge, especially in Mannheim's *Ideology and Utopia* and Popper's *The Open Society and its Enemies,* indicates that ideological and philosophical systems have a social matrix and a social implication.

PHILOSOPHY IN ACTION

Aristotle

As a representative of objectivity we might point to Aristotle. But did not Aristotle express the Athenian view of life in his love of reason? Did he not express Athenian biases in his disdain for barbarians and in his justification for slavery? Did he not represent the classical view of education in his opposition to vocational education?

Spinoza

In more modern times we might cite Spinoza as an example of a disinterested attitude in philosophy. Spinoza tried to give a mathematical basis to thinking. The same certainty which guides geometry was to dominate philosophic inquiry. Spinoza represents the bias of the mathematician who sees more order and regularity in nature than actually exists. Ultimately, is not mathematics a prelude to Spinoza's supreme value—the intellectual love of God? Spinoza believed that nature was determined by rigorous laws and thus transcended the desires of man. Did this not express the deterministic spirit of seventeenth century science, especially of the Newtonian system?

Logical empiricism

In our own time logical empiricism claims complete objectivity. Value judgments are excluded from the realm of philosophy. Reichenbach, representative of this movement, in *The Rise of Scientific Philosophy* shows how logical analysis can clarify philosophic problems. As for ethical and educational problems they usually rest upon verbal and emotional fallacies. I told Reichenbach one time that my main interest was the philosophy of education. He replied: "There is no philosophy of education!" To him education represented unverifiable value judgments. This approach narrows the domain of philosophy and would make it a mathematician's playground. But the great problems of philosophy go beyond verbal and logical meanings; they are social and cultural problems which may decide the future and destiny of man.

Science and objectivity

For the scientist, objectivity is indispensable. Unless he is guided by the logic of events, his conclusions will be fragmentary and full of error. Personal desires and personal aims thus are excluded from the domain of science. In philosophy, on the other hand, the ego of the thinker cannot be excluded. Even when he pretends to be completely objective his biases will appear. Take Descartes as an example: He claimed that his doubt would be complete; he would even doubt his own existence, yet all the time he was adhering to the canons of the church and to the moral laws of France. Complete doubt, like complete objectivity, is a pretension in philosophy.

Does this establish a dualism between objectivity and subjectivity? Will there be an inevitable conflict between our subjective desires and the disinterested, objective scientific method? The answer is in the negative. As Planck points out in *Der Kausalbegriff in der Physik,* scientific prediction depends on the *person* who carries on scientific investigation. Planck cites the example of weather forecasting. Is it not all-important that an expert would predict the weather, a trained meteorologist rather than an amateur? Personality thus enters the scientific realm. Novelty in science involves a gamble, as the life of Galileo indicates. Science like philosophy represents "progressive development," and both rest upon a faith in the rational order of nature.

Education and science

In education all this means that there can be no artificial division between subjectivity and objectivity. The teacher is not the apostle of Truth but a struggling, limited, human being engaged in *seeking* truth. The personal implications of his teaching may be more important than the subject matter which he conveys to the class. If the teacher over-emphasizes subjectivity, his classes will lack scientific precision; on the other hand, if he is too objective, his classes may lack vitality.

For education, it should be remembered, is more an art than a science. Scientific techniques, especially testing, are invaluable in education. We all owe a great debt to such pioneers as Thorndike, Terman, Thurstone, Rorschach, and many others. But education is concerned with a temporal process; the most important values are often intangible and cannot be measured. *Valuation serves only as a prelude to evaluation.* The insight of the great educator is like the insight of the great artist. Both have a sense of the unity of life; both try to overcome the gulf between objectivity and subjectivity; both search for meanings, which go beyond routine existence; both are interested in ideal possibilities.

Still we should never underestimate the importance of the scientific method in education. Without it vagueness results; without it no valid generalizations can be established. Whitehead believed that education moves from the stage of romance to that of precision, and finally to that of generalization. The neglect of science, especially of mathematics, would create an atmosphere of vague romanticism. *Science thus represents the conscience of education.*

Basic Problems of Human Existence

Philosophy and maturity

Philosophic inquiry has an animistic basis. The child at first sees himself in objects; nature to him is a friendly force; he personifies objects. But as we achieve maturity, we see nature as a force apart from man. Thus we realize that the universe goes on without our existence, that we are living on a small planet in a vast astronomical universe in which time is measured by light years. We realize that man is insignificant, perhaps a minor incident in cosmic evolution.

How should we react? What should be our attitude? We can live a life of noble despair. We can realize that our pilgrimage has no destiny and no final goal, that all our desires and all our hopes are only temporary opiates, that the universe is austere and unconscious of our existence. Thus we can look upon life as a brief interlude of unconsciousness, illuminated by the scientific method and the stimulations of reason; but our existence has no real meaning. This is the philosophy expressed so eloquently by Bertrand Russell in *A Free Man's Worship.*

We can react in the opposite way like Pascal in his *Pensées.* Pascal, like Russell, was a profound mathematician, but to Pascal, mathematics was only the overture to theology; reason, therefore, was subordinated to faith. Has not the heart reasons that reason does not know? Man may be nothingness, but he knows that he is nothingness and hence is superior to the universe. By thought, according to Pascal, *man controls life. By faith man conquers life.*

The conclusion of Pascal is a call to faith:

"What shall become of you, then, O man! You who search out what is your true condition by your natural reason? . . . Know, then, haughty man, what a paradox you are to yourself. Humble yourself, impotent reason; be silent, imbecile nature; learn that man infinitely surpasses man, and hear from your master your true condition, which you are ignorant of. Listen to God."[1]

We can evade the issue of meaning in the universe by saying, with James, that life is neither good nor bad; that, however, it can be improved. To James, the world was as incomplete as an American real estate project. By right effort and right action, man could aid in the victory of good over evil. In some ways, action was the ultimate opiate to William James.

The existential problems

Still we cannot escape certain existential problems, for man is a *meaning-seeking* creature. We are thrust into existence at a certain point in history. We play our part and then we disappear in the stream of time. In the *Upanishads* we read that the eternal self is the same as the objective self, and that the goal of life is absorption in a world principle: Moksha, in which all separateness disappears. In Buddhism likewise the goal is Nirvana—a nothingness which implies the obliteration of the self.

In my own philosophy selfhood has a different meaning. The goal of life and education is the achievement of genuine selfhood. But the self remains incomplete, often a mere fragment. As Hume

[1] *Pensées,* chap. X, Sec. 1.

pointed out, the self may be only a bundle of perceptions; and Kant was right when he maintained that we do not perceive the real self, only the empirical self, that no direct conception of the self can be achieved.

Essentials

To live meaningfully—and this implies also to teach meaningfully—we should reduce life to certain *essentials*. The test of the great individual lies in the things he can abandon, in the material goods which are expendable. Yet the direction of material civilization lies towards conspicuous consumption. Every day advertising creates new wants and new desires, from automobiles to toothpastes, from new television sets to new jet planes. The hope is that the satisfaction of these desires will create happiness, but often the contrary results can be observed. Desires multiply in a Malthusian ratio. Neuroses, rather than permanent satisfactions, are created.

The dissatisfaction is especially great when no possible means exist to satisfy desires. Take Bigger, the main character in Wright's *Native Son:* He goes to motion pictures and sees a glamorous world of butlers, swimming pools, trips to Bermuda, Cadillacs, exciting women, and here he lives in a slum section, which is incredibly ugly. How can he reconcile the two worlds? How can he achieve a balanced philosophy of life? He fails, and in the end he commits a terrible crime. Wright wonders whether Bigger, the outsider, the pariah, is to be blamed or whether society is guilty.

Many times in our existence we experience aloneness. It may be a temporary mood or a passing sensation. It may occur when we are engaged in activities or when we are idle, when no one is with us, or when we are in a crowd. This aloneness is a symbol of our fragmentary condition. We realize that perhaps on the most important occasions in life, in sickness, and in death, no one can feel with us, no one can be completely part of us. Some existentialists, like Sartre and Heidegger, believe that this sense of dread indicates the need for self-reliance leading to the autonomy of the self. Does not man create his own values? Cannot man become free by severing his ties from society and by realizing that the universe has no meaning? To the existentialists a preliminary skepticism regarding ultimate values is the foundation for man's emancipation.

The need for hope

But man *needs* hope to live meaningfully. Our hopes and expectations may be frustrated and crushed by disasters; still, having hoped and anticipated, our existence becomes more poetic and more endurable. Religion, philosophy, art, science, and education are all forms of hope. Religion is the yearning for cosmic comradeship; philosophy is the quest for a life governed by reason; art is the yearning for significant form by which the moment is eternalized; science is faith that experimentation can control both objective and subjective phenomena; and education represents the hope that man is something more than an animal, that he can solve his problems by the use of intelligence, not by the use of force.

A romantic view of education

I believe, then, in a *romantic* concept of education. Education must mold feelings and emotions just as much as reason. The educator should direct his view not to the past but to the day after tomorrow. Pessimism in education becomes a self-defeating process.

The great educators of the past were usually men of hope. When Comenius outlined a universal system of education, his contemporaries looked upon him with scorn. When Pestalozzi started to educate the children of the poor, his contemporaries regarded this as a wasteful and utopian procedure. When Froebel started the kindergarten, conservative educators looked upon him as an impractical sentimentalist. When Dewey conducted an experimental school with progressive tendencies at the University of Chicago, traditionally minded teachers felt that his system of education could not possibly succeed. But the traditionalists usually have been wrong, because they had had too low and sober an opinion of man. They have not seen the creative possibilities of humanity.

The real teacher is never overwhelmed by the despair of the present. He is transformed by his hopes. In the most somber situation he preserves an attitude of expectancy. Has he not seen creativity realized in the classroom? Has he not seen a "new birth" and the emergence of a new individual?

Hope implies self-reliance; as Marcel said, "It belongs to those who have not been hardened by life." How can we explore the capacities of others if we are unconscious of our own potentialities? Constant growth on the part of the teacher is just as important as unending growth on the part of the student. Teaching implies an overflowing of spiritual and intellectual energy. It can almost be compared to the emanation of Reason and the World-Soul in the system of Plotinus. Teaching thus is the communication of ideals to the realm of experience. *Teaching is idealism in action.*

Questions and Topics for Discussion

1. Why are premises so important in educational philosophy?
2. What is the significance of philosophical idealism?
3. What is the importance of philosophical materialism?
4. Evaluate the statement, "The world is my idea."
5. What are the educational implications of idealism?
6. Do you feel that education ought to be standard-centered? Explain your answer.
7. Why is the idealist usually tender-minded? Are you tender-minded or tough-minded?
8. What are the educational implications of materialism?
9. Explain the statement: "Life is an existential, rather than an ontological problem."
10. Can philosophy be completely objective?
11. Discuss the statement of Horne: "Mind is the highest type of reality."
12. What is the relationship between objectivity and subjectivity?
13. Explain the statement: "Valuation only serves as a prelude to evaluation."
14. Why does science "represent the conscience of education?"
15. How can we reduce life to certain essentials?
16. Why are the great educators men of hope?
17. Make a list of the educators who in your opinion have most contributed to human progress. What were their main ideals?

ASPIRATIONS AND CONDUCT

Selected References

BARRETT, C., *Philosophy*, 1925.
BECK, L. W., *Philosophical Inquiry*, 1952.
BRAMELD, T., *Patterns of Educational Philosophy*, 1950.
BROWN, F. J., *Educational Sociology*, 1947.
HOCKING, W. E., *Types of Philosophy*, 1939.
HORNE, H. H., *Philosophy of Education*, 1927.
———, *The Democratic Philosophy of Education*, 1935.
JOAD, C. E. M., *Philosophy*, 1944.
KNODE, J. C., *Foundations of an American Philosophy of Education*, 1942.
LODGE, R. C., *Philosophy of Education*, 1947.
———, *The Questioning Mind*, 1937.
MEIKLEJOHN, A., *Education between Two Worlds*, 1942.
PASCAL, B., *Thoughts*, 1670.
REICHENBACH, H., *The Rise of Scientific Philosophy*, 1951.
ROSS, J. S., *Groundwork of Educational Theory*, 1942.
RUSK, R. R., *Philosophic Bases of Education*, 1929.
TONNE, H. A., *A Realistic Philosophy of Education*, 1942.
WHITEHEAD, A. N., *Aims of Education*, 1929.
———, *Science and the Modern World*, 1925.
WILD, J. (EDITOR), *The Return to Reason*, 1953.

IX. THE SPARK OF CREATIVITY

Puritanism and Hedonism

Biology and poetry

The foundation of education is biology; the end of education is poetry. This statement implies that we must view man as a biological organism, yet man is something more than an animal; he is not defined merely by his history or by his naturalistic background, for he is a creator of mythology, a builder of culture which has not merely a factual significance, but also a symbolic and poetic meaning.

Lags of traditional education

We can never minimize the pleasure element in life. We prize the activities which give us enjoyment, and we avoid the activities which we find to be painful. Traditional education often overlooked the pleasure principle. Work and play were sharply separated. The disciplinary value of subjects was stressed. Memorization was emphasized by the teacher. Punishment was used in its most severe forms, including flogging of wayward students. The results in most cases were deplorable. Students were taught how to memorize books, but not how to think for themselves. They developed an antagonism towards education, especially towards teachers.

St. Augustine

This authoritarian view of education was the result of a pessimistic philosophy of life. Already, in St. Augustine, we have the idea that children are naturally depraved. St. Augustine, in his *Confessions*, tells about the lies he told in school, the apples he stole, and his wayward life at the University of Carthage. He believed that greed and lust start with the baby at the mother's breast. To him, original sin was the prominent feature of human existence. It was symbolized by man's pride and his fall from the bliss of the garden of Eden.

Since man, according to St. Augustine, naturally tended toward evil, education had to use disciplinary methods. The child was to abandon his natural desires; he was to be taught that the ideal existence is that of the celibate, who shuns the pleasures of the world. Education outside of the Church in reason and philosophy would be a failure, for man could not be saved by reason, only by faith in God and by membership in the Church.

Puritanism

This somber view of man was perpetuated by many Reformation leaders, although they rebelled against the Church. Thus Calvin, like Augustine, believed in predestination and emphasized the original depravity of man.

The puritanical concept of life and education has never completely disappeared from the Western World, especially in the United States. It is responsible for the tabus in many institutions of learning. In excessively puritanical communities the teacher is subjected to a host of restrictions with the result that the most vital instructors often leave the profession. The belief is that the teacher ought to be saintly and set an example in purity. No human weaknesses are tolerated! No sins are forgiven! Such rigorous standards encourage hypocrisy among teachers and laymen alike.

Results

Occasionally, the agonized puritan conscience will be stirred, and crusades will be undertaken to eliminate minor social evils. Usually the results are doubtful. The excesses of puritanism, to a great extent, were responsible for the creation of the "Lost Generation" in the 1920's—a generation which lived in a moral wasteland, which accepted no moral obligations and which had no social concern. This generation, as Lippmann indicates in *A Preface to Morals*, was prematurely sophisticated and delighted in debunking the accepted standards of civilization.

The solution to puritan excesses does not lie in a life of hedonism. Unrestrained pleasure may lead to satiation and ultimately, disgust. The hedonist often is an inverted puritan. Like the puritan, he has a somber view of man and has little faith in the future of humanity.

Education and Progress

Man's goodness

My own view of man's educational possibilities is just the opposite. If anything, I would stress the goodness of man, but not in the sense of Rousseau. Rousseau thought that man's natural instincts were excellent, but that everywhere they were corrupted by society. Reason itself paralyzed man. In a famous phrase he said, "L'homme qui médite est dépravé." He spoke about the nobility of savage life and contrasted this existence with the degradation and decadence of modern civilization.

The goodness of man, however, does not lie in the state of nature, but in the possibility of civilization. Man's mind is plastic, he can be changed, molded, and motivated. Man's goodness lies in his educability.

Still, education if it is to be successful should recognize the physical nature of man. Certain needs such as the desire for material sustenance and sexual expression must be satisfied. Social psychological needs, as outlined by Thomas, the need for security, response, new experience, and recognition likewise are important. Nor can we overlook the need for *significance* in the life of the individual. Kropotkin already pointed out that cooperation plays an important part in human culture. The needs of man are almost limitless, and they expand as civilization advances. Just compare the average material demands of the American family today with the needs of the American family in colonial times!

The significance of Epicureanism

One of the foremost needs, and one especially important in education, is the need for enjoyment. Epicurus was one of the sanest philosophers of all time, for he recognized the significance of the pleasure principle. Pleasure to Epicurus involved a life of calmness and security in a beautiful garden, surrounded by delightful friends. Epicurus, unlike Plato, thought that education should be for all, not for the few. He believed that it is never too late or too early for education. He taught young and old, the foolish and the wise. Like Kilpatrick he used the discussion method.

Unlike some of his disciples, Epicurus made it quite clear that the highest pleasure is the pleasure of the mind. Here again we can benefit from his insight. Pleasure should never be defined in a narrow context or be equated with mere physical sensation or mere activity. The fruitfulness of pleasure lies in its capacity to make us more sensitive and human, and to develop genuine concern for others.

Education as a way of life

Schools in the future should become more lifelike. In this respect they can learn from the motion picture industry and from television. The teacher should always ask himself: "How enjoyable is my instruction to the student? Will he continue to pursue his studies after school? Has education become part of his way of life?"

In the past we have developed a rather *ascetic* view of the intellectual life. This may be an echo of our medieval heritage when education was extremely authoritarian and handled in many cases by monks and nuns. We shall never overcome the distance between school and society unless we demonstrate the enjoyable nature of the intellectual life. This implies far less pompousness, far less conceit, far less concern with terminology on the part of the teacher.

In building the school more as a community center and in making education more pleasant, progressive teachers have made a major contribution to civilization. Their opponents have frequently criticized progressive educators for making school life *too* enjoyable. The criticism is unjustified, for unless education becomes a way of life, it is mere pretense. However, it should be remembered that mere pleasure is not enough, just as mere activity is not sufficient. The development of our rational capacities is just as significant as the creation of an enjoyable pattern of life.

Philosophy and life

One reason why philosophy does not prosper in our civilization lies in the fact that our approach to it is too pedantic. How different was the approach of the Athenians who looked upon the life of reason as a spontaneous activity! Philosophy was discussed at the dinner table. Did not Socrates philosophize during banquets which often lasted all night? Did not the Athenians look upon philosophy as systematic and profound conversation?

Montaigne asked how Socrates would be received in the Renaissance.

If at this moment anything of the same kind [as Socrates' teaching] should appear there are few men who would appreciate it. We can perceive no beauties that are not emphasized, puffed out and inflated by artificial means. Those which glide in their native purity and simplicity escape so gross a sight as ours. . . . Socrates makes his mind move with a natural and familiar motion. A peasant says this, a woman says that. . . . His inductions and similes are drawn from the most common and best-known activities of men; everybody understands him. Under so humble a form, we should never have recognized the nobility and splendor of his admirable ideas; we who think all ideas mean and shallow that are not set off by learning.[1]

Creativity

Obstacles to creativity

Potentially, the spark of creativity is in all individuals. The mystics speak of the light of God. The Society of Friends believes that His light is in all, regardless of race and nationality.

[1] *Essays*, III, 12, 509.

THE SPARK OF CREATIVITY

Creativity starts with self-definition, with a determination to live profoundly. Just as the great writer seeks for a multitude of experiences, so the teacher needs constant stimulation and constant inspiration. Creativity frequently is killed by routine, repetition, and monotony. Many graduate students enter the teaching profession with high hopes and after a few years become disillusioned. Often it is the fault of the administration; occasionally it is low pay; sometimes it is the discipline problem; sometimes it is over-work; occasionally it is the pressure of the community. In almost all cases teaching has ceased to be an adventure, and instead it has become a form of drudgery.

There is too much activity in our teaching professions, too many committee meetings, too many community functions, too many forms to be filled out, too many examinations to be corrected. *How can the teacher be creative when he is over-worked and living the life of organized futility?* Meditation may give the teacher new reservoirs of moral and spiritual power. Occasionally we have to withdraw from activity to find the meaning of life and education. The pressure of immediate events is so great that we lose perspective, we identify ourselves too closely with our environment. We take both our defeats and our victories too seriously. *Should not real education give humility to the strong and hope to the weak?*

Withdrawal

As we withdraw occasionally from the center of life we can ask more fundamental questions. Thus Jesus pondered about his destiny in the wilderness; thus Buddha sought in the desert for enlightenment; thus Walden became the symbol of retreat for Thoreau. Gandhi confessed he was most free when he was in jail, for now he had time to think, and meditate, and read books he had always wanted to peruse.

In solitude we are able to overcome the idols of the tribe. When we return to our work we approach it with freshness and vitality, like a stranger returning to his home after a long trip; we are more patient with our students and more conscious of the possibilities of novelty.

PHILOSOPHY IN ACTION

Teachers and creativity

We make the mistake to see often only the superficial aspects of our students: For example, how well-behaved they are; how well they pass the examination. We forget what Kilpatrick calls concomitant learnings, the implications and attitudes which arise from the educative situation. The teacher must be constantly concerned with the potentialities of his students. Perhaps in his class there may be another Kant, or another Pasteur, or another Van Gogh, or another Hemingway. Thus the teacher should be conscious of talent and nourish it. If he takes extra time and extra patience with a bright student, society will benefit and a greater culture may result.

The point is not that creativity is confined to the few; rather that all are in some degree capable of creative work. We may not be gifted in science, but we may have talents in art; we may not be very intelligent, but we may have a capacity for love. Creativity in human relationships is not to be underestimated, for is not the relationship between man and society the fundamental basis of culture? *The great tragedy of life is not merely economic want, but spiritual and intellectual poverty.* Here teachers have a vast responsibility. In the most crucial years, they can influence students in a positive or negative way. An extra word of praise and encouragement, a sign of personal interest, may mean the difference between success and failure, a constructive or a destructive life on the part of the student.

Perhaps some may feel that the role of the teacher is being overemphasized. After all, it might be stated that the great lessons are not learned in the schoolroom, but after graduation. Still, modern life, as Riesman points out, is basically lonely—the individual often lives an anonymous existence. Frequently, he goes to a large school, attends large classes, graduates with hundreds, attends a big state university with perhaps 15,000 students, receives a diploma with 3,000 students or more, and later works for a large business organization. He lives in a big city and when he goes to work, he may ride the subway with thousands of other commuters. He probably will be buried in a large cemetery which features modern advertising methods. How many will be concerned with him? His immediate family and a few friends, not many more. Hence the personal interest of the teacher will be extremely significant.

The nature of creativity

The teacher should realize that the mind is active, not inert. As Whitehead points out, no ideas are more obsolete than inert ideas. In genuine activity we live the life of adventure; we do not know the end of our pilgrimage; we discover aspects of our character which we thought never existed before. Sinclair Lewis, in writing *Babbitt,* confessed that the characters became so real that they seemed closer to him than his immediate family. To-day "Babbitt" has become part of our vocabularly. The work of art, of creativity, may be more real than nature itself.

Creative thinking

In creative thinking the preparatory stage is especially important. Before greatness can be achieved, fundamentals have to be acquired. There is no substitute for hard work and perspiration. The ability to concentrate, to exclude irrelevant details characterizes creative work both in the arts and the sciences.

Education is inadequate when it fails to develop intensity. Undoubtedly, the whole child should be educated, but actually, we know this is an ideal seldom achieved in practice. Relatively few students combine intellectual greatness with athletic competence; few athletes, on the other hand, tend to be Phi Beta Kappa's. The more we are interested in one activity, the more it tends to dominate our thinking and our view of life.

Intensity of concern develops a reason for existence and permanent interests. If a writer really wants to make a permanent contribution, literature has to become his great passion; if a painter wants to create an immortal portrait, he should dedicate himself to his art; if a scientist really desires to become great, he has to develop almost a religious fervor for research; if a teacher wants to become unforgettable, he must have almost a *missionary* faith in education. The life of creativity thus demands total loyalty.

Once the spark seizes hold of us, our life is changed radically.

PHILOSOPHY IN ACTION

Somerest Maugham in *Razor's Edge* portrays a young American who at first was rather conventional. Larry was engaged to a wealthy girl, apparently he was destined for a business career. Yet he abandoned all of this, and instead, he went to Paris to study at the Sorbonne, and later he went to India to explore the ways of Oriental mysticism. He even worked in coal mines. Few of his friends understood him; they thought that he was highly eccentric; that he should find a girl and settle down. But Larry was seeking an intense meaning in life, and ultimately he became a writer.

The spark of creativity does not seize us automatically. Occasionally a soul-shaking event takes place to change the pattern of our existence. In the case of Larry, he had participated in World War I and one of his best friends had been killed. Before that event, death had been a vague possibility; now it became dramatically real, and convinced him of the vanity of most of his endeavors. Larry wanted to leave a mark, he wanted to live fully so that at the end of his life he would have no regrets.

Creativity, then, involves a choice. We decide that we want more than a vegetative existence, that we desire more than material rewards; we strive for some principle of unity; what it is we do not know exactly.

The creative life involves stress and storm. Success seldom comes at once. Failure may discourage us; error may bewilder us; like Nietzsche, we may be tortured by physical illness. In his mature years, Nietzsche, was tormented by headaches and insomnia. Every page he wrote drained him of some of the remainder of his physical strength. At night he would pace the floor, for sleep would not come to him.

The artist often feels that a demonic power is within him. His subject will not let him rest; he has to express what is inside regardless of the cost. Creativity may involve social censorship, even loss of position, still this does not discourage the genuine artist.

Final stage

The final stage of creativity involves almost a mystic union. The stress of creation is followed by a strange calmness. For a few moments life is seen under the aspects of eternity; for a few moments the distance between ego and non-ego, between mind and nature, disappears.

We feel like Wordsworth in the first book of *The Prelude*:

> Ye Presence of Nature in the sky
> And on the earth! Ye Visions of the hills!
> And Souls of lonely places! can I think
> A vulgar hope was yours when ye employed
> Such ministry, when ye through many a year
> Haunting me thus among my boyish sports,
> On caves and trees, upon the woods and hills,
> Impressed upon all forms the characters
> Of danger or desire; and thus did make
> The surface of the universal earth,
> With triumph and delight, with hope and fear,
> Work like a sea? . . .

But this sense of the unity of life and nature is only a brief illumination; ultimately we return to the realm of actuality.

Education as a Creative Process

The active mind

What are the implications of the creative process for education? In the first place, it ought to indicate to the psychologists of education that the mind has not merely a *reacting* function as the behaviorists maintained, rather that the mind is *creative* and is constantly engaged in the reconstruction of its environment.

A new logic

In the second place, through the study of creativity we ought to pay more attention to the *way* our mind works, the way we think, and the way we achieve conclusions. Logicians in the past have been too concerned with the forms of thinking. Certainly, we owe a debt to logicians like Russell and Whitehead who have seen the equivalence of logic and mathematics; to-day however we need a closer connection between psychology and logic. In this field, Dewey, especially in *How We Think* and *Logic*, has been a pioneer. For

Dewey looks upon logic as the theory of inquiry, not as a guide to certainty or formal truth. To Dewey, thinking is problematic and involves hypothetical postulation, verification, and tentative conclusions.

If we believe that education involves training in the use of intelligence then we should know more about the contents of our thinking process. Too often we speak of the mind as an entity, instead of seeing its social matrix and its temporal and spatial connections. A study of James Harvey Robinson's *Mind in the Making* would be profitable for all those interested in the problems of the teaching profession, because it indicates how the mind depends on evolutionary features.

Desire and techniques

In the third place, more knowledge of the creative process will combine *factual precision with valuational boldness in education*. The creative process, according to Catherine Patrick, involves (1) the desire to create, (2) flashes of insight, (3) an attempt to express the mood or idea, and (4) the dynamic drive leading to the execution of the art of creation. Patrick points out that desire for creation is not enough, technique and mastery of basic skills are just as significant.[2]

Importance of imagination

In the fourth place, the study of creativity ought to convince us of the importance of imagination in education. Teachers tend to be too factual and too sober in their methods of instruction. Children often are much more imaginative than their elders. The works of art of children indicate frequently an amazing emotional horizon. The teacher should remember that correspondence to physical objects is not the sole aim of art; that art, like education, has pluralistic objectives. Esthetic imagination thus deepens experience and brings out the poetic possibilities of man.

---

[2] Cf. C. Patrick, "Creative Thoughts in Poets," *Archives of Psychology*, 178 (1935); and "Creative Thought in Artists," *Journal of Psychology*, Vol. IV, (1937), 35-73.

THE SPARK OF CREATIVITY

Questions and Topics for Discussion

1. Why is the pleasure element so important in life?
2. Compare the views of St. Augustine with those of the "lost generation" of the 1920's.
3. What are the weaknesses of an unrestrained pleasure philosophy?
4. Do you believe that man is basically good or bad? Explain.
5. Why is Epicurus so important from an educational standpoint?
6. Evaluate the statement: "Creativity starts with self-definition."
7. Why is meditation important in education?
8. Is creativity confined to the few? Justify your answer.
9. Discuss the ways creativity can be stimulated in the classroom: (a) on the primary level, (b) in high-school, (c) in college.
10. What are the traits of creative thinking?
11. Discuss the statement: "The life of creativity demands total loyalty."
12. What is the significance of Maugham's, *Razor's Edge?*
13. Why does the creative life involve stress and storm?
14. How can teachers become more creative in their approach to student problems?
15. Why do students lose occasionally their creative spark?
16. Discuss the statement: "The foundation of education is biology; the end of education is poetry."

Selected References

BAGLEY, W.C., *The Educative Process,* 1926.
BERGSON, H., *Creative Evolution,* 1912.
BLACK, M., *Critical Thinking,* 1952.
DEWEY, J., *How We Think,* 1933.
GHISELIN, B., *The Creative Process,* 1952.
HAYAKAWA, S., *Language in Thought and Action,* 1949.
HOOK, S., *Education for Modern Man,* 1946.
JONES, W. T., *A History of Western Philosophy,* 1952.
LANGER, S., *Philosophy in a New Key,* 1942.
————, *Feeling and Form,* 1953.
LOWENFELD, V., *Creative and Mental Growth,* 1949.
MALRAUX, A., *The Voices of Silence,* 1953.
MUMFORD, L., *The Conduct of Life,* 1951.
RADER, M. M., *A Modern Book of Esthetics,* 1952.
RAUP, R. B., K. D. BENNE, and G. AXTELLE, and B. O. SMITH, *The Improvement of Practical Intelligence,* 1950.

PHILOSOPHY IN ACTION

Santayana, G., *The Sense of Beauty*, 1896.
Sherrington, C., *Man and his Nature*, 1941.
Tsanoff, R., *The Moral Ideals of our Civilization*, 1942.
Welsh, M. G., *The Social Philosophy of Christian Education*, 1936.

X. THE IDEALS OF TEACHING

The Mission of the Teacher

EDUCATION is the reflection of the great teacher. For example, Athenian education reflected the impact of Socrates; medieval education was powerfully influenced by Aquinas; and modern American education has been shaped to a great extent by the ideals of James and Dewey.

This does not imply that the classroom is all-important. We should remember that one of the greatest teachers of all time—Socrates—used the market place, and appealed to all types of people; while Jesus taught under the open sky by the use of allegory and symbolism, and appealed to the lowly more than to the formally educated.

In education, as in religion, formal knowledge may be a hindrance and may develop the spirit of the Pharisee. The earmarks of the Pharisee are his smugness and self-righteousness. He is certain that he will be saved; he is proud of his virtues; he is an exhibitionist who constantly advertises his perfection. To him the superficial aspects of faith are the real substance of religion; law thus becomes a substitute for spirituality, and conformity the substitute for inwardness. Many educators likewise stress the knowledge of facts instead of wisdom, and they are so imbued by a sense of their own importance and by pride in their own knowledge that they forget the meaning of education. They become dogmatic and arrogant, and they regard all those who differ as ignorant fools; when they teach, their classroom becomes a platform for their biases; the student is not regarded as an individual, but merely as an object to be *indoctrinated*.

Tradition vs experimentation

Bergson, in *The Two Sources of Religion and Morality,* indicates that in religion a constant struggle rages between those who believe in a formalistic and traditional type of worship, and those who believe in the unending stimulation of the spirit. This essentially is the struggle between the priest and the prophet, between those who base religion on laws and commandments, and those who stress love and compassion.

In education the same struggle can be observed. On the one hand, we find the force of tradition, the view that education should only preserve the past, and *not* ask challenging questions; on the other hand, we find the view that education is a constant exploration of the inexhaustible possibilities and varieties of life.

Socrates

When Socrates was tried by the Athenians, one of the charges was that he was corrupting the youth of Athens. This may sound strange to modern observers because we regard Socrates as one of the most moral thinkers of mankind. His real crime in the eyes of his contemporaries was that he made young people think and that he challenged the biases of his environment. He believed that he was the conscience of Athens and that a divine voice was guiding him. Were not truth and righteousness more important than life itself?

Socrates realized that as a teacher he had to take a stand. He could have escaped the death penalty by appealing for mercy and by trying to sway the emotions of the Athenians. But this was not his way since he believed in the life of reason, and he lived up to his ideals till the last moments of his life. In Socrates, we find a correspondence between ideal and action. Perhaps we are impressed as much by his personality, by his daring stand, as by his words.

The greatness of Socrates was in his emphasis upon questions. He asked his contemporaries: What is justice? What is virtue? What is truth? What is wisdom? He found that those who had a reputation for wisdom were often the most ignorant, for they were guided by conceit and arrogance, and they did not challenge their basic assumptions. He visited the outstanding statesmen of his time and he found they were guided by custom; the poets trusted the force of inspiration; the scientists were interested merely in the problem of substance; while some of the Sophists would sell their services to the highest bidder and would teach any doctrine, provided it was financially profitable to them.

Socrates believed in the moral function of the teacher. *Not knowledge, but wisdom, not success, but righteousness were to govern philosophy and education.* Naturally, his doctrines were upsetting. His fellow teachers were envious of his success, the common people looked upon him as a follower of aristocracy, the aristocratic faction suspected his independent tendencies, and the orthodox suspected him of atheism. Socrates indicated that education is not tradition, but an unending struggle against tradition; that education is *not dogmatism,* but an unending rebellion against the closed mind. In theory, we give lip-service to this ideal, but in actuality most of us behave differently. Many teachers have never learned how to ask *profound* questions; they are unconscious of their own assumptions; they are too categorical in their viewpoints. How can they communicate an examined way of life when they have never examined themselves?

What strikes the modern observer is the essential sanity of Socrates. He was unafraid of death, for he felt that either death represents an eternal sleep, undisturbed by dreams and nightmares, unhindered by pain and sorrow and suffering; or else death was a pilgrimage to a happier land in which virtue and wisdom would be recognized, in which eternal peace and contentment could be found. Who would not exchange the uncertainty and agony of this life for such fulfillment? He made his decision, and the Athenians made theirs. The Athenians were convinced they had eliminated a menace to their society; they were certain their verdict was right; but history indicates the shallowness and the stupidity of their judgment. Had they not condemned to death the wisest man of Athens?

The need for independent thinking

We should not be too harsh on the Athenians. In every age great teachers have been persecuted. We have only to think of the ordeals of Abélard in the Middle Ages, who was condemned by several church councils, and of Bruno in the Renaissance, who was burned at the stake. In our time the wholesale persecution of independent thinkers and teachers by totalitarian governments, like Nazi Germany and Soviet Russia, and the drive for conformity on the part of democratic nations threatens the integrity of education.

In some ways critical intelligence is a terrifying threat to orthodoxy. Critical intelligence indicates that the old way may be wrong, that the idols of the tribe may be mistaken, that certainty may be merely a rationalization for lethargy. Critical intelligence points to the Heraclitean nature of life. The moment thus merges in the stream of history; our own insights lose the status of finality, and instead they become interludes and episodes in history. The great teacher realizes the fragmentary nature of his knowledge, but this does not discourage him, for he knows that he has found a method by which life can be transformed and reconstructed. What is this method? It is the method of experimentation, of establishing tentative solutions, of applying ideas *concretely* to the betterment of man and society.

Reason and Faith

Abélard

Abélard, like Socrates, was misunderstood by his contemporaries. Abélard lived in an age of faith, of conformity, and of traditionalism. His own method, as he indicated in *Sic et Non,* was that of doubt.

He lacked the humility of Socrates; for example, in his letters to Héloïse he constantly spoke of his own greatness; but, like Socrates, he believed in the teachability of mankind.

Wherever he taught, thousands of students followed. They felt his intensity; they were impressed by his vitality; and they appreciated his contemporary approach to knowledge. In Abélard's classroom, philosophy ceased to be a pilgrimage in vague abstraction; instead it became a drama which was more vital than concrete actuality. Even when he was only a student at Laon, Abélard's success was astounding. He was studying under a noted teacher, Anselm, but Abélard felt that Anselm's reputation was vastly over-rated. To prove it, Abélard announced he would give a talk on Ezekiel, one of the most difficult Old Testament prophets, at the same time when Anselm usually lectured. Anselm's classroom was empty, while hundreds of students thronged to her Abélard. The result was that Abélard was told to leave Laon.

Abélard had a capacity for antagonizing other teachers. He was too brilliant, too original, and too unorthodox. This has been the fate of many young teachers in history. We have only to think of Galileo at the University of Pisa. His fellow-professors looked upon him as an unsound scholar. Did not Galileo challenge the master of knowledge: Aristotle? Did he not trust his own experimentation rather than the writings of the great Greek thinkers? In more contemporary times, we can think of the fate of Kilpatrick at Mercer University. Kilpatrick was deeply religious, but he hated dogmatism and conformity. He was charged with heresy by the Board of Trustees and thus left Mercer University.

Like Abélard, Galileo, and Kilpatrick, the great teacher probably will be a *heretic*. For he is not guided by the ways of the past; he does not accept the assumptions of his environment; he makes young people think and ponder—and thinking for many is a rather painful activity.

Abélard and St. Bernard

In the case of Abélard, he incurred the enmity of St. Bernard of Clairvaux. St. Bernard was a model of purity and asceticism. He believed in mortifying his body and in turning away from the temptations of this world. He possessed every virtue except that of compassion. He was a man of faith who found himself by subordination to an absolute principle of perfection. To St. Bernard, Abélard was a danger to the unity of the Church and to his own way of life, which was based on mysticism, not reason.

The two are interesting studies in contrast. St. Bernard represented the way of conformity; Abélard was the voice of rebellion. There could be no compromise between the two, and St. Bernard saw to it that the books of Abélard were burned, and that Abélard was forbidden to teach.

Ideas cannot be destroyed

It is difficult, however, to burn ideas. Books can be destroyed; authors can be intimidated; teachers can be dismissed from their jobs; still ideas will live. Men can be killed, yet the spark of creativity will remain.

In our own time, no substitute for freedom and intelligence can be found. The struggle against intelligence is self-defeating. Such a struggle represents the spirit of the Know-Nothing Party. No nation can survive in modern times which does not value intelligence and which does not promote education. For we are living in a period of rapid technological change, of immense cultural diffusion. We can shut our eyes to change and pretend it does not exist, or we can promote only technological advancement. In either case, doom and disaster may result.

We cannot live permanently in two worlds, that of ideal and of actuality; we cannot permanently afford the lag between the physical and the social sciences, between action and morality. *Modern Man Is Obsolete* says Norman Cousins. Modern man will indeed be obsolete if he does not cultivate the arts and sciences, and if he regards education merely as a mechanical process, as a form of *tribal conditioning*.

THE IDEALS OF TEACHING

The Need for Inspiration

The "lowbrows"

Yet we are creatures of routine, and society may permit us to live on a low level. Without stimulation and motivation we tend to lapse into a state of apathy. Look at the state of culture today! To be sure, we have more libraries, publishers, and schools than ever before, but what type of books are most popular? Detective thrillers by Mickey Spillane which picture a world of incredible sadism and violence. Publishers often find it unprofitable to issue serious books which appeal to the intelligent, because so few are interested in a more profound evaluation of life. Quality magazines, like *Harper's, Atlantic Monthly*, and *Saturday Review of Literature*, find only a limited audience, while the *Confession* magazines reach millions, and the comic page has a magic attraction for the majority of children and adults. Does not this, as Clifton Fadiman points out, represent a decline of attention? Is the common man too common? asks Joseph Wood Krutch, and he answers in the affirmative.

The teacher as a prophet

The teacher, like the preacher, should awaken us from our indolence so that we become conscious of the spark within us and of the possibilities of culture in our society. Where, in education today, are we made conscious of the infinite potentialities of man? Where do ideas become living symbols of action? Where is the student stirred into activity so that he leaves all passivity behind? Where is teaching so intense and exciting a process that material concerns become secondary?

No wonder that the community often looks upon education as an unessential process, and evaluates colleges according to the type of football teams which are produced; no wonder the world of theory is looked upon with scorn, and instead the realm of action is glorified; no wonder the influence of reason does not pervade society; no wonder that a deep chasm exists between first-rate thinking, and the popular channels of communication.

PHILOSOPHY IN ACTION

Emerson's sentiment can be applied to our own age:

... By how many prophets, tell me, is man made sensible that he is an infinite Soul, that the earth and heavens are passing into his mind, that he is drinking forever the soul of God? Where now sounds the persuasion, that by its very melody imparadises my heart, and so affirms its own origin in heaven? Where shall I hear words such as in elder ages drew men to leave all and follow,—father and mother, house and land, wife and child? Where shall I hear these august laws of moral being so pronounced as to fill my ear, and I feel ennobled by the offer of my uttermost action and passion?[1]

The need for intensity

Passion and intensity, above all, are lacking in education. Teaching involves the heart and the emotions; if it only appeals to our analytical reason, it tends to be sterile; if it develops mere objectivity, it lacks in fulfillment. The life of education, like the life of religion, demands complete allegiance and complete dedication. The man who truly loves God, said Spinoza, is not interested in being loved in return; the teacher who truly loves education is uninterested in immediate results and immediate returns.

From bondage to educational freedom

We move from bondage to freedom. The uneducated man sees life according to his own desires and own wishes. The universe, thus, is contained in his own ego. The educated man sees that certain processes and ideals are greater than his own existence. By identifying himself with the source of creativity, he achieves a measure of immortality.

Aristotle held that man is composed of an active and passive reason. The passive reason is dependent on personal features, and perishes; while the active reason is impersonal, and transcends the limitations of space and time. The active reason of education is indeed immortal; *it inspires us to look beyond today, to preserve detachment and calmness in moments of crisis. Perhaps eternity is not a condition, but a perception. The perception and the inspiration of the great teacher reminds mankind that winter is not everlasting,*

[1] *The Divinity School Address.*

THE IDEALS OF TEACHING

and that spring is a constant possibility. Inspiration in education creates a constant dawn amidst the twilight of human existence.

Questions and Topics for Discussion

1. Why is education the reflection of the great teacher?
2. What is the significance of Bergson's, *Two Sources of Religion and Morality*?
3. Why was Socrates tried by the Athenians?
4. What questions did Socrates ask?
5. Why did Socrates believe in the moral function of the teacher?
6. Why did Socrates make such an impression upon world history?
7. Why have independent thinkers been so often persecuted?
8. Evaluate the statement: "Critical intelligence is a terrifying threat to orthodoxy."
9. Why is the method of experimentalism so important in education?
10. Why is Abélard significant in educational history?
11. Compare and contrast Abélard with St. Bernard.
12. Why is it difficult to destroy ideas?
13. Do you believe that books ought to be censored? Explain your answer.
14. What are the main differences between the educated and the uneducated individual?
15. Why is dedication so important in education?
16. Discuss the statement of Emerson: "God offers to every man the choice between truth and repose. Take which you please, you can never have both."

Selected References

BERGSON, H., *The Two Sources of Religion and Morality*, 1935.
BURY, J. B., *The Idea of Progress.*
CAMPAYRE, J. G. *Abélard and the Origin, and Early History of the Universities*, 1904.
CUBBERLY, E. P., *The History of Education*, 1920.
DICKINSON, G. L., *The Greek View of Life*, 1896.
DREVER, J., *Greek Education*, 1912.
DURANT, W., *The Life of Greece*, 1939.
EBY, F., and ARROWOOD, C. F., *The History and Philosophy of Education, Ancient and Medieval*, 1940.
GOMPERZ, T., *Greek Thinkers*, 1901-1911.
HAMILTON, E., *The Greek Way*, 1948.

PHILOSOPHY IN ACTION

Horne, H. H., *Jesus, the Master Teacher*, 1920.
Krutch, J. W., *The Measure of Man*, 1954.
McCallister, W. J., *The Growth of Freedom in Education*, 1931.
Mayer, F., *History of Ancient and Medieval Philosophy*, 1950.
Moore, E. C., *The Story of Instruction*, 1938.
Muller, H. J., *The Uses of the Past*, 1952.
Neutra, R., *Survival Through Design*, 1954.
Parrington, V. L., *Main Currents in American Thought*, 1930.
Santayana, G., *Dominations and Powers*, 1951.

XI. THE TEACHER AND SOCIETY

Evolution of Subject Matter

THE SUBJECT MATTER of education depends to a great extent upon the cultural environment in which it develops. For example, in an age of faith religion will play a strong role, while in an age of science the natural and physical sciences will be emphasized. In an age of stability, when few cultural changes occur, the subject matter will be relatively static, whereas in an age of rapid change and cultural diffusion, the subject matter will be fluid.

Subject-matter in education never exists as an end itself. It is always a means to an exploration of the good life. Thus philosophy was studied in Greece to achieve self-control and dignity. Theology was stressed in Calvinist Geneva to escape from the torments of hellfire and to achieve salvation. Biology is studied at contemporary universities to achieve a knowledge of evolution and to see man in his naturalistic setting. In short, the facts of the subjects are less important than their ideal values and long-range implications.

Egyptian education

In early civilizations the priests had a monopoly on education. Thus in Egypt the temple schools were taught by the priests who instructed boys in the art of writing. Other types of educational centers developed, like the departmental schools which gave instruction to future government officials, and the court schools which prepared the heirs to the throne. These schools had a more secular tendency, still the religious influence dominated Egyptian civilization, which was interested, above all, in the achievement of immortality.

Like the modern Americans, the Egyptians combined practical concerns with religious idealism. The afterlife was conceived in concrete materialistic terms which almost remind us of Evelyn Waugh's description of a Hollywood Heaven. Egyptian education taught a variety of subjects including geography, astronomy, chronology, sculpture, painting, law, medicine, arithmetic, geometry, theory of music, and morals; but all subjects were taught in a rather practical and down-to-earth manner. Truth for the sake of truth, curiosity for the sake of curiosity, was not encouraged.

Egypt never developed a genuine system of liberal education. Like the modern Americans, the Egyptians were too much interested in quantification, and they were blinded by technological advances. The lesson of Egyptian civilization is clear. A civilization is made great not so much by vocational training as by stress upon the liberal arts. Civilization is nourished by imagination more than by practical needs. Interest in theory expands our horizon and illuminates all areas of inquiry.

Athenian curriculum

In Athens the ideal of education was far broader than that of Egypt. The Athenian concept of life was based on moderation, harmony, and proportion. Education was to include both the training of the body and the cultivation of the mind. The main subjects of the Athenian curriculum included gymnastics, music, and literary instruction. Athens neglected vocational education and thus went to the opposite extreme from that of Egypt. Vocational instruction, according to the Athenians, would be unworthy of the man of contemplation and would only degrade education. Whenever this concept of education has prevailed, it has produced a parasitical leisure class. *The ideal system of education makes the liberal arts central, without however neglecting vocational instruction.*

THE TEACHER AND SOCIETY

Medieval curriculum

During the Middle Ages education had a supernatural foundation. Many thinkers followed Augustine and believed there could be no compromise between Athens and Jerusalem, and that revelation as given by the Church was more important than natural reason. The study of science for the sake of science was discouraged. All education was to have a religious value and was to lead man to the knowledge of God.

The curriculum in the Middle Ages stressed the Seven Liberal Arts. By writers like Cassiodorus, Isidore of Seville, and Boethius, they were divided into the trivium (grammar, rhetoric, and dialectic) and the quadrivium (arithmetic, astronomy, geometry and music). Medieval education was dominated by the ideals of scholasticism which tried to harmonize Aristotle and the teachings of the Church. The most important study was theology, the queen of the sciences.

Neglect of theology

Some modern thinkers, like Hutchins, decry the decline of theology in contemporary life. Does this neglect not give us a narrow view of civilization? Does this not lead to an exaggerated emphasis on science? Does it not give a schizoid tendency to modern learning? The answer is that it all depends on how we approach the study of theology. If we regard it in a medieval manner, as a subject revealing absolute truth, it has little value in the modern curriculum. However, if we see the poetic and cultural significance of theology, if we understand its *symbolic* values, then it should be stressed in higher education. For example, today some of the most profound observations on the dilemmas of modern man can be found in the works of Maritain, Tillich, Berdyaev, Niebuhr, and Barth.

Renaissance revolt

During the Renaissance a revolt against scholasticism took place. Humanists, like Erasmus, Colet, Ficino, Rabelais, Ramus, and Montaigne, indicated the inadequacy of scholasticism and instead urged more stress upon the classics. In humanistic education the primary schools emphasized such subjects as reading, spelling, arithmetic, Latin and Greek vocabularly, religion, and ethics. The secondary schools expanded the curriculum by including Greek and Roman literature, composition, and rhetoric; while in higher education grammar, literature, and rhetoric received most attention, and logic lost its place of preëminence. Scientific studies were generally neglected by the humanists.

The humanistic ideal was to produce a new man. He was to be versed in the classics; he was to be a gentleman in his behavior towards ladies; knowledge was a prelude to universality, but few achieved this ideal. Like medieval education, the humanistic education over-emphasized the importance of the past.

Latin and Greek formed the center of the humanistic curriculum. Some scholars believe that the weakness of contemporary education is due to its neglect of classical languages. Do they not train the intellect? Do they not produce intellectual precision and discipline? Unfortunately, in the past, the grammatical aspects of the classics have been over-emphasized and thus the student has developed antagonism toward them. One of the most valuable parts of any curriculum can be "Classics in Translation." When Wilder taught this course at the University of Chicago, hundreds of students attended, and they were fascinated by his humanization of Homer, Aeschylus, Sophocles, and Plato.

Modern Trends

The revolt against classicism

The revolt against the classics was spearheaded by the scientists. Sir Francis Bacon already had pointed out that knowledge should be applied concretely. John Locke in the seventeenth century recommended the study of practical subjects, rather than Latin and Greek. In the twentieth century, science dominates the curriculum in most Western nations. This is due both to the rapid advance of scientific technology and invention, and to the work of thinkers like Spencer, Hall, James, and Dewey.

The twentieth century curriculum

The twentieth century has witnessed an immense expansion of the curriculum. In the modern American high school courses range from typing to family relations, from motion-picture appreciation to the electric shop. Likewise, in higher education hundreds of courses can be taken by the student. Lately the tendency has been to decrease the number of elective subjects, and to widen the range of required courses for college students.

Self-examination is stressed in higher education, as is indicated by the Harvard report, *General Education in a Free Society,* and by the funds given by the Ford Foundation for the purpose of institutional self-evaluation. Most of the time, however, self-examination means only a rearrangement of courses, instead of a change in basic educational philosophy.

Extremes

Some extremists in education have over-emphasized the interests of students. Dewey already pointed out that no artificial dualism is to be established between interest and subject matter. Progressive education fails when it reduces the teacher to a *minor* role. Subject matter has within itself seeds of creativity. Study of a great book can change the life of the individual. Kant confesses how the study of Rousseau's *Émile* changed his entire concept of philosophy; Nietzsche testifies to the almost overwhelming effect of Schopenhauer's *The World as Will and Idea;* Richard Wright in his autobiography, *Black Boy,* tells of the intense impact of writers like Dreiser and Lewis upon his thinking.

Need for balance

Modern education must never encourage vagueness and superficial thinking. When we go to a physician, we want a specific diagnosis, and we desire that he should know his subject thoroughly. When we go to an architect and have a house built, we rely upon his expert knowledge; when an engineer builds a bridge, we trust that he should know his mathematics and that the bridge will not collapse. When we hire a teacher, we want not only dedication and inspiration, but also *factual competence.*

This does not imply external control on the part of the teacher. He can never be a dictator. Authoritarianism defeats the true end of education; namely, the development of genuine individuality. The task of the teacher is that of a guide and a mediator. He brings out the creative possibilities of subject matter, so that it penetrates the life of the student, and so that the gulf between the culture and the individual is narrowed.

We certainly should not equate factual knowledge with educational insight. A student may know, for example all the presidents of the United States, the details of the party system, the structure of the federal and local governments, and still be misinformed. What matters is *how* we approach the subject matter. Do we regard it as an end and as an isolated study, or as a prelude to further inquiry? Does the study only confirm our biases or does it develop an open mind? Do we approach it in an *a priori* manner, or in a scientific way? The ideal of education is not to impart facts, but to create permanent interests, so that the student ultimately becomes his own teacher; in Spencer's words, *"a self-governing being."*

General Education

One of the remarkable developments of our period lies in the growth of general education. In the primary schools general education has always been stressed, especially in experience-centered schools. On the secondary level general education has lagged behind, for here departmentalization has a strong influence. On the college level general education has been stimulated especially by the Chicago experiment under Hutchins. The tendency today is to expand general education on the senior level. Thus seniors at Dartmouth are introduced to the contemporary world in a course dealing with critical issues; furthermore, general education is invading graduate studies, especially in the field of humanities.

Basic philosophy

The basic philosophy of general education stresses that man reacts to his environment as a total being. Too often education creates fragmentation. The scientist thus sees only the laboratory; the artist sees only the sphere of beauty; and the theologian is only conscious of religious values. In the seventeenth century, Leibnitz, in his *Monadology*, pictured the basic units of the universe as monads, which are windowless and have no communication with the outside world. Is not the condition of the scholar in the modern world like that of the monad? Are we not becoming victims of our own specialization? Is not excessive specialization a symptom of decadence in civilization, as Ortegà y Gasset points out? Does not excessive specialization lead to a narrow culture and a narrow society?

It cannot be forgotten that the advance of knowledge lies in two directions. First, it lies in the direction of smaller areas of knowledge. Specialists in medicine, for example, will devote most of their time to one organ; specialists in education may select a field like administration or psychology; specialists in philosophy may select an area such as logic or ethics, or they may give their major attention to one man, like Kant or Wittgenstein. Secondly, the advance of knowledge creates fundamental relationships. New fields have been created such as astrophysics, mathematical biology, and psychosomatic medicine. The development of nuclear physics indicates the equivalence of matter and energy. Psychosomatic medicine tells us about the impact of the mind on physiological functions. Perhaps, as Heisenberg pointed out, science can be reduced to a few fundamental force-concepts.

The development of the theory of relativity indicates progressive simplification in the physical laws of science. This simplification is not on a quantitative, but rather on a qualitative level; it represents a "form of etherealization," to use Toynbee's term.

The same change can be observed in the social sciences. Some of the most illuminating studies of our times have been carried on by men like Popper, Sorokin, Toynbee, Croce, Spengler, Lamprecht, Dilthey, and Pareto, who have tried to see history as a whole and who have attempted to correlate art and science, religion and social studies. Gestalt psychology attempts to see the wholeness of man's havior. Political scientists, like Laski and MacIver, have come to the conclusion that political studies are not ends in themselves, but need the illumination of philosophy, religion, and psychology. The development of economics has been furthered by a stress upon its religious matrix, especially in the works of Tawney and Weber. All this implies a need for more unification of knowledge and more general education.

Many students who have graduated from high school and college complain that they have had too much specialization, and that they have missed the cultural values of education. Education that merely stresses specific knowledge is incomplete. Do we not all need an understanding of generalization? Do we not all have to make general judgments? Are we not all parts of an esthetic as well as a scientific continuum?

General education and graduate studies

General education is desperately needed in graduate studies. Too often the dissertations deal with trivial subjects. Instead of contemporary problems, graduate education centers upon the past. Frequently, the graduate student has wide gaps in his cultural background. When he goes into college or high-school teaching, he tends to see the world according to his own subject, instead of seeing the interrelationship of all inquiries.

Certainly, graduate work does not train us for college teaching. The graduate student usually attends seminars, gives a report on specialized problems to a bored audience, writes a multitude of papers, and finally a dissertation.

I believe that a new type of graduate school should be developed for the liberal arts, one which would stress the humanities. All the courses of such a school should be staff-taught on a collaborative basis. The method of presentation might be as follows:

A. From the very beginning students should be carefully trained in the art of teaching and in the technique of leading discussion groups.

B. The graduate institute should publish a journal which would serve as a platform for the major contributions of the students and faculty members of the institute.

C. Once a month at least, all the students and faculty members should meet to discuss significant problems of education.

D. The graduate school should be based upon the consideration of ten problems; two problems a semester. The last semester should be for internship and the thesis.

Sample problems:
1. The problem of truth
2. The problem of morals
3. The problem of self-knowledge
4. The problem of esthetic criticism
5. The problem of education
6. The problem of freedom
7. The problem of revolution
8. The problem of civilization
9. The problem of war and peace
10. The problem of God

E. Tutors would take care of specialization. The student would have a special tutor who would assign readings and papers and who would see to it that the students made up any lags in general education.

F. The final examination would be in five parts:
1. A written examination in the great ideas of liberal arts
2. A written examination in the student's area of specialization
3. An oral examination of the student's general education background and his thesis
4. A public lecture by the student, followed by a general discussion
5. The student would have to lead a discussion group

G. The thesis should deal with one of the ten fundamental problems and should indicate creative ability. The thesis ought to have contemporary relevance.

PHILOSOPHY IN ACTION

Teaching is primary

Most universities demand that their professors publish books or articles if they want professional advancement. Deans often evaluate their instructors according to the number of books they have produced. This quantitative measurement is ridiculous. Too much emphasis on literary production not only wears out the instructor, but takes away from his teaching duties. Teaching should never be conducted as a subordinate activity; it should always be the central interest of the instructor.

Survey courses

Survey courses are among the most inadequate in the field of general education. At large universities a professor will give the lecture to perhaps a thousand students, and then they will be divided into discussion sections, usually guided by assistants. At some universities only a year is devoted to an introduction to world civilization. For example, in talking to a freshman at X University, I asked him what he was studying. He replied: "We are covering Rome this week. Last week we covered Greece." Such an approach encourages vagueness, superficiality, and faulty generalization. Survey courses too frequently use only anthologies which give a cafeteria impression of literature. Thus from a selection of ten pages the student is supposed to understand Plato's *Republic;* Aristotle may rate fifteen pages, and Dewey five.

Cooperative teaching

What is needed in general education most desperately is an *integration* of the staff. Cooperative teaching should definitely be encouraged on all levels. For example, in high school, members of the literature, science, English, art, civics, home economics, history, and speech departments should combine and present a course in Social Living. They and the students should plan the course cooperatively. The instructors should alternate in lecturing and in leading small discussion sections. Such a course should be made as dramatic as possible through the use of audio-visual means, especially television.

One of my most treasured educational experiences has been my participation in the humanities course at the University of Redlands, in which members of seven departments took part. We planned the course together; every week we met for three hours; we attended all the lectures; and all of us led discussion sections. We criticized each other frankly. We even graded the tests cooperatively. The impressive aspect of this course was that professors continued to learn and expand their horizon. The historian actually became interested in philosophy, instead of looking down on the abstractions of theoretical thinking. The philosopher was forced to clarify his terminology. The literature professor took up art, and the artist read books on physical science. The theologian made a concentrated study of anthropology, and the professor of European civilization became imbued with the importance of Oriental culture.

Guidance

More emphasis in general education should be given to the problem of guidance. We are told by psychiatrists that one out of ten will have some type of serious psychological maladjustment. Our prison population is alarmingly high; juvenile delinquency is a national problem. Adults have been shocked by revelation of drug addiction among high-school and even junior-high-school youngsters. Skillful counseling will not be merely preventive, but positive. It will stress not merely the problem child, but the exceptional child. The Wickman study indicates the need for special counseling for children who tend to withdraw. Frequently, teachers are too conscious of aggressive behavior in the classroom, and they neglect the passive and introspective child.

Counseling, it is hoped, will be done more on a cooperative basis, with the aid of the home, clergy, social workers, teachers, administrators, psychologists, physicians, and psychiatrists. In the future every school, if possible, ought to employ a psychologist not just for testing, but for clinical purposes. Guidance is a continuous function of education from the nursery school to graduate school.

PHILOSOPHY IN ACTION

Core work

Kilpatrick makes an excellent suggestion when he proposes that in high school about one half the time should be devoted to core work. This core curriculum, he believes, should be under the guidance of one teacher, who would have about twenty-five students under him. The studies devised would be fluid, and would be experience-centered. My feeling is that the core work should involve several teachers from various departments and that it should be more subject-centered; still the guidance values of either approach are important.

Television as a form of education

The advent of television promises a new era in education. Within fifty years half the teaching in our primary and secondary schools may be through television. Some teachers probably will shudder. Are not most television programs extremely poor? Does not television exaggerate the infantile traits of our culture? Still the educational possibilities of television are unlimited. Through television great teachers can reach a nationwide audience. Through television the child will actually see history in the making. Television will stimulate the imagination of both students and teachers, and ultimately may create a real renaissance of education.

Teachers will make a grave mistake if they take an isolationist attitude regarding television. Here is an instrument which can spread education to all levels and all classes of society. Here is an invention which can make education truly dramatic and lifelike. In ignoring television, teachers will broaden the gap between school and society; in exploring the educational vistas of television and making it part of classroom instruction, teachers will make a formidable contribution to the betterment of our civilization.

Questions and Topics for Discussion

1. Why did the priests have a monopoly of education in primitive civilizations?

2. Discuss the educational system of ancient Egypt.
3. What were the advantages and disadvantages of medieval education?
4. What can theology contribute to modern life? What is the difference between philosophy and theology?
5. What was the humanistic ideal of education?
6. Should there be a greater emphasis upon classical languages in American education? Justify your answer.
7. Why is factual competence so important in education?
8. Should there be more or fewer requirements in college? Justify your answer.
9. What is the significance of general education?
10. What are the basic aims of general education?
11. Why is general education needed in graduate studies?
12. What are some of the main lags in your own educational development?
13. Why is guidance such an important problem on *all* levels of education?
14. In your opinion, how can children be taught better habits of mental hygiene?
15. How can education contribute to the solution of the juvenile delinquency problem?
16. Show how television can improve instruction in various subjects.

Selected References

BOBBITT, J. F., *The Curriculum of Modern Education*, 1941.
BUTTS, R., *The College Charts its Course*, 1939.
CARROLL, H. H., *Mental Hygiene*, 1949.
COE, G., *Educating for Citizenships*, 1932.
CROW, L. D., and A. Crow, *Introduction to Education*, 1950.
COUNTS, G. S., *The Prospects of American Democracy*, 1938.
DALE, E., *Audio-Visual Methods in Teaching*, 1949.
HARVARD COMMITTEE, *General Education in a Free Society*, 1945.
JONES, H. M., *Primer of Intellectual Freedom*, 1949.
KANDEL, I. L., *Comparative Education*, 1933.
KAPLAN, O. J., (EDITOR), *Encyclopedia of Vocational Guidance*, 1948.
KILPATRICK, W. H., *Education and the Social Crisis*, 1932.
———, *Philosophy of Education*, 1951.
LEIGHTON, J. A., *Individuality and Education*, 1928.
MUMFORD, L., *Values for Survival*, 1946.
———, *The Story of Utopias*, 1933.
MONROE, P., *Source-Book of the History of Education*, 1901.
NASH, H. S., *The University and the Modern World*, 1943.

PHILOSOPHY IN ACTION

NEWMAN, J. H., *The Idea of University*, (sixth edition), 1886.
PATER, W., *The Renaissance*, 1873.
PRESIDENT'S COMMISSION ON HIGHER EDUCATION, *Higher Education for American Democracy*, 1948.
STANLEY, W. O., *Education and Social Integration*, 1953.
WARTERS, J., *Achieving Maturity*, 1950.
WILSON, H. E., *Universities and World Affairs*, 1951.

XII. MORAL VALUES IN EDUCATION

Ethical Conflicts

THE MORAL CONFUSION of modern man is one of the dominant facts of our time. We are caught by dilemmas and paradoxes which arise out of the uncertainty of our existence. While nineteenth century thinkers looked forward to a brave new world of science and progress, many twentieth century thinkers, like Spengler and T. S. Eliot, can only see doom and disaster ahead.

The optimistic feeling of the nineteenth century has been shaken by major world wars, by the atomic bomb, dictatorships, the Nazi and the Soviet Regimes, as well as by the dissatisfaction regarding the use of scientific technology. The cruelty of this century has been almost unparalled; we have only to think of the terrors of the Nazi concentration camps, which cost millions of lives.

Gandhi

Great spiritual leaders of our time have attempted to define a new ideal of life. Thus Gandhi in India preached a gospel of absolute non-violence, together with a universal type of religion. To Gandhi the triumphs of industrialism were only superficial; man's real problem was his relationship to his neighbor and to God. Like Thoreau,

PHILOSOPHY IN ACTION

Gandhi believed in the simple life, and, like Thoreau, Gandhi was skeptical of the advantages of civilization.

Radhakrishnan

Another great Indian Leader, Radhakrishnan preached a perennial gospel based upon the *Upanishads*. To Radhakrishnan, change is an illusion; behind every event, behind all flux, behind the world of phenomena, is an absolute principle. Once we concentrate upon this realm we see life more calmly and with greater perspective. Radhakrishnan hoped that India would mediate between East and West and thus aid in the survival of world civilization.

Rufus Jones

Rufus Jones, the great Quaker leader, believed, likewise, in the ideal of non-violence, and in the equivalence of ends and means. A conscientious objector to war, Jones tried to help the victims of World War I and World War II. Furthermore, he did heroic work in the relief for refugees of the Nazi regime.

Schweitzer's ideals

Albert Schweitzer, another great moral leader of our time, has impressed the conscience of the Western World by his medical missionary work in Africa. Schweitzer abandoned the comforts of civilization to aid the natives in Africa. Had they not been exploited by the white man? Had they not suffered from Western callousness? To Schweitzer, Jesus was an absolute guide; the ideals of Jesus were not impractical; on the contrary, they were the only valid rules for living.

The Yogi and the Commissar

Koestler one time said that the ultimate conflict of today will be between the Yogi and the Commissar. The saint, or the Yogi, sees life from a qualitative viewpoint; he believes in human possibilities, while the Commissar stresses exact measurement and objectivity. The realm of subjectivity is excluded by the Commissar, who has no use for private feelings and private emotions. *1984*, as pictured by Orwell, is almost the inevitable outcome of the triumph of the Commissar.

Education and social change

The educator cannot evade the fundamental moral problems of our time, for education is concerned with values and ideal concepts. The work of the educator is incomplete as long as suffering, frustration, and want prevail. This is not a time for smugness or self-righteousness on the part of the educator.

Can education by itself bring about Utopia? Should education directly change society? Some thinkers, like Brameld, would like educators to take a more active part in social reconstruction. Undoubtedly, educators owe an obligation to society to present a vision of man's possibilities and to create an affirmative view of our future, but education cannot and should not agitate for one system of morals, or politics, or economics.

Such agitation would be opposed to the open-minded spirit so important in education. The change which can be accomplished by education is much more fundamental than that envisioned by political, economic, and social reformers. It is a change in the habits of thinking of mankind, so that dogmatism and fanaticism can be avoided, and so that we can live together in peace and harmony. If we are able to apply scientific techniques to social and moral problems, we may be able to solve them in an experimental manner. But the difficulty is that it is easier to control objects than human beings, who are subject to a thousand forms of irrationality. It is certain that scientific experimentation alone is inadequate, and that good-will and humanitarianism go together with a hypothetical, scientific attitude.

Dangers of absolutism

The danger is that we shall return to an absolute form of morality. Whenever absolutistic morals have governed humanity—be it in the Middle Ages, during the Inquisition, in Calvin's Geneva, or the Boston of Jonathan Edwards—regression and intolerance resulted. The problem of moral nihilism cannot be solved by a re-

PHILOSOPHY IN ACTION

turn to Puritanism. *Goodness cannot be coerced; morals cannot be established through categorical commandments.*

Moral Enlightenment

Platonism

The struggle between those who favor a categorical concept of morality and those who believe in a relative view of ethical standards is an ancient one. In Greece, Platonism favored a puritanical form of morals, while Epicureanism had a more humanistic concept of life. It must be remembered that Plato tended to be intolerant of heretics and in his last dialogue, *The Laws,* he even advocated the death penalty for certain forms of heresy. In his ideal Utopia, Plato would not allow poets like Homer. Had not Homer portrayed the gods in a fallible manner? Had not Homer exaggerated the human traits of the gods? What was worse, according to Plato, was Homer's opposition to war. The brave do not always win the battle, nor do the good gain final victory. Apparently, a blind fate governs life, which makes mockery out of conventional moral standards.

Plato, like many modern totalitarians, believed in the use of the lie. This is to keep the common people satisfied with their lowly status. False propaganda has been frequently used in the history of education. Thus, the modern Nazis introduced a course in racial science in all German schools. This course was designed to teach German youth that the Aryan race was the greatest and must sublime race in the world and that racial impurity created the downfall of culture. Modern history books of most nations are full of semi-truths, distortions, and exaggerations, so that the virtues of one country are emphasized as against the weaknesses of another.

Morality in Plato had a hierarchical nature. Different virtues were needed for the ruler, the soldier, and the common people. In modern education, likewise, we often accept various standards of morality: One ideal for the administrator, another for the student, and a third for the teacher. Needless to say, such a view of morality creates hypocrisy and confusion. The same standards that are applied to the administrator should be applied to the teacher and the student. All should be a part of the democratic process, which has respect for the integrity of the individual.

Epicurus

Epicurus, unlike Plato, had a more humanitarian concept of morality. To Epicurus philosophy and education were guides to *conduct*. The problem of life was foremost in Epicureanism. All men seek pleasure, according to this philosophy, but they frequently follow the wrong path. Instead of cultivating detachment and tranquillity, they lose themselves in society. Instead of seeking the highest pleasure, the pleasure of the mind, they cultivate sensuality. Instead of living the life of reason, they put their faith in material goods.

One of the cardinal problems of education in any period is the problem of human existence. For we desire not only to know deeply, but also to live meaningfully. Too often education fills us only with unrelated meanings; too often intellectuals are less happy than common people. Does this not indicate that they have missed the central meaning of education?

Epicurus anticipated the conclusions of modern psychology. The greatest fears, he held, are those which arise in the mind. Anxiety is a constant danger to man. Let man see reality as it is. The universe, according to Epicurus, is made up of atoms; their changes and movements produce different world systems; even man is composed of atoms. The gods exist, but they live far away and are unconcerned with human destiny. As for immortality, that is an illusion. We are part of the atomic whirl and after our death, our bodies return to the material substratum.

Philosophy and education, according to Epicurus, could give us a better knowledge of pleasure. They could give us a sense of moderation so that we would not be overcome by blind passion. In adversity, they would give us hope; in prosperity, they could imbue us with a sense of limitation. Here, indeed, was one of the most livable philosophies ever propounded. It may have lacked the poetry and beauty of Platonism, but it was far more civilized and far more humane than Platonism.

Dangers of Nihilism

Nietzsche's ideas

Still, if we abandon an external sanction for morality, we are caught by uncertainty and often by confusion. Few individuals are willing to live the calm life Epicurus advocated. Instead, like Nietzsche, they search for power. In the Prologue of Nietzsche's *Thus Spake Zarathustra* the dilemmas of contemporary morality are outlined. Zarathustra is the new prophet of power who is preparing to spread his teachings among humanity. He has lived in the wilderness and now wants to "enlighten" civilized man. With vigor, Zarathustra asserted that God is *dead*.

Pitfalls of atheism

The danger always is that we may set up our own egos as the standards of history. Atheism, as in Nietzsche and Nazi Germany, may lead to the worship of the infallible leader. The function of religion in civilization is to give us a sense of limitation, so that we realize our insufficiency. The tyranny of orthodox religion is mild compared with the tyranny of political systems like National Socialism and Communism. Man apparently needs some type of metaphysical integration. What matters is how he approaches his quest for certainty. If it becomes a compulsive quest, then it loses its value; on the other hand, if it broadens his horizons, and if it deepens his imagination, it adds to his creativity.

Farewell to Arms

The inadequacy of just living for the moment is perhaps best described in *Farewell to Arms* by Hemingway. The central character, a young American lieutenant, has come to Italy to fight with the Italians against the Austrians. He is a man without illusions. He has joined because of a sense of adventure, but that was soon destroyed by the violence and terror of the war.

He has no faith in religion. In a revealing conversation with a priest, he indicates that he believes in God only when he is afraid. He finds a type of religion when he falls in love with Catherine, a British nurse. At first, he resists love, because it would upset him, and he has no time or use for sentimentality. But when he falls in love with her, she becomes the center of his life. Now he hates the war and his great desire is to quit. When the Italian army is defeated, he has a real opportunity to flee the country. Together they escape to Switzerland. At first they feel overjoyed, but then Catherine becomes very ill. She is taken to a hospital. As she is being operated on, he becomes conscious of the irony of life. He prays to God to let her live; that he will do anything if she will live; he thinks of life as a mechanistic process in which man is just an animal constantly exposed to destruction. Then the doctor comes out of the operating room. The operation has been a failure. After a while he asks permission to see Catherine's body; but in death she looks lifeless, almost as if she had never existed. The doctor explains that he had done his best, but she is dead, nevertheless. The story ends with the young hero walking out into the rain—a symbol of the hopelessness of life.

Skepticism in twentieth century literature

The skepticism of Hemingway is duplicated by some of the most gifted American writers. We have only to mention Faulkner, Jeffers, Capote, Mailer, Jones, Williams, and O'Neill. Does this indicate that we are living in a moral wasteland? Does it mean that our civilization is decadent? Does it imply that education has failed?

Education as a Moral Process

Three attitudes

Education can aid morality by stressing three attitudes, above all: (1) sensitivity, (2) self-reliance, and (3) social concern. Some thinkers believe that man is born with a conscience and that he has an innate sense of duty. Thus Kant speaks about a categorical imperative, which is to be the guide to right action. History, however, indicates how plastic man's conscience is. Thus during the Inquisition few consciences were bothered by the persecution of heretics. In the period of the Nazi persecution, few Germans were disturbed by Hitler's atrocities; what is worse, only relatively few in other nations took notice of the ravages of the Nazi regime. The other day I saw a picture on the front page of a tabloid. It showed a man who had been shot in a barroom brawl. His body was lying on the floor; the customers apparently were indifferent, and they were busy with their drinks.

The problem of moral awareness is the same as that of esthetic sensitivity. The more we are conscious of the rhythms of nature, the more meaning existence has for us. Moral sensitivity can be increased in the classroom by unfailing consideration for the feelings of others.

I remember an interesting incident in my class in educational philosophies last summer. A student was reporting on Santayana, and he mentioned the fact that Santayana regarded slavery as a minor evil. The student added that in his own personal opinion certain people needed education before they could be free, and that slavery in the past had positive aspects. Had it not produced a formidable culture in the South before the Civil War?

The situation was rather critical, for several colored students were in the class, and I could see that they were indignant, and rightly so. At the same time I wanted to reason with the student, not indoctrinate him. I asked him whether he wanted to be a slave. He replied that he never thought in those terms. I told him to read Pierre Van Paassen's *Days of Our Years,* which shows the influence of slavery upon Africa, and to peruse Paton's *Cry, the Beloved Country;* also I recommended Wright's *Black Boy* to him. I indicated how the concept of slavery was incompatible with our ideals of freedom and our basic religious beliefs. In the end he realized that he had *not* been sensitive to the feelings of the class and that he had accepted an irrational bias.

Sensitivity

The cultivation of sensitivity is a life-long process. By becoming sensitive, we cultivate an attitude of understanding, and we become fully civilized. Without moral awareness, life is a Darwinian jungle, in which might is right, and in which no moral laws prevail.

Sensitivity cannot be created by rules. External authority is not the answer to moral dilemmas. It is a mistake to believe that merely by establishing regulations we educate individuals in a creative manner. For example, in certain colleges cheating may be regarded as a serious crime. Students are warned that if they are caught cheating, they will be expelled from school. The result is that cheating has a great fascination, it is forbidden, and we all know that youth loves to defy authority.

Self-reliance

A much better way is to establish as few rules as possible, and to develop *self-reliance* and a genuine honor system on the part of youth. *Morality is an inward feeling, not outward conformity; morality demands self-determination, rather than external determination.*

The teacher cannot play the role of Providence. He fails when he tries to set up his own standards as ultimate, or when he tries to show that he is perfect, while the student is a sinner. Youth appreciates frankness and is not easily deceived by pretense. This does not imply that mere pleasure-seeking is to be encouraged. The student often will say: "I don't care about others; I am only interested in my own welfare. Are not most people basically selfish? Does not everyone think of himself first? It not altruism an illusion?"

The larger self

The answer is that we find ourselves only by identification, by seeing a more inclusive Self. This cannot be achieved merely by an intellectual attitude, but it involves positive work and positive sacrifice. One of the great educational experiences for a wealthy student may be a summer in a Quaker work camp. In this way he learns the greatness of sharing and of social concern. He meets all classes and all types; he is engaged in a meaningful activity; and, like Schweitzer, he has followed a call which goes beyond expediency.

Questions and Topics for Discussion

1. What causes the confusion of twentieth century man?
2. Why has the optimism of the nineteenth century been shaken?
3. Why is Gandhi so important for our time?
4. Who is Radhakrishnan? Do you agree with his ideas?
5. What are Schweitzer's moral views?
6. Do you agree with Koestler that the ultimate conflict will be between the Yogi and the commissar?
7. Should education directly change society?
8. Discuss the statement: "Morality cannot be coerced."
9. What was Plato's view of morality?
10. What is the significance of Nietzsche's *Thus Spake Zarathustra*?
11. Why is *Farewell to Arms* a modern classic? How does it illustrate our contemporary moral values?
12. How can education aid morality?
13. Discuss the statement: "The problem of moral awareness is the same as that of esthetic sensitivity."
14. Why do many students cheat on examintions? Do you believe in an honor system?
15. What to you are the main moral problems of our time?

Selected References

BOSANQUET, B., (Translator), *The Education of the Young in the Republic of Plato*, 1917.
CHILDS, J. L., *Education and Morals*, 1950.
COE, G. A., *Law and Freedom in the School*, 1924.
DEWEY, J., *Ethical Principles Underlying Education*, 1903.
———, *Moral Principles in Education*, 1909.
FISCHER, L., *Gandhi*, 1955.
HARTSHORNE, H., *Character and Human Relations*, 1932.
HEMINGWAY, E., *A Farewell to Arms*, 1929.
LIPPMANN, W., *A Preface to Morals*, 1929.
MASON, R. E., *Moral Values and Secular Education*, 1950.
NORTHROP, F. S. C., *The Meeting of East and West*, 1946.
PALMER, G. H., *Ethical and Moral Instruction in the Schools*, 1909.
PATON, A., *Cry, the Beloved Country*, 1948.
PERRY, R. B., *Realms of Value*, 1954.
RANDALL, J. H., JR., *The Making of the Modern Mind*, 1940.
RUGG, H., *Foundations for American Education*, 1947.

MORAL VALUES IN EDUCATION

RUSSELL, B., *Unpopular Essays*, 1950.
SCHWEITZER, A., *The Philosophy of Civilization*, 2 parts, 1923.
SPENCER, H., *Education: Intellectual, Moral and Physical*, 1861.
WASHBURNE, C., *The World's Good: Education for World Mindedness*, 1954.
WRIGHT, R., *Black Boy*, 1945.

XIII. THE GOALS OF EDUCATION

Obstacles in Education

BEFORE A RECONSTRUCTION can be achieved in education, certain obstacles will have to be overcome. It appears that our thinking is dominated by perenniel idols such as authoritarianism, traditionalism, anthropomorphism, and dogmatism, which usually arose in a pre-scientific age. In this way our mental habits contrast with our technological methods. In technology the basic question is: Does the invention work? If not, it is abandoned. In our intellectual life, however, workability is of secondary consequence, for we are often overcome by the attractions of irrational gospels and irrational views of existence.

Traditionalism

The most pernicious idol, in some ways, is that of *traditionalism* in education. We tend to look back, instead of forward, we worship ancient culture, and we forget that the standards of Greece and Rome cannot be applied to modern civilization. As Korzybski indicates, the influence of Aristotelian logic has created a false valuation, an either-or viewpoint, and has led to an over-emphasis upon formal, deductive logic in our educational system. In many colleges Aristotelian logic is still being upheld as the best system of thought. To some, Aristotle is still the master of knowledge.

Contemporary logic, if it is to have a constructive influence upon education, should stress the reality of *change* and should be guided by the tentativeness of the scientific method. Static categories, absolute standards, and syllogistic reasoning will only impede the progress of knowledge and the advancement of learning. We should be more conscious of our initial assumptions and should examine our motives in establishing conclusions. Psychology thus can illuminate the field of logic and can indicate that eternal truth may be only a rationalization for the imperfections of the present.

Freudian psychology has indicated only too well that man's reason is not pure, and that often we disguise the real purposes behind our conclusions. But many thinkers are still dominated by Kantian philosophy, and hence accept the autonomy of reason and the formal conditions of knowledge.

Traditionalism in education leads to an over-emphasis upon past literature and past history. In many literature courses, the present is overlooked or regarded as being insignificant; in many world history courses the twentieth century plays a minor role. Historians often will say that the present is too controversial and that it cannot be evaluated objectively. Undoubtedly, this statement contains an element of truth, but is not the ultimate test of knowledge its contemporary relevance? Is not the task of the scholar to use his education for the advancement of the present?

Many traditionalists in education are convinced that the new emphases in education are perverted because they differ from the system of education in vogue during their childhood. We constantly hear that in the 19th century children had a better grasp of fundamentals, the 3 R's, and that greater discipline prevailed in the schools. It is forgotten that today we educate far more children than ever before, and that we are just beginning the experiment in mass education.

The 3-R's are not the kingdom of heaven in education; modern society cannot be saved merely by a return to them, as some critics appear to believe. The 3-R's are only preludes to creative thinking and a creative way of life; they are an overture to *sensitivity, self-reliance, and social concern.*

While the Great Books program generally has a healthy effect upon American education, the need today is for more stress upon contemporary literature; to develop a cultural audience that can appreciate the serious novels, essays, dramas, and poetry produced in our time. If we are unable to develop this audience, our culture will suffer, and it will be dominated by cheap vulgarity and sensationalism.

Authoritarianism

Besides traditionalism, authoritarianism is a constant danger in education. The autocratic spirit prevails too often among some administrators who regard the teaching staff as being part of the hired help. A hierarchical spirit in education is contrary to the ideals of democracy, and it creates frozen individuals on the top and fearful persons on the bottom of the scale. The democratic spirit ought to develop more patterns of genuine cooperation between administrators, teachers, and the community. It ought to include even the custodians who share in the educative process.

The authoritarian teacher demands conformity on the part of his students. They thus are not required to think for themselves, but to accept the word of the teacher as absolute truth. Undoubtedly, the authoritarian spirit of German learning contributed to the rise of National Socialism. In German schools the teacher was often regarded as an idol; to contradict him was a form of heresy.

Authoritarian rulers in the past have realized the importance of iron control in education. Thus Frederick William IV of Prussia reformed the teacher-training schools so that philosophy of education was reduced to "school knowledge"; instruction in religion was confined to the Catechism, which the future teacher had to memorize. Independent thinking was not allowed, for the King realized that it would undermine his own rule and lay the seeds for democracy. Thomas Alexander in *The Prussian Elementary School* tells us about his visit to hundreds of German primary schools and his impression was that the pupils were taught to be docile and not to

THE GOALS OF EDUCATION

think independently. In our own time, as Hans Habe asserts, the poison of National Socialism has not been completely eliminated from the German school system. Many teachers are only lukewarm supporters of democratic ideals and they still use the traditional autocratic method in public instruction.

The way we teach, the way we approach our students, may affect the future of our civilization. If we stress in education preconceived truths, absolute standards, memorization and drill, if we discourage independent decisions, we create students who lack initiative and self-reliance, and who are always potential tools for dictatorships.

Anthropomorphism

Another road-block in education is anthropomorphism. In Greece, Xenophanes pointed out that man conceives of the gods according to his own background. Thus the Athenian gods loved life and were as delightfully immoral as the average Athenian citizen. Anthropomorphism implies that we regard our own standards, ideals, views, and beliefs as ultimate and project them upon the universe.

Now anthropomorphism indicates a lack of sophistication. For as we travel more widely, and as we meet various customs and ideals, we find that *relativity* prevails in the world. Many Athenians were shocked when Sophists, like Protagoras, asserted that truth is relative. For what may be true to an Athenian may not be true to a Spartan; and what may be true at one time, may be false at another time.

If we regard our own standards as being infallible, as criteria for the universe, we are unteachable. For in effect, we claim that we already have the key to wisdom and perfection. Why should we try to improve ourselves? Why should we ever change our minds? Why should we listen to others?

The comparative approach in education is especially valuable in counteracting the idol of anthropomorphism. In becoming acquainted with world culture, especially Oriental civilization, we become more humble, less exclusive, and we make fewer claims of perfection. We realize that many contributions, which we thought came from the West, were really derived from the East.

The chosen-people concept is as dangerous in our own time as it was in Hebrew civilization. No nation has a monopoly on virtue; no nation has the key to wisdom; no nation is so perfect that it cannot learn from others. In the past, culture has advanced through diffusion and amalgamation of diverse philosophies and ideals. The United States has progressed by being a melting pot of diverse races and nationalities who accepted a framework of unity within diversity. The hope is that the United Nations also can become a genuine family of nations, in which diversity can be combined within a common framework of tolerance and understanding. The task is vastly more difficult, but not hopeless; and education can play an important part in developing genuine world-mindedness, instead of social anthropomorphism.

Dogmatism

All this implies the avoidance of dogmatism. The advancement of education indicates that the absolute truths of yesterday are the relative theories of today. Dogmatism in the past has been the insistent enemy of science. We have only to think of the persecution of Galileo by those who thought his heliocentric theory of the universe was both impious and unscientific. Medicine for centuries was held back by the belief that disease is caused by sin. In more recent times science has been impeded by the growth of national dogmatism. Thus the Germans under Hitler spoke of German science and tried to ignore Freud and Einstein because they were Jewish, and hence "obviously wrong." In Soviet Russia, scientific principles are subordinated to political expediency. For example, the controversy in genetics was settled by political decree. Scientists have to conform to the basic tenets of Marxism, otherwise they lose their jobs and may even end in the concentration camp.

The great conflict in education is ultimately between those who believe in fallibility and those who regard themselves as being infallible. As long as we realize that our conclusions are subject to error and that our standards are not final, we can be persuaded by rational means and we can be taught; but when we feel that we have a private communication to the sources of truth, then we cease to be creative and we become *fanatics* instead.

Enlightenment in Education

The goal of education is the creation of enlightened human beings. To be enlightened implies that we abandon all claims to finality and that we try to overcome all forms of prejudice.

Buddha

Here we can benefit from the insight of Buddha. As a young man Buddha had lived a sensual life; he had enjoyed political and economic power. He was a prince with a beautiful wife, but still he was dissatisfied. He wanted to conquer not only life, but death. Thus he abandoned his kingdom and sought salvation. He first practiced the most severe types of asceticism and mortified his flesh, but he was still dissatisfied. Psychologically, he had just inverted the pleasure principle; he was still a serf to his emotions. Enlightenment came to Buddha when he realized the importance of the Middle Road, to avoid extremes and to see the significance of *compassion*.

The need for compassion

Compassion, it should be realized, overcomes the sense of alienation; compassion creates a feeling of unity in a world of isolation; compassion makes us morally sensitive to the sufferings of others; compassion is love, with a sense of gentle melancholy.

As we become enlightened, we are struck like Lucretius, in *De Rerum Natura*, by the follies of mankind. What a striving for futility! What a madness for activity! What a pilgrimage in triviality! Was not Erasmus correct when he maintained that most individuals are governed by Folly? Has modern man really advanced so much over his primitive ancestors?

Progress

Yet basic in the philosophy of enlightenment is a belief in the possibility of progress. We realize that progress is uneven, and that the eighteenth century thinkers, like Diderot, were too optimistic when they felt that the old prejudices of mankind had been permanently conquered. We know that progress has to be guarded in every generation, and that intellectual advancement depends on economic security.

The great ages of education have usually been ages of prosperity. This holds true for the Athens of Phidias, the Renaissance of Leonardo, and the eighteenth century of Voltaire. In times of poverty, like the Thirty Years War, education has lagged behind. To be sure, prosperity is not an inevitable source of progress and genuine education. Prosperity, as we all realize, can develop an idolization of material goods, and it can reduce everything to a quantitative level. In that case, education becomes a business enterprise, rather than a *spiritual and moral concern*.

Some theologians, like Niebuhr, assert that progress is an illusion. Is not human nature the same everywhere? Are we not all subject to sin? Is not enlightenment a sign of pride? Does it not alienate us from God? The answer is that if we see only sin in the world, the educational task is hopeless. The challenge of education is just the opposite. It lies in seeing the affirmative possibilities of every situation and every person; in regarding man not as a creature of sin, but as a creative child of God.

Basic to the philosophy of enlightenment is faith in freedom. Freedom is never complete or absolute; freedom, like education, is a process. The enlightened individual realizes that freedom depends on responsibility.

The contributions of various subjects

The various subjects of the curriculum can greatly contribute to an enlightened view of life. The study of citizenship and social problems can imbue us with a sense of social responsibility; it can remind us of the need for being informed, for overcoming tribalism, and for developing a world perspective. Democracy ceases to be merely an ideal faith and becomes a way of acting and reacting. It imbues all our activities and prevents the creation of an authoritarian personality. We should furthermore develop a better knowledge of personal and social phychology. Courses in mental hygiene should start in junior high school. We cannot become enlightened when we suffer from fundamental behavior and personality problems. Serious neuroses interfere not only with our effectiveness, but also with our joy of life. The effectiveness of the schools can be measured by their capacity to develop a sense of fulfillment and self-realization on the part of the student and teacher.

The arts, literature, music, and drama can aid the process of enlightenment. Do not the arts increase our enjoyment of life? Do they not make us more sensitive? Do they not give color and emotional depth to our existence? Do they not develop a feeling of intensity? The important fact is that we view the arts not merely from the standpoint of spectators, but as *participants*, so that our existence receives both a new depth and a new significance. The discovery of great books, great paintings, great musical compositions, great dramas, and great poetry should be a *climactic* experience for the child, involving both a sense of passionate joy and intense wonder.

A sense of values

However, the process of enlightenment is incomplete without a sense of values, perhaps best achieved through the study of philosophy. Traditionally, technical theories have been stressed in philosophy; the student has been taught about great thinkers instead of developing his own view of life. A much better approach would be *existential*, so that the student sees the personal matrix and significance of philosophy; that it has important social implications; and that it inevitably refers to the present. All this involves a *humanization* of philosophy with a stress upon education rather than epistemology.

Enlightenment as a process

Enlightenment, however, is not an entity; it is never completely achieved. This realization ought to imbue the student with a sense of limitation. It also ought to encourage him to apply his ideas and ideals so that society becomes more rational, humane, and compassionate. We fail as educators if our high-school and college graduates are interested only in making a living, instead of improving the quality of life for themselves and others.

Culture Change

War and revolution

In the past, cultural change has been attained mainly through war and revolution. Heraclitus said that war is the father of all things. Does not war add to culture diffusion? Does not war encourage invention? Does not war promote quantitative growth?

But the effects of war upon human civilization are negative, rather than positive. War promotes the cause of dictatorship; it develops regimentation and, in the long run, creates a permanent emergency. It develops biases and hatreds, inconsistent with a moral view of civilization. The promise usually is that war will lead to peace, but in history it has only led to more wars. War creates iron personalities who lack human warmth and sensitivity. We have only to think of the various characters described so ably and eloquently by Mailer in *The Naked and the Dead*.

In education war usually promotes the physical sciences and obstructs the humanities. During World War II a wholesale exodus from the humanities and social sciences took place. War accelerates the advancement of applied science, but it retards the progress of pure science. In the atomic age, it is clear, war threatens the survival of civilization.

Darkness at Noon

The method of revolution is just as destructive as that of war. Revolutions create the type of personality described so eloquently by Koestler in *Darkness at Noon*. The two main protagonists are Rubashov and Gletkin. Rubashov is a Commissar who has been imprisoned by the Russian authorities. He took part in the revolution with a faith that a better world would be established. He had made sacrifices for the cause of his Party. But after the victory was won, his faith was shaken. He began to doubt the righteousness of the

THE GOALS OF EDUCATION

cause. Could man live by obedience alone? Could human feeling be eliminated? Did the means justify the ends in history? Was murder excusable in the defense of a social cause? Could man live without freedom? Was security more important than liberty? Was heresy the worst political crime?

Rubashov was in jail, not so much for overt acts, although he was accused of plotting to assassinate the head of the State, but for his doubts and skepticism. A revolutionary movement, whether of the right or the left, cannot tolerate *loss of faith*.

The antagonist of Rubashov is Gletkin, the prosecutor, who admits no subjective standards, who has submerged his own individuality in the service of the State. To Gletkin, the world is divided into two camps; those who accept the cause, and those who rebel against it; those who believe in the dogmas of the Party and those who attack them. To Gletkin, compromise is an impossibility; a middle-ground cannot be achieved. The fact that Rubashov doubted the official dogmas, that he admitted humanitarian standards, made him an enemy, a potential danger to the Party and the State.

Gletkin is the prototype of the modern Machiavelli; he can justify any act, any betrayal of morality, any crime, because it serves his cause. He regards education not as a tool of rationality, but as a form of social conditioning. Is it not the task of education to eliminate independence on the part of the individual?

Gletkin realized that Rubashov could not be re-educated and so Rubashov had to die. Rubashov had to be made an example. His last service to the Party was to be a confession of crimes he had *not* committed. This was to be a symbol of the futility of his acts, and the failure of his opposition. Rubashov's fate was to be a warning to others who might rebel against the power of the Soviet state.

The important point in *Darkness at Noon* is that revolutionary movements usually start by proclaiming faith in freedom, and end by destroying freedom in an atmosphere of total conformity. Education under those circumstances cannot prosper, for freedom of inquiry is basic; there is no substitute for it. To be sure, vocational education can flourish in a totalitarian regime, be it Mussolini's Italy, Peron's Argentina, or Khrushchev's Russia, but vocational education is not the substance and core of culture; it is only a prelude to the life of enlightenment.

Education as a living faith

Our faith, then, is that an enlightened system of education provides the best method of cultural change. Now such a system works gradually; it stresses intangible values as well as tangible facts; it takes advantage of the resources of the scientific method and the inventions of technology. It appeals to the emotions and to the mind of man. It provides for no external authority, gives no magic formulas, and no intoxicating slogans. It promises no perfection in the distant future. It makes clear that no immoral means shall be used to achieve moral ends; and, most important of all, it regards the individual as an end, rather than as a tool of an all-powerful organization.

Questions and Topics for Discussion

1. Why is traditionalism such an obstacle in education?
2. What is the relationship between psychology and education?
3. Do you agree or disagree with Freud's concept of reason?
4. Do you feel that the 3 R's are slighted in our schools? Defend your viewpoint.
5. Why is authoritarianism a constant danger in education?
6. How did the German educational system contribute to the growth of National Socialism?
7. What is anthropomorphism and why is it an important concept?
8. What is the meaning of enlightenment?
9. Do you believe that progress is inevitable? Explain.
10. What, in your opinion, constitutes progress in education?
11. How can the arts contribute to the process of enlightenment?
12. Why is self-realization such an important value?
13. Why does war impede the advance of the humanities?
14. What is the relationship between war and education?
15. What is the significance of *Darkness at Noon*?

Selected References

ALBERTY, H., *Reorganizing the High School Curriculum*, 1947.
BODE, B. H., *Fundamentals of Education*, 1931.

THE GOALS OF EDUCATION

BRUBACHER, J. S., *A History of the Problems of Education,* 1947.
———, *Modern Philosophies of Education,* 1950.
———, *Eclectic Philosophy of Education,* 1951.
BUTLER, J. D., *Four Philosophies and Their Practice in Education and Religion,* 1951.
BUTTS, F., *The American Tradition in Religion and Education,* 1950.
EATON, T. H., *An Approach to a Philosophy of Education,* 1938.
FINNEY, R., *A Sociological Philosophy of Education,* 1928.
FITZPATRICK, E. A., *Readings in the Philosophy of Education,* 1936.
HENDERSON, S., *Introduction to Philosophy of Education,* 1947.
KOESTLER, A., *Darkness at Noon,* 1941.
LEARY, D. B., *Living and Learning,* 1931.
READ, H., *Education for Peace,* 1949.
TUTTLE, H. S., *A Social Basis of Education,* 1934.
WHITEHEAD, A. N., *Aims of Education,* 1929.

XIV. THE QUEST FOR THE GOOD LIFE

Foundations of the Good Life

Education and the good life

EDUCATION represents the yearning for the good life. In every generation it will be interpreted in a different way, for as man advances new needs and new possibilities arise. One hundred sixty years ago, it would have been thought impossible that millions of students would go to college in the United States, and that high-school education would become almost universal; two hundred years from now, if not sooner, college education may become as prevalent as high-school education is today.

This does not imply that mere extension of education will create happiness or automatic progress. Quantitative expansion of education does not prevent dictatorship, as the experiences of the Germans under Hitler indicate. The Germans, before Hitler, represented one of the most civilized nations in the world, yet they succumbed to the temptations of dictatorship. Education to be successful must be qualitative as well as quantitative, must touch our sense of morality as well as our intellect. How can the good life be found? No magic formula can be given, but it appears clear that a well-functioning body is the foundation. Those educators who ignore the biological basis of man, just do not observe sharply, and they are unrealistic.

Physical well-being adds to zest in our strivings and gives us a feeling of completeness. We have never explored completely the resources of our senses. Few of us are able to observe sharply; few of us are completely sensitive to the beauties of nature.

Asceticism

Often, the joy of life is inhibited by the medieval perspective which looked with disdain upon the world of matter and which regarded the body as a source of imperfection. Was not the body the seed of sin? Was not the body subject to a thousand temptations? Had not the great saints lived a life of celibacy? Yet, St. Francis has already pointed out that salvation and spirituality depend on love, not on the negation of the joys of life.

Zest for life

This zest for existence is eloquently represented in Walt Whitman's "When Lilacs Last in the Dooryard Bloomed":

Lo, body and soul—this land,
My own Manhattan with spires, and the sparkling and hurrying tides, and the ships,
The varied and ample land, the South and the North in the light, Ohio's shores and flashing Missouri,
And ever the far-spreading prairies cover'd with grass and corn.

Lo, the most excellent sun so calm and haughty,
The violet and purple morn with just-felt breezes,
The gentle soft-born measureless light,
The miracle spreading bathing all, the fulfill'd noon,
The coming eve delicious, the welcome night and the stars,
Over my cities shining all, enveloping man and land.

In search of sanity

Educators ought to create a perspective of sanity, and they ought to be conscious of the principles of mental hygiene. Schools fail when they do not give a balanced program, when they establish no creative outlets for children, and when they over-emphasize work, keeping play to a minimum. Traditionally, in our educational system the spirit of competition has been cherished; today we favor more the ideal of cooperation. Critics of the new educational approach have often said that such a concept of life is unrealistic, that when the student enters the adult world he will have to get used to a world in which only the strong can survive. But in business also, we are learning the importance of human relations, and if the influence of our schools is strong enough, then society will feel their idealistic impact. *Our task in life is not merely to adjust; we should struggle against premature adjustment and adjustment on a low plane; rather our task is to live profoundly and meaningfully.*

Social factors

Such an existence cannot be realized without understanding society. We become fully human only through social relationships. At first, when we are very young, we are only concerned with our own needs; we tend to be egocentric; some, of course, never outgrow this condition; but, as we become more mature, we recognize the joys of sharing, and we strive for mutuality and reciprocity. Many individuals live a twisted life because they are frustrated in their personal relationships; our marriage problems, as the divorce rate indicates, are indeed complex. Here again education can help by clarifying values, by overcoming ignorance, by increasing economic efficiency, by more scientific studies, and, above all, by better personal counseling.

Guidance for happiness

Many educators believe that if more money were spent for the prevention of juvenile delinquency and for better guidance facilities, our crime bill could be cut in half. We usually try to change the criminal offender when he is an adult; we treat psycho-neurotic problems when they have become serious, instead of starting therapy when children are young and plastic and when their behavior can be reconstructed.

A mature understanding of the self will avoid the extremes of egoism and submergence in a social group. The egotist is a blind man, for he can see only his own interests, and he is callous toward others. But it is just as dangerous, as existentialist thinkers point out, to try to lose oneself in a cause or to submerge one's personality in a group. Unless individuality is fully cultivated, we lose the essential joy of living and we constantly escape into forms of unreality.

Too many, today, have jobs which they dislike thoroughly and which offer no challenge to their creative talents. Vocational counseling, thus, is especialy important in our school system. What could be worse than an existence of monotony, of going to work at nine o'clock, looking at the time-clock every hour, taking an hour off for lunch, and then returning home at five o'clock, weary and dissatisfied. The teaching profession may be under-paid, but it is a welcome relief from drudgery. The good teacher has the satisfaction of seeing novelty in his class-room, of discovering original talents, of helping others, and thus building a better future for society.

The need for esthetic activities

Our life is incomplete without esthetic activity. Did not Nietzsche say that life would be tragedy without music? Did not Schopenhauer assert that art is a direct key to reality? In our esthetic life we achieve both more objectivity and more subjectivity. Thus, a great writer, like Dante, could achieve almost a universal perspective in his *Divine Comedy;* his personal sorrows and defeats could be forgotten in his vision of heaven, hell, and purgatory. At the same time he could become more conscious of his own personality, his own desires, and his own love for Beatrice, the symbol of perfection.

As we become interested in art, not only as spectators, but as participants, life has a new meaning for us. As Kokoschka said, a blade of grass may be more significant than a king, a landscape may have greater depth than a big mansion. This means, as Blake wrote in *Auguries of Innocence*:

> To see the world in a grain of sand,
> And a heaven in a wild flower;
> Hold infinity in the palm of your hand,
> And eternity in an hour.

We notice as we study the history of civilization how art characterizes the soul of man. Material remains often are more transitory than the works of painting, sculpture, music, and architecture. In the United States as in ancient Rome, we borrow too much from other nations and we are too utilitarian in our concept of art. We do not patronize creative artists sufficiently.

The reader may object, and point to our sponsorship of symphony orchestras, our magnificent museums, and our vast attendance at concerts of various types. Still we are interested mainly in the technician, rather than the creator of art. Poets have a difficult time finding an audience; American composers usually are neglected by their contemporaries. The drama of ideas suffers, because the audience wants action and sex, and is impatient with abstractions. In this respect, our schools have not been too successful in raising the taste of the public, or in improving our level of culture.

Science, Religion, and Philosophy

Science

Science gives a quantitative basis for culture. It reduces qualities to mathematical units, and thus nature can be controlled by man. Science teaches us that reason must be used concretely, and that it is expanded through the use of invention. Science is a social matter. We usually think only of spectacular scientists, like Pasteur, Planck, and Einstein, and we forget that their researches depended on the collaboration of thousands of unknown scientists who came before them.

The world of the scientist is in many ways like the universe of Spinoza. It allows no place for individual bias and desire; it is subject to laws which go beyond caprice. Does it reveal a completely deterministic structure? The answer is in the negative, as Peirce has pointed out. To be sure, the law of causality can be applied to the investigation of nature, but there is no necessity in causality, and indeterminism plays, according to Heisenberg, a large role in nuclear science. We use scientific laws as *postulates* to control nature for the benefit of man.

The changes which science has created in the United States are indeed breath-taking. Our life has become mechanized. We travel, today, to New York faster than our ancestors traveled to Philadelphia. Distant countries have become our neighbors; through radio and television we become spectators of the most important events of our time. Scientific understanding has eliminated much superstition; no one, today, would believe in witchcraft; still not all superstitions have been eliminated; now they occur more along political, social, and economic lines.

As more and more secrets of the universe are uncovered, man feels a new sense of power and a new exaltation. He believes that he can comprehend the structure of the world. According to P. W. Bridgman, this faith "is the most important gift of science to civilization."

Education and scientific progress

Education can promote the progress of science by humanizing it, by training the scientist, not only in his own field, but in the humanities, by teaching him a sense of social responsibility, and by emphasizing the constructive, rather than the destructive uses of science. Nationalism in almost every country threatens the advancement of science. Education ought to stress the international basis of science and that freedom of inquiry is essential if scientific research is to be promoted.

No student should graduate from high school or college without understanding the meaning of the scientific method. Should not the tentativeness, the hypothetical spirit, and the strict regard for truth, which we have in science, be applied to our social institutions? Should we not avoid in our political and economic thinking *a priori* theories? Should we not examine beliefs according to their evidence?

Religion

Religion adds to science by its stress upon ideal values and by indicating that ideals are not impractical but *essential* for successful living. Many of us live by expediency, with a dual standard; one for ourselves and one for society. Many of us worship tribal idols; others are serfs to an omnipotent party. Some regard religion as a form of coercion, and feel that anyone who differs is bound for damnation.

Faith and action must combine. *If religion is only theology, it becomes an escape from reality. If religion is only ritual, it becomes a metaphysical form of poetry.* When religion is applied to our daily life, when it transforms social institutions, it fulfills a central function in civilization and narrows the gap between Utopia and actuality.

Search for an affirmative philosophy

We need, above all, in our quest for a good life, a constructive philosophy. Pessimists may say that our existence is futile, that an evil will governs the universe, and that all is vanity; but such a view is basically insincere. For example, Schopenhauer, the great German pessimist, said that fame is vanity and then asked his disciples to save all the reviews of his books. To Schopenhauer, life was tragedy, but when he was ill he went to a doctor, trying to prolong "the tragedy."

This criticism of pessimism does not mean that we should all become confirmed optimists and overlook the evils of human existence. Most contemporary writers, like Faulkner, Sartre, Berto, Moravia, Capote, Mailer, Bowles, and T. S. Eliot, are rather somber about the prospects for the future. They picture man's inhumanity to man, and man's failure to adjust to civilization. Tragedy in art may deepen our understanding and may give us a more realistic basis for our faith.

The teacher as optimist

Still the teacher ought to be an optimist. His attitude toward his students ought to be one of encouragement and hopefulness. Life will present enough obstacles, discouragement will come later, and perhaps even defeat. Thus the schoolroom ought *to be an oasis of hope.* When the teacher sees the spark of creativity in his students, his faith radiates, and it contributes to a new perspective. The teacher can never be a defeatist, for is he not the surgeon of the spirit?

THE QUEST FOR THE GOOD LIFE

Questions and Topics for Discussion

1. Why is physical well-being so important in the good life?
2. What does Whitman say about man's existence?
3. Why is the new educational approach so important?
4. Why are human relations paramount in our school system?
5. How can education aid in the preparation for marriage?
6. What, in your opinion, are the qualities of the good counselor?
7. Why is our life incomplete without esthetic activities? How, in your opinion, can the program of art appreciation be strengthened on the primary and secondary level?
8. Discuss the statement: "Art characterizes the soul of man."
9. How can we develop a truly appreciative audience in our school system?
10. What are some of the changes that science has accomplished in twentieth century America?
11. How can education promote the progress of science?
12. Do you believe that more students should study mathematics? Explain.
13. Why does nationalism threaten the advancement of science?
14. What are the weaknesses of a pessimistic philosophy of life?
15. Why are ideals essential for successful living? Why are ideals so important in teaching?
16. What, to you, are the elements of the good life?

Selected References

ASHLEY, MONTAGU, M. F., *On Being Human*, 1950.
BERNAL, J. D., *The Social Function of Science*, 1939.
BROWN, H., *The Challenge of Man's Future*, 1954.
CHASE, S., *Roads to Agreement*, 1951.
CONANT, J. B., *On Understanding Science*, 1947.
FROMM, E., *Man for Himself*, 1947.
——, *The Sane Society*, 1955.
MAY, R., *Man's Search for Himself*, 1953.
MAYER, F., *Education and the Good Life*, 1957.
MONTAGUE, W. P., *Great Visions of Philosophy*, 1950.
MUMFORD, L., *The Conduct of Life*, 1951.
MURPHY, G., *Personality*, 1947.
NIEBUHR, R., *Moral Man and Immoral Society*, 1932.
SULLIVAN, H. S., *Conceptions of Modern Psychiatry*, 1947.

PHILOSOPHY IN ACTION

TEAD, O., *Character Building and Higher Education*, 1953.
TEMPLE, W., *Christianity and the Social Order*, 1942.
TRILLING, L., *The Liberal Imagination*, 1950.
WHITMAN, W., *Democratic Vistas*, 1921.
———, *Leaves of Grass*, 1921.
WILSON, E., *Shores of Light*, 1952.

XV. THE PROBLEM OF TRUTH

The Meaning of Truth

A basic problem

BASIC IN THE PHILOSOPHY of education is the problem of truth. For we desire not merely knowledge, but coherence of ideas, not merely facts, but an understanding of significance. Man thus is a system-builder. Philosophers in the past have attempted to give us an understanding of eternal truth, a final evaluation of the meaning of the universe. Yet the great systems of classic philosophy, like those of Kant and Hegel, are in decline today because we believe more in a specific and tentative approach to life and we are suspicious of large-scale assumptions. We smile when we read Hegel's dictum that the real is rational and that the rational is real; for what is real and what is rational?

Having been exposed to the rigorous labors of psychology, we tend to be more conscious of our prejudices in the search of truth. We realize with Freud that some of our cherished beliefs may be only rationalizations, excuses for our biases; we accept with Pareto the viewpoint that our ideals may be only derivations of fundamental patterns of existence and organization. We cannot escape the existential problem in our search for truth; for knowledge exists not as a thing-in-itself, but as a living relationship to fragmentary individuals.

The teacher thus loses his position of absolute authority. He becomes instead a dramatist of ideas, who explores with his students the possibilities of the intellectual life; he can never stand still; he can never relax his efforts; he can never assume omnipotent knowledge. As soon as he repeats the past, as soon as he discovers *only* sameness in the classroom, his creativity will be exhausted.

Meister Eckhart, one of the great medieval mystics, prayed for poverty so that the love of God would penetrate his soul. Eckhart wanted to abandon all forms of externality. The teacher likewise should avoid all preconceptions and empty his mind of formal rules; instead he should be guided by the dialectic and atmosphere of the class. Like the artist, he should try to give emotional color to analytical facts.

No final answer

To be more specific, in teaching, the digression may be more valuable than the formal subject matter. We are often annoyed when students interrupt us with questions, for we are intent upon covering a certain topic. Occasionally, the questions appear to be immature; perhaps we have heard them before. The mediocre teacher will express his annoyance and will give a superficial answer, while the superior teacher will explore the meaning of the question, clarify it and discuss its ramifications, somewhat as Plato discussed the problem of Ideas in the *Parmenides*. The superior teacher will not suggest that a final answer exists, rather he will ask a question in return so that the students will be constantly stimulated.

Need for inwardness

We make the mistake in education of hurrying through the process of knowledge, like an American traveler trying to see the world in two weeks. This only results in vagueness, superficiality, and a nodding acquaintance with precision and factual competence. The search for truth demands a leisurely spirit. In college we fail when we give too many assignments or when we regiment our students so that they have not enough leisure time for the exploration of their own interests. A dean of a reputable school of music, which prided itself on its high standards, one time told me that his students worked so hard that some of them had nervous breakdowns. He was very proud of that fact, for he thought the unfit would be eliminated in this fashion. But the life of creativity suffers when we establish too many barriers. *Often we gain knowledge of techniques and abandon spontaneity; we learn about rules and we forget the reason for their existence; we become proficient, but we lose the spark of individuality.* A South American composer recently told me, "Your musicians are great technically, but they lack a soul." This may be an exaggeration and an unwarranted generalization, but the statement contains an element of truth. We tend to be too much concerned with externality, instead of inwardness.

Various standards

In trying to define the meaning of truth philosophers have established various standards. The idealists look upon truth as the expression of an eternal mind, as an absolute principle, which governs the flux of everyday existence. As Sir Edward Dyer wrote:

> My mind to me a kingdom is;
>   Such present joys therein I find
> That it excels all other bliss
>   That earth affords or grows by kind:
> Though much I want which most would have,
> Yet still my mind forbids to crave.
>
> No princely pomp, no wealthy store,
>   No force to win the victory,
> No wily wit to salve a sore,
>   No shape to feed a loving eye;
> To none of these I yield as thrall:
> For why? My mind doth serve for all.

Idealism and truth

Certainty, clarity, and coherence govern the idealistic philosophers. For example, Descartes would accept only those standards of knowledge which possessed the certainty of mathematics; while Hegel felt that all parts of the universe were involved with each other and could be understood dialectically.

The weakness of the idealistic view of truth is that it often leads to solipsism, the theory that only my own private world, my own private desires have reality. For if to be is to be perceived, and if we are only conscious of our own sensations and ideas, we can have no trustworthy knowledge of the ideas of others. In modern novels, the solipsistic tendency is extremely strong. Thus Joyce was mainly interested in his own reactions and passions, and his characters, as in *Ulysses*, have almost lost touch with the external world. Kafka, in *The Castle* and *The Trial*, reduces literature to subjective interludes and introspective episodes in which symbolism replaces external facts.

The idealist in philosophy suffers from the same deficiences as the idealist in politics who makes beautiful statements about the "Four Freedoms." We may agree in theory and we may approve these noble objectives, but disagreeement results when we try to define the method or attempt to develop the means whereby great aims are to be realized.

Avoidance of extremes

In education we are often overwhelmed by two extremes. Some educators who follow the idealistic tradition are only interested in ultimate goals, and they neglect methodology. They speak of the perfection of the spiritual life and the greatness of eternal truth. When specific means are mentioned, they are somewhat disinterested, for they look upon methodology as a temporal process, while ultimate goals go beyond the dictates of space and time. On the other hand, we find some pragmatists who only stress methodology, who confess that no ultimate aims exist and that the concept of growth is to govern all of life. But methodology without a vision of goals may be a self-defeating process and may lead to irrationality. The purpose of a project is just as important as the execution of it. A purpose exists not as an isolated idea, but in a social matrix. A purpose thus becomes a postulate for action.

The mistake of traditional idealism was to imbue the universe with a final purpose. For example, Aristotle thought that man was a rational animal and that cultivation of reason was man's greatest achievement. The universe itself, according to the Greek thinker, was striving to achieve the perfection of God, who governed the world not as an actual ruler, but as a pattern of perfection.

No single purpose

It is doubtful whether mankind has a single purpose; the more we observe life, the more we realize that purposes are diverse and that they are determined by historical accidents. The purpose of Greek civilization thus was more intellectual than the purpose of American civilization; Goethe's *Faust* may be an excellent prototype for German culture, but may be inadequate in American civilization, which may be expressed more fully by Sinclair Lewis's *Babbitt*. A purpose, consequently, is tentative and gives only a temporary sense of unity. It performs the same function as the ego of the individual, imbuing us with a sense of centrality without negating empirical diversity.

Direction in education

The great value of a teleological philosophy in education is that through it we obtain a sense of *direction*. If we believe only in growth, we may identify it with physical activity and we may claim that material expansion is the equivalent of educative advancement. We may believe that the more buildings we establish, the more courses we teach, the more progress will be achieved. But expansion merely for the sake of expansion creates a wasteland of spiritual emptiness. An individual achieves greatness through concentration. Thus Somerset Maugham, in *The Summing Up*, confessed that he was a writer almost twenty-four hours a day, that all of his activities had a significant relationship to his novels, short stories, and plays. The educator, like the artist, should undertake a phenomenological purge and should attempt fewer activities in a more *profound* manner.

To be more concrete, universities make a mistake when they imitate business organizations and when they organize too many colleges and departments. The result often is that mediocrity, instead of greatness, is achieved. Courses in cosmetology and mortuary science may have a sales value for the public, and may attract students, but they cheapen higher education. Not all subjects have the same educative value; not all ideas have the same consequences. Acquaintance with first-rate ideas and first-rate teachers creates a great center of learning, while association with mediocre instructors and uninspiring subjects creates a school which lives by expediency and materialism.

The Pragmatic Viewpoint

Evaluation of pragmatic truth

The pragmatic viewpoint, that truth is determined by consequences, has both advantages and disadvantages. The advantage is that we see more the incomplete nature of life and that we usually avoid dogmatism. In this way we subject our ideas to exact methods of scientific proof.

The disadvantage may be the development of the cult of immediacy. An idea may work now, but it may have deplorable consequences in the future. A teacher, for example, may be extremely popular, and yet be rather shallow, or he may attract only a handful of students as Santayana did at Harvard and still make a great impression upon the university. Santayana in *Persons and Places* tells us how dismayed the president of Harvard was when he found out that only four students had enrolled in Santayana's philosophy class. Was this not a sign of incompetence? Was this not a symbol of failure?

Man a weaver of fictions

As we become more sophisticated in knowledge, we realize that what is true may not be beautiful or what is good may not necessarily be true. As a weaver of fictions, man is a poetic creature, and he often escapes to a realm which has no factual existence, but which, nevertheless, adds color to his life. The outward fact, or even the consequence of the fact, is less important than the symbolism behind it. Religion itself points to a realm beyond facts and beyond immediacy. The truth of the spiritual life is less important than its poetic beauty and its support to human hopes and human aspirations.

Need for poetry

Education fails when it becomes too sober a process and when it does not stir our sense of poetry. The teacher who always asks for empirical evidence and who is merely interested in verification of ideas reduces education to a mechanical enterprise. His objectivity tends to be barren; he eliminates what is perhaps most precious in man—subjective depth and poetic imagination.

The Essence of Truth

The realist position

The realistic concept of truth, as championed by Russell, sees the deterministic structure of the universe. The realist looks upon the pragmatist as being too sentimental. Truth, the realist asserts, exists independently of man. Relations are external. Our views tend to be false when we base them upon our own desires; they tend to be valid when they are subordinated to the structure of facts.

The keynote of realism is resignation. Nature, we are told, is governed by laws and is not concerned with man. The universe is blind to our needs and desires.

In ancient philosophy the Stoics preached a philosophy of acquiescence. Was not nature law-abiding? Was not nature the expression of deterministic laws? Unlike the Stoics, modern realists, like Russell, stress the dualism between man and nature and assert that the objective and subjective poles of existence are far apart.

The teacher who is dominated by the gospel of realism usually emphasizes precise facts and exact measurements. He tends to regard mathematics as the most important science and as the model for the study of human behavior. The danger is that he may overlook the *uniqueness* of individuals. We should realize that intellectual capacities depend upon emotional conditions, and that such non-quantitative attitudes as determination and curiosity may decide our intellectual effectiveness. *Stress upon quantification without a knowledge of motivation results in empty formalism in education.*

The realist, like the ancient Eleatics, is too much interested in the problem of being. He often overlooks the reality of change and the implications of possibility. Bergson, in *Introduction to Metaphysics*, points out that the universe is in a constant state of flux. Even on a warm summer day, when we are in the country and when we contemplate the stillness of life, our existence is being transformed. Time passes, nature is at work, and a multitude of sensations pass through our mind.

Truth as a process

It is impossible then to define the essence of truth, for truth is a complex process; it involves the past and the present, and it points to an unexplored future; it depends upon both antecedents and consequences. Truth is not an autonomous realm; it involves an understanding of beauty and goodness.

The teacher and truth

The teacher who is genuinely interested in the pursuit of truth will always welcome new insights and new viewpoints. Novelty thus will be cherished, instead of being regarded with suspicion. Such a teacher will imbue his students with a solid regard for facts, without developing a scientific form of fatalism; such a teacher will be interested in establishing a correspondence between knowledge and action so that society becomes more humane.

The human predicament

It is true that, except for rare moments, human beings think mostly of their own interest and welfare. Our thoughts and reveries tend to be on an ego-centric plane. To most of us life is a drama with only one central character. As Sir Walter Raleigh wrote in "The Lie":

Go, Soul, the body's guest,
Upon a thankless arrant:
Fear not to touch the best;
The *truth* shall be thy warrant:
Go, since I needs must die,
And give the world the lie.

Tell zeal it wants devoting;
Tell love it is but lust:
Tell time it is but motion;
Tell flesh it is but dust:
And wish them not reply,
For thou must give the lie.

Tell age it daily wasteth;
Tell honour how it alters;
Tell beauty how she blasteth;
Tell favour how it falters:
And as they shall reply,
Give every one the lie.

Questions and Topics for Discussion

1. Why is the problem of truth basic in the philosophy of education?
2. Can there be a final explanation of the universe? Justify your answer.
3. Why is the teacher a dramatist of ideas?
4. Why is the digression so important in teaching?
5. Discuss the statement: "The search for truth demands a leisurely spirit."
6. How does the idealist look upon truth?
7. What are the weaknesses of the idealistic view of truth?
8. Do you believe that life has a cosmic purpose? Justify your answer.
9. Why is a sense of direction so important in education?
10. What are the advantages and limitations of the pragmatic concept of truth?
11. What is the realistic concept of truth?
12. Discuss the statement: "It is impossible to define the essence of truth."
13. Why should the teacher be a constant learner?
14. Why is poetic imagination so significant in education?
15. Do you believe that the universe is governed by invariable laws? Explain your answer.

PHILOSOPHY IN ACTION

Selected References

BERKSON, I. B., *Preface to an Educational Philosophy*, 1940.
BODE, B. H., *Progressive Education at the Crossroads*, 1938.
BRAMELD, T., *Philosophies of Education in Cultural Perspective*, 1955.
BREED, F. S., *Education and the New Realism*, 1939.
CHILDS, J. L., *Education and the Philosophy of Experimentalism*, 1931.
HORNE, H. H., *The Democratic Philosophy of Education*, 1935.
KILPATRICK, W. H., *The Educational Frontier*, 1933.
LODGE, R. C., *Philosophy of Education*, 1947.
MAUGHAM, W. S., *The Summing Up*, 1938.
MOORE, E. C., *What is Education*, 1915.
RANDALL, J., H. and J. BUCHLER, *Philosophy*, 1942.
ROGERS, H. K., *A Student's History of Philosophy*, 1907.
ROYCE, J., *The Spirit of Modern Philosophy*, 1892.
SARTRE, J. P., *Existentialism*, 1947.
SKINNER, C. E. and R. E. LANGFITT, *An Introduction to Modern Education*, 1937.
THOMPSON, G. H., *A Modern Philosophy of Education*, 1929.

XVI. MAN, FREEDOM, AND CULTURE

The Ideals of Democracy

THE MEANING of democracy is one of the great problems of our time. Just as in the colonial period, a strong conflict is being waged between those who, like Hamilton, are opposed to democracy, and those who, like Jefferson, believe in the unlimited possibilities of freedom.

We constantly hear the term "democracy in education." Is it merely a slogan or does it have an actual meaning? Does it imply equal educational opportunity for all or only for the most brilliant? What is the social function of education? These questions are pressing and of utmost importance, and they cannot be answered without an understanding of the essential meaning of democracy.

Democracy as a faith

Democracy represents a living faith. It stresses the fact that every individual counts, that regardless of class, race, or nationality he has inalienable rights of which he may not be deprived. These rights have been gained only after a long historical struggle and they are never completely won. They are in jeopardy especially in times of crisis and war. Thinkers like Locke, Montesquieu, and Jefferson

PHILOSOPHY IN ACTION

have contributed to the expansion of these rights. All three had a passionate faith in freedom and they believed that man could fully develop only in a free society.

Freedom

Freedom at first was defined in rather narrow terms. Locke, for example, was more concerned with freedom for property holders than freedom for the common people. In colonial times only a small minority was eligible to vote. The Puritans, who made a great contribution to the expansion of democracy, believed that their opponents, especially the Catholics and Quakers, should not be tolerated. As a matter of fact several Quakers were put to death in Puritan Boston.

Protection of freedom, it should be remembered, depends not merely on legal sanctions, but on community attitudes. It implies faith in reasonableness, a willingness to tolerate various views of life and various concepts of politics and religion.

To protect freedom, it is necessary to curb the power of the state. The experience of history indicates that whenever one organization has gained absolute dominance, it has curtailed fundamental freedoms. A pluralistic concept of society, including separation of state and church, is the best defense against totalitarianism.

Laws

In democracy, the ideal is that laws are superior to men. Laws provide for stability and for continuity in culture. Laws are in some ways the best protection against arbitrary authority. But laws are not absolutes. When they are viewed in a rigid manner, when they are enforced without vision, they become chains, and develop the frozen bureaucratic mind so prevalent in modern civilization.

Peaceful evolution

While totalitarian governments depend on violent change and encourage revolutions, democratic governments depend on peaceful evolution. Legislation, elections, and education are the main forces which promote a gradual change in a democracy. The ideal is to protect both the rights of the majority and the rights of the minority. When only one party exists, the will of the people cannot be expressed.

The enemies of democracy

The two great enemies of democracy have been war and economic insecurity. Wars have created an attitude of despair and chaos in which totalitarianism could flourish. Depressions likewise have weakened the hold of democracy, for in times of need the individual will listen to any demagogue and he will abandon his freedom for security. He usually finds out that once he has given up certain fundamental rights, they are not easily regained. Did not Jefferson say, *Malo periculosam libertatem quam quietam servitutem (I prefer freedom, though fraught with dangers, to servitude with security)?*

Leadership

Freedom of inquiry

Democracy cannot exist without freedom of inquiry. Once we close the door to independent research and freedom of discussion, we have entered the path of totalitarianism. Since the sovereignty of the individual is the ideal of democracy and since the citizen makes the ultimate decisions, he must be informed, otherwise he will act according to prejudice and bias.

Lack of information creates a condition already envisaged by Washington. The individual will be unstable in his allegiance. Today he will favor one party; tomorrow another. In foreign policy this will mean friendship for one nation and hostility for another. Emotions and hysteria, instead of rationality, will guide the individual and the nation.

Experts

Especially important today is the need for expert leadership. Too often democracies have had too much faith in the common touch.

Too often distrust has been shown towards the expert. It is true that experts without humanitarianism are of doubtful value, but the issues of the modern world are too complex to be solved by mere emotionalism.

Education for democracy

What can educators do to strengthen democracy? How can they aid the cause of freedom? No categorical formula can be given, but certain attitudes can be created. Education itself, as Dewey points out, should represent the best aspects of democracy. This means equality of opportunity, more emphasis on student government, protection of the rights of minorities, and freedom of expression for both student and teacher. Unless democracy becomes a way of life in the schoolroom, it has little chance in the adult world.

The student in the classroom should be taught respect for the opinions of others. This does not imply that all opinions are on the same level or of equal value. Some are based on factual evidence, while others represent merely a blind faith. The student should learn how to weigh opinions, how to judge issues and then make a tentative decision. Others may disagree with him, and he should learn to protect their right to dissent.

One of the tasks of contemporary education is to develop intelligent leadership and a responsible audience. Not all can be leaders, but all can appreciate effective leadership. The schools ought to train students so that they will regard government service as an honor. Unfortunately, parents frequently maintain that politics would be the last occupation they would recommend to their children. In this way the victory of the ignorant and the unscrupulous in political life may be brought about.

Ethical ideals

The schools should imbue students with high ideals of honor and integrity. This does not imply formal teaching about honor or integrity, but making these concepts part of the life of the student. For example, an honor system should be developed in the primary grades and should continue until graduate shool. As long as the teacher acts as a policeman, who has to *enforce* certain standards, the schools have failed in providing for higher standards of morality.

Cooperation

Modern life requires enormous cooperation on the part of various groups. The old type of school usually stressed competition between students, while the new school emphasizes the spirit of cooperation. It is easy to cooperate with those who agree with us; it is much more difficult to create cooperation when fundamental differences exist. Nevertheless, education should indicate the need for harmonious mutuality even in an atmosphere of diversity.

Nazi education

While schools in a democratic society emphasize cooperation, the child-centered approach, respect for reason, and freedom of inquiry, in totalitarian countries like Nazi Germany the school favored the leadership principle, thought control, and preparation for war. The teacher became merely a propagandist for the state. It was his task to indoctrinate children in blind allegiance to their nation and hate for their enemies. Truth for the sake of truth was not respected; rather truth in a Machiavellian manner was subordinated to political expediency.

Under the Nazi regime, action was glorified, and the intellectual was regarded with scorn. Was not the man of reason too objective? Was he not aloof from political emotion? Was he not often a potential opponent of National Socialism? Students in Nazi schools were urged to join the Hitler youth organization; in this way they would be promoted more easily; in this way they would have an easier time at the university; and later they could obtain better jobs. Educational standards disintegrated completely; professors did not dare to fail a student who was a faithful party member.

Criticism of the regime was not tolerated. A professor who was scornful of National Socialism could expect dire consequences. In a mild case, just the loss of his position; in a severe case, the tortures of a concentration camp.

The entire direction of education in such a system was towards

PHILOSOPHY IN ACTION

war. The student was trained in the arts of war, and he was told by his teachers how glorious it was to die for the fatherland. Physical virtues were emphasized, especially bravery in battle; intellectual virtues such as love of reason and truthfulness were regarded as being entirely secondary.

Democratic vs. Totalitarian Education

The struggle between democratic and totalitarian ideals of education is of ancient origin. For example, the conflict between Sparta and Athens was not only a political struggle, but a conflict of educational aims.

Spartan education

In Sparta the ideal of education was to create strong soldiers. According to Plutarch, students were early exposed to a rigorous way of life. Boys wore only scant clothing. Usually they had only one coat; in this way, it was thought, their bodies would be hardened. If they failed the tests of endurance, they were flogged in a merciless manner. Even music was used to stimulate military virtue. Only the august Doric rhythms were allowed; all effeminate types of music were outlawed.

Girls, likewise, were subjected to stringent physical exercises. The Spartan ideal was to produce strong mothers who would produce strong children. Weak or malformed children were not allowed to live.

Interest in culture for the sake of culture was discouraged; contact with foreigners was not allowed. The Spartan state was organized for war, both against external and internal enemies. Occasionally, the helots, the serfs, were slaughtered by the Spartans. This was done to keep the serfs in check and also to promote military *efficiency*.

Athenian education

In Athens, on the other hand, physical virtues were subordinated to intellectual excellence. It was thought that education should train the whole man, not just his body. The Athenian loved the life of reason, and so he patronized philosophy, the arts, and drama. Beauty became the keynote to the Athenian temperament. Even moral standards were evaluated in esthetic terms. Thus the evil man was thought to be lacking in taste, while the good man exercised the highest forms of sensitivity. Intellectual tolerance was shown by the Athenians, although occasionally, thinkers, like Socrates and Anaxagoras, were persecuted. Compared with Sparta, Athens was an educational paradise.

The ideals of Athenian education were beautifully summarized by Pericles as quoted in Thucydides:

> We are lovers of the beautiful, yet simple in our tastes, and we cultivate the mind without loss of manliness. . . . The great impediment to action is, in our opinion, not discussion, but the want of that knowledge which is gained by discussion preparatory to action. For we have a peculiar power of thinking before we act and of acting too, whereas other men are *courageous from ignorance but hesitate upon reflection.*

American education and Athenian ideals

Modern American education has a broader base than Athenian education; its buildings and techniques are far more imposing; its scientific accomplishments are greater, but where is the love of reason which the Athenians had? Where is philosophy as a natural way of life? Where is faith in careful deliberation? Where are the great teachers like Socrates and Epicurus? Where is the sense of moderation and balance? Where is the pursuit of beauty as an intense passion? To be sure, we are not lacking in beauty, philosophy, and perhaps even great teachers; still our intellectual accomplishments do not compare with those of Athens. The Athenian experiment, in short, presents a constant challenge to American education.

Philosophy and Democracy

Idealist contribution

Various philosophies have contributed to a genuine democratic view of education. The idealist, like Horne, has shown the importance of moral and spiritual aspirations. To the idealist, selfhood is ultimate. While the facts of nature may change, selfhood unites past, present, and future. In seeking an absolute standard, the idealist has found a principle by which change can be evaluated. Some idealists, like Ulich and Croce, have been the most insistent opponents of totalitarianism.

The realists' achievement

The realist in education, like Breed and Russell, shows that scientific advancement depends on objectivity and that man is not the center of the universe. The more man understands nature and the more he realizes the independent structure of the external world, the more he escapes from his ego-centric bondage. Does not democracy imply a respect for facts regardless of individual desires? Does not the future of democracy depend on the promotion of scientific knowledge?

Pragmatism and democracy

The pragmatist, like James, Bode, Mead, Kilpatrick, and Dewey, appeals to concreteness. He is impatient with old standards, absolute assertions, and *a priori* viewpoints. He has faith in the pluralistic possibilities of experience. Knowledge becomes not a mirror of reality, but a way of adjustment. Education and philosophy are equated; the quality of living and doing, rather than theorizing, is stressed.

In its tentative, experimental spirit pragmatism best expresses the ideals of democracy. The implications of pragmatism are vast for all fields of inquiry, as Dewey brought out in *Reconstruction in Philosophy*. But pragmatism must be constantly redefined; otherwise it becomes a dogma, rather than a *living vision*.

Romantic pragmatism

My own educational philosophy is a romantic version of pragmatism. It is a new version of pragmatism and differs from Dewey just as Dewey differed from James. Yet all of us have a certain spirit in common: We believe in the open-mind, in the scientific method, and in a philosophy with vast social and educational implications.

The educational philosophy which I have outlined stresses the centrality of the teacher, not as an authoritarian force, but as an unending source of inspiration and dedication. It regards liberal education as the center of life. It emphasizes that we learn best through insight. It believes in an optimistic philosophy of life, that a creative spark exists in every individual, and that poetry is just as important as the scientific method. It advocates a core program from kindergarten to graduate school. It regards culture not as a luxury for a few, but as a desperate need for all. It stresses the moral implications of education, as Schweitzer does in his *Ethics and Civilization*.

The aim of such an educational philosophy is to help create another renaissance: *Athens slightly Americanized*. We certainly have the material resources and the technological strength; *all we need is the determination, and the moral vigor, and a collective enthusiasm for the possibilities of education.*

Questions and Topics for Discussion

1. What is the essential meaning of democracy?
2. What was the colonial concept of democracy?
3. Compare the ideals of democracy with those of totalitarianism.
4. What is the role of the elite in education? Should there be special schools for superior students?
5. How can education strengthen democracy?
6. Should the schools stress the ideals of co-operation or those of competition?
7. Discuss the ways in which teachers can contribute to community affairs.
8. Do you believe that teachers should take an active part in political campaigns? Justify your answer.
9. Why was the struggle between Sparta and Athens significant from an educational standpoint?
10. What was the Spartan ideal of education?
11. Why is selfhood ultimate to the idealist?
12. Why does the pragmatist appeal to concreteness? Compare pragmatism with idealism.
13. Discuss the statement: "Knowledge in pragmatism becomes not a mirror of reality, but a way of adjustment."

PHILOSOPHY IN ACTION

14. What does the author mean by romantic pragmatism?
15. Can education bring about a new renaissance of American culture?

Selected References

ADAMSON, J. W., *A Short History of Education*, 1920.
COLE, P. R., *A History of Educational Thought*, 1931.
COUNTS, G. S., *Education and American Civilization*, 1952.
DEWEY, J., *Democracy and Education*, 1916.
DOOB, L., *Propaganda*, 1935.
EBENSTEIN, W., (Editor), *Man and the State*, 1947.
KOHN, H., *The Twentieth Century*, 1949.
LASKI, H. J., *The American Democracy*, 1948.
LILGE, F., *The Abuse of Learning*, 1948.
MAYER, F., *Education for Maturity*, 1956.
MELBY, E. O., *Freedom and Public Education*, 1953.
NATIONAL SOCIETY FOR THE STUDY OF EDUCATION, *Modern Philosophies and Education*, 1955.
RATNER, J., (Editor), *Intelligence in the Modern World: John Dewey's Philosophy*, 1939.
RAUP, R. B., *Education and Organized Interests in America*, 1936.
ULICH, R., *Fundamentals of Democratic Education*, 1940.

XVII. THIS I BELIEVE

I BELIEVE in the values of public education, the foundation of democracy. Within this structure we must realize the importance of diversity. Admitting that public education needs criticism for its own improvement, I still feel that the main hope for America and for democracy lies in the perfection of public education.

I believe that the American teacher is the most solid supporter of democracy, and that education ought to be teacher-centered as well as child-centered. Teaching can never be mediocre or it becomes self-defeating. Teaching must be great, yet greatness has many dimensions. It is not a possession, but a pilgrimage. It is measured by consequences—its influence on the lives of students and on culture.

I believe that the teacher is the servant of the future, of the day after tomorrow. I believe in self-criticism in education. Smugness and self-righteousness are as dangerous in education as in religion. We can never consider the problems of education outside of the social matrix. There is a fundamental difference between education and indoctrination. I feel that the teacher's function is not that of a propagandist, but that of an analytical scientist with a sense of actuality.

I believe that a philosophy of life is basic in education, that one cannot teach profoundly and constructively without such a philosophy. Our educational philosophy ought to be humane, guided by the spirit of compassion and mercy.

PHILOSOPHY IN ACTION

I believe that standards are secondary, for man forms his own values. Every generation will create its own standards, thus forever reforming the future.

I believe that every student has a creative spark. The development of this spark is our most *sacred* task. This spark makes us truly human, gives continuity to existence, and gives hope for the future. What it is we do not know, for ultimately man remains a secret to himself. Man sees himself only in manifestations, not as an essence. Perhaps this spark indicates that nothing is impossible if we have the necessary patience and intelligence.

I believe in the creative possibilities of subject matter.

I believe in competence in the basic skills, but they are only preludes to genuine creativity.

I believe that the center of education is the present, that the twentieth century is the underlying problem of all problems. The study of the past for the sake of the past is intellectual archeology.

I believe in the liberal arts as the core of education. By the liberal arts I mean those studies which make us humane, compassionate, and develop our critical attitude.

I believe in the value of "unessential" studies. The arts, especially music, should be part of every classroom.

I believe that administration and teaching are interdependent. Administrators ought to be concerned, not with trivial details, but with the philosophy of the program they administer. Education will advance in proportion to our ability to produce great administrators and great teachers.

I believe in men rather than buildings—in values rather than statistics. I do not believe that poverty among teachers adds to civilization. I feel that all levels of education are the same, that, if anything, the primary teacher is more important than the college professor.

I believe that teaching is the most important vocation of mankind. Teaching must be dramatic, profound, and enjoyable. If it is not, our philosophy is inadequate.

I believe that the discussion method is the heart of education. Discussion implies the convertibility of both student and teacher, that neither takes a dogmatic position, but that both maintain a position of fallibility.

I believe that the teacher must be willing to accept novelty. Teaching indicates the fallacy of a cyclical view of life. Teaching demonstrates that life is not vanity, but an invitation to creativity.

I believe in the *integrity* of the teaching profession. It is undignified and unwise for the teacher to succumb to every political storm.

I believe that education can prosper only in an atmosphere of freedom, and that freedom can never be maintained by authoritarian means.

I believe in the future of American democracy, for dictatorship is ultimately destroyed because it does not recognize the creative spark in the individual.

I believe that provincialism is the greatest enemy of education. As we broaden our horizons and expand our viewpoints, we see life under the aspect of universality.

I believe there are no poor teachers, only *unawakened* teachers.

I believe there are no poor students, only *unmotivated* students.

I believe that education will change drastically within our own lifetime, especially in the use of audio-visual techniques and television in our schools.

I believe that the use of psychiatric methods will expand in education, with ultimately a psychologist in every school.

I believe in scientific measurement as means, not as an end, in education.

I believe that the possibilities of adult education are one of the unfulfilled promises of our democracy.

I believe that morality can never be legislated, but must be exemplified.

I believe that ignorance in our time is perhaps the worst form of immorality. Morality demands constant self-examination on the part of the teacher and the student. There is a close relationship between education and religion, education being one of the great signs of the spiritual nature of man.

I believe that the authoritarian attitude is as dangerous in morality as in education.

PHILOSOPHY IN ACTION

I believe in the scientific method illuminated by poetry.

I believe that we are approaching a golden age in education, and that education will prosper more in the future than in the past.

I believe in the *total* approach in education, with emphasis on intensity, for totality must have a direction and a purpose.

I believe in the centrality of literature in education, for literature forms man's mirror of himself.

I believe in respect for facts; they are the matter of education, just as values represent the form of education.

I believe that free universal public education is our greatest contribution to civilization.

I believe, in short, that education represents the kingdom of God on earth.

Glossary of Names

ABÉLARD, P. (1079-1142). French philosopher whose *Sic et Non* is an example of his independent spirit. He was suspected of heresy and some of his works were burned. He is famous for his love affair with Héloïse.

ACTON, LORD (1834-1902). Professor of history at Cambridge University and a discerning critic of modern civilization. He concentrated especially upon the problem of power.

ADAMS, H. B. (1838-1918). American historian famous especially for his autobiography, *Education of Henry Adams*. Adams yearned for the certainty of medieval culture and had contempt for modern machine civilization.

ADLER, M. Contemporary philosopher who for many years taught at the University of Chicago. Among his books we find *How to Read a Book*. He is noted as a caustic critic of progressive education.

AESCHYLUS (525-426 B.C.). Greek dramatist whose works, such as *The Persians* and *Prometheus Bound*, exhibit a strong moral sense.

ALBERTUS MAGNUS (1193-1280). As teacher of Aquinas he laid the foundations of a synthesis between Aristotle and the teachings of the Church.

ALCOTT, A. B., (1799-1888). American transcendentalist whose theories of education shocked his contemporaries. Author of *Ralph Waldo Emerson* (1865).

ALEXANDER, T. 19th century writer on educational problems. Author of *The Prussian Elementary School*.

ALLEN, E. (1738-1789). American revolutionary soldier who was also a philosopher. As a deist he was opposed to religious orthodoxy.

GLOSSARY OF NAMES

Anaxagoras (500?-428 B.C.). Greek thinker who taught in Athens. He was accused of impiety by the Athenians because he gave a naturalistic account of the planets.

Anselm of Laon. A twelfth century contemporary of Abélard who was a supporter of orthodoxy. Anselm was head of a school at Laon.

Aquinas, Saint Thomas (1225?-1274). Greatest medieval theologian whose work *Summa Theologica* is a masterpiece and authoritative for the Catholic Church.

Aristotle (384-322 B.C.). Probably the greatest Greek thinker. He founded the Lyceum. Among his many works are *Politics, Rhetoric, Metaphysics,* and *Nichomachean Ethics.* He stressed the importance of moderation.

Augustine (354-430). Bishop of Hippo who in the *City of God* gave a classic expression of Catholic thought. His personal life and his religious conversion are recorded in *The Confessions.*

Bacon, Sir Francis (1561-1626). English Renaissance scientist who developed new concepts of logic and who opposed the influence of Aristotelianism. Among his works are *Essays, New Atlantis,* and *Novum Organum.*

Barnard, H. (1811-1900). First commissioner of education of the United States who was also editor of the *American Journal of Education.*

Barth, K. (1886—). He is one of the great theologians of our time. Author of *Christian Dogma.* He now lives in Switzerland.

Berdyaev, N. A., (1874-1948). Russian theologian, author of *Spirit and Reality* and *Solitude and Society.*

Bergson, H. (1859-1941). French philosopher who gave a spiritual interpretation of evolution. His best known work is *Creative Evolution.*

Berkeley, G. (1685-1753). Irish philosopher who represented the viewpoint of idealism. Author of *Principles of Human Knowledge.*

Bernard of Clairvaux (1091-1153). French saint who opposed Abélard and was formative in the second crusade. He wrote theological treatises like *De Contemptu Dei, De Consideratione,* which exhibit his mystical spirit.

Berto, G. (1914—). He represents the realistic spirit of contemporary Italian literature as can be seen in his *The Sky is Red.*

Blake, W. (1757-1827). English artist and poet whose works are extremely mystical as in his *Songs of Innocence* and *Auguries of Innocence.*

Bode, B. H. One of the twentieth century leaders in pragmatic philosophy. He taught for many years at Ohio State University. Among his works are *Fundamentals of Education* and *Progressive Education at the Crossroads.*

GLOSSARY OF NAMES

BOETHIUS, A. M. (480-524). Roman philosopher whose *Consolation of Philosophy* is his greatest work.

BOWLES, P. (1910—). He is active in literature as well as in music. His most thought-provoking book is *The Sheltering Sky* (1949).

BRAMELD, T. B. Noted contemporary philosopher of education; author of *Patterns of Educational Philosophy* and *Towards a Reconstructed Philosophy of Education*. He favors a utopian approach to education and believes that a reconstruction of our schools is needed.

BREED, F. S. One of the leaders in the realistic school of educational philosophy.

BRIDGMAN, P. W. (1882—). He won the Nobel prize for physics in 1946. He has been especially interested in the relationship between philosophy and science.

BRUNNER, E. (1889—). This Swiss theologian expresses the spirit of Protestant orthodoxy. Among his works are *Our Faith* and *The Divine Imperative*.

BRUNO, G. (1548?-1600). Italian thinker who opposed Aristotelianism and who was a heretic. He was burned at the stake in 1600.

BÜCHNER, C. L. (1824-1899). A physician who stressed a scientific philosophy and opposed orthodox religion.

CALVIN, J. (1509-1564). Author of the *Institutes of the Christian Religion* and one of the most brilliant theologians of all time. He contributed to the development of Protestantism and his concepts of religion have influenced many denominations, especially Presbyterianism.

CAMUS, A. Contemporary French novelist and essayist who reflects the influence of existentialism. Among his books are *The Fall* and *The Stranger*.

CAPOTE, T. (1924—). He is a novelist, short-story writer and playwright. One of his best works is *Other Rooms, Other Voices*.

CARLYLE, T. (1795-1881). Scottish historian and essayist who developed the great man theory of history in *Heroes and Hero Worship*. Carlyle was especially influenced by German idealism.

CARR, P. One of the friends and correspondents of Thomas Jefferson.

CASSIODORUS, F. M. He lived in the sixth century A.D. and was a founder of monasteries which aided in preserving ancient learning.

CASSIRER, E. (1874-1945). German philosopher and author of such works as *Essay On Man* and *Philosophy of Symbolic Forms*. He reflects the influence of Kant.

CERVANTES, M. (1547-1616). Spanish author of *Don Quixote*, which is one of the immortal satires of the ideals of knighthood.

CHATEAUBRIAND, F. (1768-1848). French writer and statesman who expressed the spirit of romanticism, especially in his *René*.

GLOSSARY OF NAMES

CHAUCER, G. (1340?-1400). English poet and author of *The Canterbury Tales*, a satire on medieval society.

CICERO, M. T. (106-43 B.C.).Roman statesman and author whose letters have a timeless beauty. He was an eclectic in philosophy who appreciated both Platonism and Aristotelianism.

COLERIDGE, S. T. (1772-1834). English romantic poet and critic best known for his *Ancient Mariner*.

COLET, J. (1467?-1519). One of the foremost scholars of the Renaissance. He popularized the ideals of humanism.

COMENIUS, J. A. (1592-1670). Czech educator and theologian who developed a progressive system of education.

COPERNICUS, N. (1473-1543). Polish astronomer who developed the heliocentric theory. His main work is *On The Revolution of Heavenly Bodies*.

COOPER, T. (1759-1839). American scientist and political philosopher whose *Political Essays* reflect a naturalistic spirit. He had extremely unorthodox views in religion. He taught at the University of Pennsylvania and at Dickinson College.

COUSIN, V. (1792-1867). French philosopher who specialized in German thought and who was minister of public instruction.

COUSINS, N. Born in 1912. Editor of the *Saturday Review* and one of the most eloquent critics of our time. Noteworthy are his *Who Speaks for Man?* and *Modern Man is Obsolete*.

CROCE, B. (1866-1952). Italian philosopher and statesman. An idealist, he reflects the influence of Hegel. Among his works is *Politics and Morals*.

DANTE (1265-1321). Italian poet whose *Divine Comedy* is a summary of medieval ideals. In education he stressed the importance of the vernacular and urged a better system of instruction for the underprivileged.

DARWIN, C. R. (1809-1882). Author of *The Origin of Species* and *Descent of Man*, which revolutionized science. His theory of evolution caused both philosophical and scientific controversy.

DESCARTES, R. (1596-1650). French thinker who has been called father of modern philosophy. His works include *Meditations, Discourse on Method*, and *Passions of the Soul*.

DEWEY, J. (1859-1952). Probably the outstanding American philosopher of the twentieth century. A pragmatist, he laid the philosophical foundations of progressive education. His *Democracy and Education* became one of the most influential books of our time.

DE WITT CLINTON (1769-1828). Leader in the spread of democratic education in the United States. He was active in the state of New

GLOSSARY OF NAMES

York and was president of "The Society for Establishing a Free School in the city of New York."

DILTHEY, W. (1833-1911). German thinker who was especially interested in the philosophy of history. He wrote an important book on pedagogy.

DONNE, J. (1573-1631). English poet of the metaphysical school who was both an eloquent author and a powerful preacher.

DREISER, T. (1871-1945). American naturalistic novelist whose *American Tragedy* has become a classic.

DURKHEIM, E. (1858-1917). A French sociologist who was especially interested in primitive behavior. Author of *De La Division du Travail Social* (1893) and *Les Formes Elementaires de la Vie Religieuse.*

DYER, SIR EDWARD (c1550-1607). English writer and poet who was a close friend of Sir Philip Sidney.

ECKHART, MEISTER (1260?-1327). German Dominican priest known for his mystical sermons. Especially eloquent was his sermon on poverty. He was suspected of heresy by the Church authorities.

EDWARDS, J. (1703-1758). Puritan preacher and philosopher who popularized the ideas of Calvin in the United States. Among his works his treatise on freedom of the will is especially noteworthy.

EINSTEIN, A. (1879-1956). He became famous for his theory of relativity and in 1922 won the Nobel prize for physics. He left Germany because of Hitler and became an American citizen. He lectured at the Institute of Advanced Studies at Princeton.

EL GRECO. (1548?-1614). Spanish painter of the Renaissance whose works express the mysticism of that nation.

ELIOT, T. S. (1888—). Born in the United States, he has migrated to England. He is one of the best-known modern poets and critics, and as a proponent of tradition he shows the futility of contemporary culture. His *Wasteland* has become a modern classic.

EMERSON, R. W. (1803-1882). American poet and essayist whose works, such as *The American Scholar, Self-Reliance,* and *Compensation,* embody his ideals of transcendentalism.

EPICURUS (342?-270 B.C.), Greek thinker who stressed the importance of pleasure and who gave a scientific account of man.

ERASMUS, D. (1466?-1536). A Dutch humanist who satirized the follies of mankind. He is best known for *In Praise of Folly.*

EUCKEN, R. C. (1846-1926). German philosopher of the idealistic school who in 1908 received the Nobel prize in literature.

EUCLID (c300 B.C.). Greek mathematician who developed the foundations of geometry and whose contributions are still studied today.

EZEKIEL. He lived in the sixth century B.C. and was one of the major Hebrew prophets.

GLOSSARY OF NAMES

FADIMAN, C. (1904—). For many years he was book editor of *The New Yorker*. His principal work is *Party of One*.

FAULKNER, W. (1897—). Faulkner's novels deal with the South. He won the Nobel prize in 1955.

FEUERBACH, L. H. (1804-1872). A naturalist, Feuerbach attacked orthodox Christianity in *The Essence of Christianity* (1840).

FICINO, M. (1433-1499). Italian philosopher of the Renaissance who spread the concepts of Platonism.

FRANCKE, A. H. (1663-1727). German pietist and educator who founded a teacher-training school.

FRANKLIN, B. (1706-1790). He was eminent as statesman, inventor, and philosopher. His autobiography has become a classic. As a deist, he stressed a rational approach to religion. In education he emphasized moral virtues.

FREDERICK WILLIAM IV (1795-1861). Son of Frederick William III, he represented a reactionary spirit in Prussia.

FREUD, S. (1856-1939). Austrian neurologist whose theories of sex caused a scientific revolution. He developed the science of psychoanalysis. He taught at the University of Vienna and when the Nazis came to Austria he fled to London. From an educational standpoint his lectures on psychoanalysis and his *Civilization and its Discontents* are especially important.

FRÖBEL, F. (1782-1852). German educator who founded the kindergarten. He was an idealist and stressed the spiritual possibilities of man. Author of *Die Menschenerziehung* (1826) and other works.

GALILEO (1564-1642). Italian astronomer who supported the Copernican hypotheses and who taught at Padua.

GANDHI, M. K. (1869-1948). Indian leader who fought for the independence of his nation. He believed in non-violence and inspired millions of followers.

GAUTAMA BUDDHA (563?-483 B.C.). Indian thinker who founded a new religion based on overcoming desire and thereby finding emancipation (Nirvana).

GOETHE, J. W. (1749-1832). German poet who in *Faust* attempted to summarize the dilemmas and temptations of man. He was especially influenced by Spinoza.

GOGH, V. VAN (1853-1890). Dutch painter whose expressionism stamps him as one of the masters of the nineteenth century.

HABE, H. (1911—). He is a German-American novelist whose principal work is *A Thousand Shall Fall*.

HALL, G. STANLEY (1844-1924). American psychologist and educator, he was the first president of the American Psychological Association.

GLOSSARY OF NAMES

Hamilton, A. (1757-1804). American statesman who represented the Federalist viewpoint and opposed the democratic ideas of Jefferson.

Harris, W. T. (1835-1909). Noted American philosopher and educator who was an idealist in his theory of education. He became United States Commissioner of Education. Harris stressed the importance of discipline in education.

Hegel, G. W. (1770-1831). German philosopher whose *Phenomenology of Spirit* is an example of his absolute idealism. Hegel's philosophy of history influenced the development of Marxism. Hegel's famous dictum was: "The real is rational and the rational is real." Encyclopedic in his interests, he also wrote *Philosophy of Art, Logic, History of Philosophy*.

Heidegger, M. Contemporary German philosopher who is an existentialist and whose main work, *Being and Time*, displays his atheism and subjectivity. Heidegger had a profound influence upon the famous French existentialist, Jean Paul Sartre.

Heine, H. (1797-1856). German poet who gave voice to the ideals of romanticism, especially in his *Buch der Lieder*.

Hemingway, E. (1898—). He has become the spokesman of the "lost generation." His greatest work is generally considered to be *A Farewell to Arms*.

Heraclitus. (c535-c475 b.c.). Greek thinker whose philosophy stressed the importance of change.

Herbart, J. F. (1776-1841). German thinker and educator who laid the foundations of educational psychology in such works as *General Pedagogy* (1806).

Herbert, G. (1593-1633). English clergyman and poet. He belonged to the metaphysical school.

Heisenberg, W. (1901—). He won the Nobel prize in physics in 1933. He developed the theory of indeterminacy which limits the application of causal relations to atomic particles.

Hitler, A. (1889-1945). Born in Austria, he became chancellor of Germany in 1933. His political ideas are expressed in *Mein Kampf*. His theory of national socialism emphasized extreme chauvinism and anti-semitism.

Hobbes, T. (1588-1679). English philosopher whose materialism is expressed in his *Leviathan*.

Holbach, P. H. (1723-1789). French materialistic philosopher who opposed conventional religion.

Homer (c10th century b.c.). Traditional Greek poet who is thought to be the author of *The Iliad* and *The Odyssey*.

Horne, H. H. Twentieth century philosopher of education; author of *The Democratic Philosophy of Education* and *The Philosophy of*

GLOSSARY OF NAMES

Education. An idealist, he was vigorously opposed to Dewey's pragmatism.

HUME, D. (1711-1776). Scottish philosopher who became famous because of his skepticism. His works include *A Treatise of Human Nature* and *Enquiry Concerning Human Understanding*.

HUTCHINS, R. M. (1899—). A vigorous critic of Dewey, he favored a philosophy of perennialism. He has had a notable career in education as dean of Yale Law School and president of the University of Chicago. Among his books are *Education for Freedom*, *University of Utopia*, and *No Friendly Voice*.

HUTCHINSON, A. (1591-1643). A religious radical, she rebelled against Puritanism and advocated freedom of conscience.

ISIDORE OF SEVILLE (560?-636). Spanish scholar who specialized in encyclopedic labors. His main work is entitled *Etymologies*.

JACKSON, A. (1767-1845). Seventh president of the United States. He tried to expand American democracy.

JAMES, W. (1842-1910). Developed the philosophy of pragmatism. He was eminent both in philosophy and in psychology. Author of *Pragmatism* and *Varieties of Religious Experience*. In education he is noted for his *Talks to Teachers*.

JEFFERS, R. (1887—). He is a poet in the classical tradition, as can be seen in his *Tower Beyond Tragedy*. Noteworthy in his poetry is his pessimism and penetrating indictment of twentieth century culture.

JEFFERSON, T. (1743-1826). American statesman and writer whose ideas were formative in developing the American concepts of freedom and education.

JONES, R. M. (1863—). He became one of the leaders of the Quakers. He taught at Haverford College and wrote many books on mysticism.

JOYCE, J. (1882-1941). Irish writer best known for his *Ulysses*, which utilizes a stream of consciousness technique.

KAFKA, F. (1883-1924). Austrian writer who specialized in philosophical novels such as *The Trial* and *The Castle*.

KANT, I. (1724-1804). German philosopher who taught at the University of Königsberg. His main works are *The Critique of Pure Reason*, *The Critique of Practical Reason*, and *The Critique of Judgment*.

KIERKEGAARD, S. (1813-1855). Danish existentialist who opposed Hegelianism. He stressed a personal approach to philosophy and education. His main work is *Concluding Unscientific Postscript*. He has been called the Socrates of Denmark.

KILPATRICK, W. H. (1871—). He popularized the educational theories of John Dewey. For many years he taught at Teachers College, Columbia. Among his books are *Philosophy of Education* and *Foundations of Method*.

GLOSSARY OF NAMES

KOESTLER, A. (1905—). Born in Budapest, Koestler became in his youth a Communist. Later he gave up the party and became one of its most acute critics. He is best known for his *Darkness at Noon*.

KÖHLER, W. (1887—). Born in the Baltic provinces, Köhler became a professor at Frankfurt. He specialized in the study of apes.

KOKOSCHKA, O. (1886—). He is an Austrian expressionist painter and dramatist. He specializes in portraits and landscapes.

KORZYBSKI, A. 20th century pioneer in the study of semantics (the meaning of meaning); author of *Science and Sanity* and *The Manhood of Humanity*. He fought against the influence of Aristotelian logic and developed a system based on a non-Aristotelian viewpoint.

KROPOTKIN, P. A. (1842-1921). Russian social philosopher who stressed the importance of co-operation. He wrote *Memoirs of a Revolutionist* and *Science and Anarchism*.

KRUTCH, J. W. (1893—). He taught literature at Columbia and is one of the most acute American critics, as can be seen in his *Measure of Man*.

LAMPRECHT, K. (1856-1915). German historian who gave a social-psychological account of man.

LANGER, S. Contemporary American thinker who won fame for her *Philosophy in a New Key*.

LASKI, H. J. (1893-1950). British political scientist who favored the Labor party; among his works are *Democracy in Crisis* and *The Problem of Sovereignty*.

LEIBNITZ, G. W. (1646-1716). German thinker especially known for his *Monadology*. He believed that the universe is composed of monads (spiritual force-centers). An optimist, he taught that this is the best of all possible worlds.

LEONARDO DA VINCI. (1452-1519). Great artist and scholar of the Renaissance who anticipated many of the inventions of our time.

LESSING, G. E. (1729-1781). German critic and dramatist best known for his *Nathan the Wise*. He expresses the tolerant spirit of the German Enlightenment.

LEWIN, K. (1890-1947). A German psychologist, he came to the United States and taught at Massachusetts Institute of Technology. Among his works is *A Dynamic Theory of Personality*. He was a pioneer in group dynamics.

LEWIS, S. (1885-1951). American novelist whose books, such as *Babbitt* and *Arrowsmith*, gained world-wide recognition. He satirized the behavior of the American middle class.

LIPPMANN, WALTER. (1889—). One of the keenest writers on political science, government, and ethics of our time, as can be seen by his *Preface to Politics* and *A Preface to Morals*.

GLOSSARY OF NAMES

LOCKE, J. (1632-1704). An English philosopher whose ideas influenced the American revolution. In education his thoughts were opposed to classicism. He favored moral education and vocational training. His main work is *Essay Concerning Human Understanding*.

LUCRETIUS, (96-55 B.C.). Roman epicurean author best known for his philosophical poem *De Rerum Natura (On the Nature of Things)*.

LYND, R. (1892—). He is a sociologist and taught at Columbia. His best-known works are *Middletown* and *Middletown in Transition*, which he wrote with his wife.

MACH, E. (1838-1916). Austrian physicist and philosopher who developed a philosophy of realism. He was especially interested in the analysis of sensations.

MACHIAVELLI, N. (1469-1527). Italian political theorist whose *The Prince* has become one of the masterpieces of social science. In his cynicism he mirrored the mood of the Renaissance.

MACIVER, R. M. (1882—). This Scottish American sociologist now teaches at Columbia. He is especially interested in political thought as he expressed it in *The Modern State*.

MADISON, J. (1751-1836). Fourth President of the United States and one of the authors of the Federalist papers.

MAILER, N. (1923—). He belongs to the naturalistic school of novelists as is exhibited in *The Naked and the Dead* and *The Deer-Park*.

MALTHUS, T. R. (1766-1834). English clergyman who wrote a historic essay on population. He maintained that population increases in a geometric ratio while food supply increases only in an arithemetic ratio with the result that poverty becomes inevitable for mankind.

MANN, H. (1796-1859). American educator whose reforms in Massachusetts aided the cause of public education.

MANN, T. (1875-1955). Thomas Mann achieved fame as a writer of novels and essays. Among his works especially noteworthy are *Bruddenbrooks* and *Magic Mountain*.

MANNHEIM, K. (1893-1947). German sociologist whose main work is *Ideology and Utopia*. He believed in the principle of social planning, but he was suspicious of bureaucracy.

MARCEL, G. Contemporary French philosopher who believes in a religious version of existentialism.

MARITAIN, J. (1882—). He is one of the most noted French thinkers. A Catholic, he represents the viewpoint of neoscholasticism in such works as *True Humanism* and *Religion in the Modern World*.

MARQUAND, J. P. (1893—). He is a noted author who describes especially the New England scene. In 1941 he wrote *H. M. Pulham, Esq.*

MARX, K. (1818-1883). German thinker who in *Das Kapital* developed the foundations of modern Communism. He held that history is guided

GLOSSARY OF NAMES

by economic factors and that a class struggle exists between the bourgeoisie and the proletariat. He opposed traditional education because it was based upon aristocratic privilege.

MATHER, C. (1663-1728). He was the son of Increase Mather and for a time supported witchcraft trials. Author of *Wonders of the Invisible World* and other works.

MATHER, I. (1693-1723). American clergyman who was a spokesman for Congregationalism.

MAUGHAM, W. S. (1874—). One of the most popular novelists of our time. His principal work is *Of Human Bondage*.

MEAD, G. H. (1863-1931). He taught at the University of Chicago and was an adherent of pragmatism. One of his best works is *Mind, Self and Society*.

MEAD, M. (1901—). American anthropologist whose researches have changed our attitude regarding primitive behavior. Among her books are *Male and Female* and *Coming of Age in Samoa*.

MENCKEN, H. L. (1880-1956). American author who wrote burning satires of Puritanism and who was influenced by Nietzsche. He was called the sage of Baltimore.

MONTAIGNE, M. (1533-1592). Author of *Essays*, which stamped him as a skeptic. His *Essays* influenced many modern French writers, including A. Camus and J. P. Sartre.

MONTESQUIEU, BARON (1689-1755). French philosopher and lawyer who believed in a representative government. Best known for his *Persian Letters* and *The Spirit of Laws*.

MORAVIA, A. (1907—). He won fame for his *Woman of Rome*. Like Berto's, his novels are naturalistic.

MUSSOLINI, B. (1883-1945). Italian dictator who started as a socialist and later turned to Fascism. He supported Hitler in World War II. Like Hitler, Mussolini believed in the leadership principle in education and used the schools as training-grounds for war.

NAPOLEON I (1769-1821). French ruler who started as a follower of the revolution and ended as Emperor. He died on St. Helena.

NICHOLAS OF CUSA (1401-1464). He anticipated the ideas of Copernicus. He was a Catholic bishop who wrote both on mathematics and philosophy.

NIEBUHR, R. (1892—). American theologian who stresses man's sinfulness. He teaches at Union Theological Seminary and is author of the monumental *Nature and Destiny of Man*.

NIETZSCHE, F. (1844-1900). German philosopher whose best known work is *Thus Spake Zarathustra*. He is especially noted for his theory of the Superman. He called for a "transvaluation of values"—a radical reconstruction of ethical ideals.

GLOSSARY OF NAMES

O'Neill, E. (1888-1953). One of the great dramatists of all time whose last plays were enthusiastically received on Broadway. *The Iceman Cometh* is regarded by some critics as his best play.

Ortega y Gasset, J. (1883-1955). He represents an existential viewpoint in his philosophy. His best known work is *The Revolt of the Masses*.

Orwell, G. (1903-1950). English author who opposed totalitarianism and whose *1984* is a frightening example of a modern Utopia.

Paine, T. (1737-1809). American political philosopher whose writings inveighed against all forms of tyranny. His philosophy is contained in *The Age of Reason*.

Pareto, V. (1848-1923). Italian sociologist who developed the philosophic bases of Fascism. Among his works are *The Mind and Society*.

Pascal, B. (1623-1662). French thinker famous in both science and philosophy. His *Pensées* have become a classic.

Pasteur, L. (1822-1895). French scientist who made fundamental contributions to medicine, especially in the prevention of hydrophobia.

Paton, A. (1903—). This South African novelist has given a realistic account of his nation's racial problems. His best-known work is *Cry, the Beloved Country*.

Patrick, C. A contemporary writer who specializes in the psychology of creativity.

Pavlov, I. P. (1849-1936). Famed Russian psychologist known for his behaviorism and his attempt to base psychology upon physiological phenomena. He was especially interested in the exploration of reflexes.

Peirce, C. S. (1839-1914). He developed the foundations of pragmatism. He was especially interested in mathematics and logic.

Pericles (c490-429 B.C.). Athenian statesman under whose reign Athens experienced a golden age.

Perry, R. B. (1876—). He has been especially interested in pragmatic philosophy. For many years he taught philosophy at Harvard. Among his works is *Realms of Value* (1954).

Pestalozzi, J. (1746-1827). Swiss educational thinker who was influenced by Rousseau. He believed in a dynamic, individualistic system of education. He wrote a novel, *Leonard and Gertrude*, which embodies his educational philosophy.

Phidias. (c500-c432 B.C.). Greek sculptor who did much to beautify the Parthenon.

Pico della Mirandola, G. (1463-1494). One of the leading humanists of the Renaissance who was suspected of heresy by the Church.

Planck, M. K. (1858-1947). German physicist who won the Nobel prize. His contributions to thermodynamics and to the quantum theory are especially noteworthy.

Plato (427?-347 B.C.). Noted student of Socrates who wrote the

GLOSSARY OF NAMES

Republic and other dialogues which stamp him as one of the most original thinkers of all time. He stressed the importance of universal concepts and believed in the immortality of the soul.

PLOTINUS (205?-270 A.D.). Roman thinker who gave a mystical version of Platonism in his *Enneads*.

PLUTARCH (46?-120 A.D.). Greek biographer and philosopher whose best work is his *Parallel Lives*.

POINCARÉ, J. H. (1854-1912). French scientist and mathematician who held that scientific "laws" are only hypotheses, not absolutes.

POPPER, K. R. (1902—). He is active in philosophy and in social science. His main work is *The Open Society and its Enemies*, which is a vigorous attack upon totalitarianism.

PRIESTLEY, J. (1733-1804). English clergyman and chemist who was in sympathy with the French Revolution and who influenced Unitarianism.

PROTAGORAS (c481-411 B.C.). Greek Sophist who taught that all values are relative. He contributed to a humanization of the Greek curriculum.

PYLE, E. (1900-1945). One of the best-loved American journalists, who was killed in World War II. His *Brave Men* has become a classic.

RABELAIS, F. (1494?-1553). One of the immortal humanists who is known especially for his *Gargantua*.

RADHAKRISHNAN, S. (1888—). Radhakrishnan has had a brilliant career both in politics and in philosophy. His *History of Indian Philosophy* is of inestimable value to the Western student.

RALEIGH, SIR W. (1552?-1618). English writer and courtier who was an inveterate explorer and whose poems include *The Lie*.

RAMUS, P. (1515-1572). He was a French scientist who opposed Aristotelianism. He was killed in the Massacre of St. Bartholomew.

REICHENBACH, H. One of the leaders of the twentieth century school of logical empiricism. For many years he taught at U.C.L.A. Author of *The Rise of Scientific Philosophy*.

REUCHLIN, J. (1455-1522). A German humanist, he was especially interested in promoting knowledge of the classical languages.

RIESMAN, D. (1909—). He won fame for his *The Lonely Crowd*, an excellent study of middle-class America.

ROBINSON, J. H. (1863-1936). A celebrated historian who stressed the human aspects of history. He is known especially for his *Mind in the Making*.

RORSCHACH, H. (1884-1922). A Swiss pioneer in the development of psycho-diagnostic tests.

ROUSSEAU, J. J. (1712-1778). French thinker whose *Émile* has become a milestone in education. In politics his *Social Contract* is especially

GLOSSARY OF NAMES

important. His *Confessions* reveal his neurotic tendencies. Rousseau favored the life of nature and opposed all forms of discipline.

RUSSELL, B. (1872—). Russell has achieved eminence both in philosophy and in mathematics. He has been awarded the Nobel prize. Among his many works are *The Analysis of Matter* and *History of Western Philosophy*.

ST. FRANCIS (1182-1226). Best-loved saint of the Middle Ages. He started an order which emphasized charity for the poor.

SANTAYANA, G. (1863-1952). He was born in Spain but spent many years in the United States. As a philosopher he combined faith and reason; among his major works is *The Life of Reason* (5 vols.).

SARTRE, J. P. Contemporary French dramatist and philosopher whose *Age of Reason* is a summary of his existential philosophy. The most concise introduction to his ideas is his *Existentialism* (1947). Sartre stresses man's aloneness in the universe and holds that man must create his own values and ideals.

SARTON, G. A. (1884—). Born in Belgium, he later settled in the United States and became a Professor at Harvard. He has been especially interested in the history of science.

SCHELER, M. (1874-1928). German philosopher who taught at Cologne and at Frankfurt and who was especially interested in an analysis of ethics. He collaborated with Husserl in developing the ideas of phenomenology, a theory which tries to divorce philosophy from psychology.

SCHLEIERMACHER, F. E. D. (1768-1834). German theologian who stressed man's dependence on God. Among his works we find *Speeches on Religion* (1799) and *The Christian Faith* (1821).

SCHOPENHAUER, A. (1788-1860). German philosopher known for his pessimism. His main work is *World as Will and Idea*.

SCHWEITZER, A. (1875—). He is one of the best-known thinkers of our time. He is notable not only in philosophy but also in medicine, biology, and music; his missionary labors in French Equatorial Africa have been rewarded with the Nobel Prize.

SENECA, M. (54 B.C.-39 A.D.). He was a noted rhetorician and he popularized the ideals of Greek thought. He wrote tragedies and philosophical essays; among his books are *De Vita Beata* and *De Providentia*.

SHELDON, E. A. Nineteenth century superintendent of schools at Oswego, New York, who was influenced by the ideas of Pestalozzi.

SHELLEY, P. B. (1792-1822). British romantic poet whose "Mont Blanc" is an excellent example of his lyrical gifts.

SOCRATES (470-399 B.C.). Outstanding Greek philosopher who was the

GLOSSARY OF NAMES

gadfly of Athens and who taught that the unexamined life is not worth living.

SOPHOCLES (496?-406 B.C.). Greek dramatist who ranks with Aeschylus and who wrote more than 120 plays. He was mainly concerned with psychological problems.

SOROKIN, P. A. (1889—). Sorokin came to the United States from Russia after the Soviet Revolution and for many years taught at Harvard. He is author of *Social and Cultural Dynamics* (4 vols.).

SPENCER, H. (1820-1903). English thinker who tried to give a complete account of cosmic phenomena. Especially important is his *First Principles*. Spencer developed a sociological version of Darwinism.

SPENGLER, O. (1880-1936). German philosopher of history who held that the West was in a state of decay. His *Decline of the West* became one of the most influential books of our time.

SPINOZA, B. (1632-1677). Dutch philosopher of Jewish parentage whose *Ethics* is one of the masterpieces of philosophy. Spinoza taught the doctrine of pantheism, that man and God are one. He believed that man should see life under the aspect of eternity.

STALIN, J. (1879-1953). Russian dictator noted for his purges and autocratic spirit.

STEELE, SIR R. (1672-1729). British essayist and dramatist who wrote on the morals of his time. In 1709 he founded the *Tatler*, a journal of politics.

STEWART, D. (1753-1828). Scottish philosopher, author of *Tracts, Physical and Mathematical*, and a proponent of common-sense realism.

STOWE, C. American educator of the nineteenth century who in 1837 reported to the Ohio legislature on his impressions of European education.

STURM, J. (1507-1589). German educator who stressed discipline and classicism in his school at Strassburg.

TAWNEY, R. H. (1880—). English historian and economist who shows the influence of Calvinism upon capitalism. His major work is *Religion and the Rise of Capitalism*.

TERMAN, L. M. (1877—). He is best known for his intelligence tests. For many years he taught psychology at Stanford.

THOMAS, W. J. Contemporary American sociologist who with Znaniecki wrote *The Polish Peasant in Europe and America*.

THOREAU, H. D. (1817-1862). American thinker who championed the life of nature in *Walden*.

THORNDIKE, E. L. (1874-1949). Famous American psychologist who taught at Teachers College. He specialized in the psychology of learning.

GLOSSARY OF NAMES

THUCYDIDES (c460-c400 B.C.). Greek historian who wrote about the Peloponnesian war. He is regarded as one of the first scientific historians.

THURSTONE, L. L. Famed psychologist at the University of Chicago who specialized in factor analysis and who contributed to the exploration of personality.

TILLICH, P. (1886—). Born in Germany, he came to the United States in his mature years. He is regarded as one of the great theologians of our time. One of his most popular books is *The Courage To Be.*

TOWNSEND, H. G. In 1926 he became a professor at the University of Oregon. Author of *Philosophical Ideas in the United States.*

TOYNBEE, A. Contemporary British historian whose *Study of History* is based on a psychological view of man's destiny. He is a professor at the University of London and has lectured in the United States, where his books are best-sellers.

ULICH, R. S. One of the noted contemporary philosophers of education who for many years has been at Harvard. He reflects the influence of German idealism in his philosophy. Among his works are *Fundamentals of Democratic Education* and *History of Educational Thought.*

UNAMUNO, M. (1864-1936). Spanish philosopher celebrated for his *Tragic Sense of Life.*

VAN PAASSEN, P. (1895—). He is noted as a writer and minister. His main work is *Days of Our Years.*

VIVES, J. L. (1492-1540). A Spanish humanist, Vives was a friend of Erasmus. He was especially interested in the problems of education.

VOLTAIRE (1694-1778). French author who dominated the Age of Reason. His main work is *Candide,* a satire on morals. Voltaire was a proponent of tolerance and freedom of thought.

WAGNER, R. (1813-1883). German composer who expressed the spirit of romanticism in such works as *Lohengrin* and *Siegfried.*

WAUGH, E. (1903—). He is one of the most satirical novelists of our time, as can be seen in *The Loved Ones.*

WEBER, M. (1864-1920). German sociologist and political economist whose masterpiece is *Wirtschaft und Gesellschaft.*

WERTHEIMER, M. (1880-1934). German psychologist who developed the theories of Gestalt psychology.

WHITEHEAD, A. N. (1861-1947). British mathematician and philosopher who with Russell wrote *Principia Mathematica.* His main work is *Process and Reality.* His *Aims of Education* is especially important for the teacher.

WHITMAN, W. (1819-1892). One of the best-loved American poets whose *Leaves of Grass* has become a classic.

WIENER, N. Contemporary American mathematician who teaches at

GLOSSARY OF NAMES

Massachusetts Institute of Technology and is the author of *Cybernetics*.

WILDER, T. N. (1897—). He is one of the most noted novelists and playwrights of our time. Won the Pulitzer Prize for *The Bridge of San Luis Rey* (1927).

WILLIAMS, R. (1603-1683). Baptist clergyman who rebelled against Puritanism and who advocated separation of state and church.

WILLIAMS, T. (1914—). He writes in his plays about decay and dissolution. Most famous of his plays is *A Streetcar Named Desire*.

WITTGENSTEIN, L. Contemporary philosopher who has developed the foundations of logical positivism in his *Tractatus Logicus-Philosophicus*.

WOODBRIDGE, W. C. A nineteenth century educational reformer who wrote articles on European schools for the *American Journal of Education*.

WOOLMAN, J. (1720-1772). American Quaker who was a preacher and a philosophical writer. His *Journal* is an excellent example of his love for mankind.

WORDSWORTH, W. (1770-1850). English poet who was influenced by German romanticism.

WRIGHT, R. (1908—). He is regarded as one of the most brilliant Negro novelists. Especially impressive are *Native Son* and *Black Boy*.

XENOPHANES. (c570-c480 B.C.). Greek thinker who believed that man pictures God according to his own prejudices.

ZOROASTER or ZARATHUSTRA (about sixth century B.C.). Persian prophet who developed a religion of dualism. His ideas are contained in the *Zend-Avesta*.

Glossary of Terms

Agnosticism—First used by Herbert Spencer and popularized by Huxley. It indicates that no definite knowledge can be obtained of certain subjects. Applied to theology, it means that we can have no certain assurance of either the existence or the non-existence of God.
Altruism—The belief in the transcendence of the self and the possibility of compassionate moral actions.
Anthropomorphism—Viewing God and reality according to human parallels.
A posteriori—Stands for knowledge based upon experience. It is the opposite of *a priori* reasoning, which is reasoning prior to experience. In logic, *a priori* reasoning is deductive, whereas *a posteriori* reasoning is inductive.
Atheism—A concept in philosophy which stands for the negation of the belief in a supreme being.
Atman—A term frequently used in the *Upanishads*, which stands for man's essential self which transcends the categories of space and time. While the empirical self is constantly changing and shifting and is dependent on individual manifestations, Atman is truly universal.
Augustinianism—Applies to the philosophy of Augustine (354-430), who stressed the majesty of God and the reality of original sin and who developed a Christian philosophy of history.
Authoritarianism—A term in philosophy which states that the source of knowledge can be found in an absolute standard; this standard can be represented by an ecclesiastical organization, a sacred book, the personal will of a god, history, or the laws of society. In education this implies a stress upon formal standards.

GLOSSARY OF TERMS

Axiology—The organized and systematic consideration of values; especially important in this subject is the relationship between values and reality.

Brahma—An important god of Hinduism; also used to describe the personal form of the World Soul.

Brahman—The impersonal essence of the universe; also used to describe the members of the priestly class.

Calvinism—The religious movement initiated by John Calvin, who stressed the perfection of God, predestination, puritanism, and the wickedness of man.

Categorical imperative—The basis of Kant's moral philosophy; it stands for the absolute, unconditioned moral law.

Cosmological argument—An argument which attempts to prove the existence of God by postulating the necessity of a first cause. All causes are based upon prior causes which depend upon something which is absolute and uncaused, namely God.

Cyrenaicism—A school of philosophy founded by Aristippus, who stressed the importance of physical pleasures.

Deduction—The process of reasoning whereby conclusions are made on the basis of assumed premises. Aristotelian logic is generally deductive, while Baconian logic is inductive. Medieval religious philosophy, which followed Aristotle, is generally deductive. Modern religious philosophy, especially in Protestantism, is inductive.

Deism—A term which stands for the religious philosophy of the 18th century and interprets religion according to the principles of reason. Deism is opposed to fervent emotionalism and revelation and regards God as a supreme scientist who does not intervene directly in the affairs of the universe.

Determinism—The doctrine that all events in the universe can be understood according to their causal relationships. It is opposed to indeterminism, which believes in the freedom of the will. Determinism upholds the view that human behavior is governed by laws—physical or psychic.

Dialectic—Stands for a thorough examination of the categories and presuppositions of knowledge. Dialectic reasoning has been used in various ways by Kant, Hegel, and Marx. It is especially important in modern Communism which believes that knowledge reflects social conditions and applies Hegelian principles to institutional problems.

Eclectic—A synthetic approach to intellectual problems. In education it implies an attempt to combine various viewpoints.

Élan vital—A concept used by Bergson to describe vital impulse in evolution; this impulse is the source of creative activity.

Empiricism—The type of philosophy which claims that knowledge is

GLOSSARY OF TERMS

based on experience and denies the knowledge of innate truth. The classic exponent of this school of philosophy is John Locke, who considered man's mind a blank tablet with no capacity to understand concepts transcending experience. In education this viewpoint stresses verifiable hypotheses.

Epicureanism—The school of philosophy which maintains that the highest pleasures are those of the mind. Opposed to supernaturalism, Epicureanism believes in a scientific interpretation of the universe and tries to get away from the fear of God and the dread of death. The founder of this school was Epicurus (342-270 B.C.) whose theories were popularized by Lucretius in the poem *On the Nature of Things*.

Epistemology—The subject in philosophy which deals with the analysis of the grounds, content, and limitations of human knowledge.

Eternal recurrence—The view of Nietzsche that reality is part of a cosmic cycle.

Existentialism—The philosophical viewpoint which stresses a subjective view of life and which emphasizes intuition and indeterminism. In education it implies a stress upon the personal relationship between teacher and student.

Formalism—The belief in a categorical principle of ethics; a view often identified with the philosophy of Kant.

Hedonism—The doctrine that all human behavior is motivated by pleasure. There are two types of hedonism: (a) ethical hedonism which regards pleasure as the absolute value; and (b) psychological hedonism which holds that all conduct is guided by the quest for pleasure and the avoidance of pain.

Humanism—A term which has various meanings in philosophy. It generally stands for an opposition to supernaturalism and regards man as the main factor in the universe. In education it stresses a secular approach to knowledge.

Idealism—Used popularly to describe the spiritual content of life and to denote a faith in ultimate values. Technically, it holds the view that existence is dependent on thought. It has various forms such as in Hegel (experience is reduced to an Absolute Mind) and in Berkeley (experience depends upon perception, a pluralistic concept of reality). In education it stresses discipline and rigorous standards.

Immanence—Sometimes used as though synonymous with pantheism. It holds that God is an indwelling principle in the universe. It is opposed to the viewpoint of transcendence which claims that God is beyond the universe.

Instrumentalism—A school of philosophy associated with John Dewey, who regards ideas as instruments and tools whose main function is to clarify social issues. Instrumentalism is based on the pragmatism of

GLOSSARY OF TERMS

William James and looks with disdain on metaphysical reasoning. In education this implies a stress upon growth as the basic criterion of value.

Intuition—The view that reality can only be comprehended through supra-rational vision or insight.

Machiavellianism—Applies to the theories of Machiavelli, who thought that might makes right and who held that the end justifies the means.

Materialism—A school of thought which holds that all events in life can be reduced to their material origin. According to Hobbes, there are only two realities: matter and motion. Materialism denies the independent existence of spiritual values; it views ideals according to their physiological origin. A distinction should be made between ancient materialism as in Democritus, which is concerned mainly with a consideration of cosmology, and modern materialism as championed by Marx, which is dialectic and tries to change the universe rather than interpreting it.

Maya—A term in Indian philosophy which stands for illusion. The veil of Maya is everything which obscures reality.

Meliorism—A concept which tries to mediate between optimism and pessimism. It holds that life can be improved through concentrated human effort, especially through education.

Metaphysics—A study of reality, of "what comes after physics." The term is used in various contexts. To Descartes it stood for knowledge of immaterial entities, to Kant it dealt with things-in-themselves and objects of faith, to Aquinas it was the subject which dealt with supernatural ideals.

Modernism—The view in theology which tries to combine science and religious ideals.

Mysticism—The view that reason is inadequate when it comes to the search for the ultimate principle of reality. Mysticism appeals to intuition and holds that the highest state of knowledge is beyond all intellectual categories.

Neoplatonism—A school of philosophy established by Plotinus, who believed in the transcendence of the One, mysticism, and the non-reality of evil.

Nirvana—A term in Indian philosophy which has various meanings. On the psychological side it stands for the extinction of lust, hatred, covetousness, and craving. Metaphysically, it stands for the extinction of finitude or of all becoming.

Noumenon—A term representing Kant's view that a thing-in-itself exists. This term is used in opposition to the concept of phenomenon, which stands for the appearance of things.

Ontological argument—Was first used by Anselm (CA. 1100), who held

GLOSSARY OF TERMS

that the idea of God as greatest being presupposes his existence. It was subjected to a strong criticism by Kant in the *Critique of Pure Reason*.

Personalism—A shool of philosophy with a theistic orientation and which stresses the reality of the self.

Positivism—A doctrine developed by Comte, who held that knowledge does not extend to ultimate principles but only to phenomena. Positivism rests on the scientific method and is opposed to metaphysical reasoning.

Pragmatism—A school of philosophy associated with James, Dewey, Mead, and F. C. S. Schiller. It believes that knowledge should deal with man's adaptation to his environment and that it is to be tested by practical consequences. It is concerned with the effects rather than the motives of men. It encouraged the development of progressive education.

Progressive education—The movement which believes in a child-centered system of instruction and which stresses interest as the motive for learning. Dewey and Kilpatrick gave impetus to this movement in the United States.

Puritanism—The moral and religious philosophy which believes in rigorous ethical standards and is opposed to all types of hedonism.

Rationalism—A school of thought which holds that reason is the standard of truth and that knowledge is to be verified by intellectual rather than empirical factors. It was popular on the Continent with such thinkers as Leibnitz, Descartes, and Spinoza; in England, however empiricism was more important than rationalism.

Realism—A philosophical concept which stresses the actual existence of the external world. In educational thought realism stresses the importance of objective facts.

Reconstructionism—An educational philosophy developed by T. Brameld, who stresses utopianism and social action in education.

Relativism—The view that no absolute truth exists; in education it implies an emphasis on the flux and change of moral standards.

Self-realization—The ethical view that perfection lies in the cultivation of the potentialities of the self.

Stoicism—One of the important ethical schools of philosophy which emphasizes self-discipline, the rational nature of the universe, resignation, and control of emotions. This school holds that it is man's task to follow the laws of the universe. Metaphysically, Stoicism owed much to the philosophy of Heraclitus.

Summum bonum—Applies to the Supreme Good. Various values are regarded as the highest good, such as pleasure, reason, self-sufficiency, classless society, etc.

GLOSSARY OF TERMS

Supernaturalism—In opposition to naturalism, this view maintains that the universe represents the creation of a supreme being. It regards man's life as an interlude in the cosmic process and affirms the reality of heaven and hell.

Taoism—A Chinese philosophy developed by Lao-tse, who looked upon Tao (Nature) as the criterion of all values. Opposed to city life, Taoism glorified simple virtues and upheld an ethical system of nonassertion and compassion.

Teleological argument—Tries to prove the existence of God by the concept of design. It holds that the universe reveals a purposeful structure which must be ascribed to a supreme being.

Theism—The doctrine that the universe is guided by a personal God who is eternal and all-powerful and that there is a personal relationship between man and his Creator.

Thomism—The philosophy of St. Thomas Aquinas, who tried to synthesize the teachings of Aristotle and those of the Church. In education Aquinas stressed the importance of discipline and the role of the teacher.

Transvaluation of values—The view of Nietzsche, who desired a new code of ethics based on the will to power.

Utilitarianism—The theory that all actions should be judged according to the principle of the greatest good for the greatest number. The chief exponents of this belief were Jeremy Bentham and John Stuart Mill, who were more concerned with social legislation than with metaphysical reasoning.

Value—Applied to anything which possesses significance. Persistent controversies are carried on regarding such subjects as the objectivity and relativity of values.

Vedas—The Hindu holy books. The *Vedas* are divided into the following parts: Rigveda, Yajurveda, Samaveda, and Arthavaveda.

Vitalism—A biological concept which holds that the events of life are not to be explained by materialistic assumptions but only by postulating an independent substance which is essentially unknowable and immaterial. Various names for this substance are Élan Vital, Vital Principle, etc.

Voluntarism—The position in philosophy which emphasizes the will as the fundamental part of life and reality.

Selected Bibliography

Bagley, W. C., *Education, Crime and Social Progress*, 1930.
―――, *Education and Emergent Man*, 1934.
―――, *The Educative Process*, 1926.
Beale, H. K., *Are American Teachers Free?* 1936.
Berkson, I. B., *Education Faces the Future*, 1943.
Bode, B. H., *Conflicting Psychologies of Learning*, 1929.
―――, *How We Learn*, 1940.
―――, *Modern Educational Theories*, 1927.
Bogoslavsky, B., *The Technique of Controversy*, 1928.
Boas, F., *The Mind of Primitive Man*, 1938.
Brameld, T. B., *Patterns of Educational Philosophy*, 1950.
―――, *The Battle for Free Schools*, 1951.
―――, *Ends and Means in Education: A Midcentury Appraisal*, 1950.
―――, *Philosophies of Education*, 1955.
Breed, F. S., *Education and the New Realism*, 1939.
Briggs, T. H., *The Great Investment*, 1930.
Brown, F. J., *Educational Sociology*, 1947.
Brubacher, J. S., *Eclectic Philosophy of Education*, 1951.
―――, *Modern Philosophies of Education*, 1939.
Burnet, J., *Higher Education and the War*, 1917.
Butler, N. M., *The Meaning of Education*, 1915.
Bury, J. B., *The Idea of Progress*, 1932.
Chancellor, W. E., *Motives, Ideals, and Values in Education*, 1907.
Chapman, J. C., and G. S. Counts, *Principles of Education*, 1924.
Charters, W., *Curriculum Construction*, 1929.

SELECTED BIBLIOGRAPHY

Childs, J. L., *Education and Morals*, 1950.
———, *Education and the Philosophy of Experimentalism*, 1931
Choy, J., *Étude Comparative*, 1926.
Coe, G. A., *Educating for Citizenship*, 1932.
———, *Education in Religion and Morals*, 1911.
———, *Law and Freedom in the School*, 1924.
———, *What is Christian Education?* 1930.
Conference on the Scientific Spirit and Democratic Faith, *The Authoritarian Attempt to Capture Education*, 1945.
Counts, G. S., *Dare the School Build a New Social Order?* 1932.
———, *The Prospects of American Democracy*, 1938.
———, *The American Road to Culture*, 1930.
Cunningham, W. F., *The Pivotal Problems of Education*, 1940.
Curti, M., *The Social Ideas of American Education*, 1935.
DeHovre, F., *Catholicism in Education*, 1934.
Demiashkevich, M., *An Introduction to the Philosophy of Education*, 1935.
Dewey, J., *Art and Education*, 1929.
———, *Child and Curriculum*, 1902.
———, *Democracy and Education*, 1916.
———, *Education Today*, 1940.
———, *Ethical Principles Underlying Education*, 1903.
———, *Experience and Education*, 1938.
———, *How We Think*, 1938.
———, *Human Nature and Conduct*, 1922.
———, *Ideals, Aims, and Methods in Education*, 1922.
———, *Moral Principles in Education*, 1909.
———, *Reconstruction in Philosophy*, 1920.
———, *The School and Society*, 1900.
———, *The Sources of a Science of Education*, 1931.
———, and J. L. Childs, in W. H. Kilpatrick (ed.), *Educational Frontier*, 1938.
Doughton, I., *Modern Public Education*, 1935.
Everett, S., *A Challenge to Secondary Education*, 1935.
Finney, R. L., *A Sociological Philosophy of Education*, 1928.
Fleshman, A. C., *The Educational Process*, 1908.
———, *The Metaphysics of Education*, 1914.
Froebel, F. W. A., in S. Fletcher and J. Welton, *Froebel's Chief Writings on Education*, 1912.
Gentilé, G., *The Reform of Education*, 1922.
Gideonse, H. D., *The Higher Learning in a Democracy*, 1927.
Gilio-Tos, M. T., *Il Pensiero di Giovanni Dewey*, 1938.
Hardie, D. C., *Truth and Fallacy in Educational Theory*, 1942.

SELECTED BIBLIOGRAPHY

Hartshorne, H., *Character in Human Relations*, 1932.
Harvard Committee, *General Education in a Free Society*, 1945.
Henderson, E. N., *A Textbook in the Principles of Education*, 1950.
Hocking, W. E., *Human Nature and Its Remaking*, 1923.
Hogben, L., *The Retreat from Reason*, 1936.
Hook, S., *Education for Modern Man*, 1946.
Horne, H. H., *The Democratic Philosophy of Education*, 1935.
———, *Idealism in Education*, 1923.
———, *The Philosophy of Education*, 1927.
———, *This New Education*, 1931.
Hopkins, L. T., *Integration—Its Meaning and Application*, 1937.
Howerth, I. W., *The Theory of Education*, 1926.
Hutchins, R. M., *The Higher Learning in America*, 1936.
———, *The University of Utopia*, 1954.
Huxley, J., *Unesco: Its Purpose and Philosophy*, 1947.
Hyde, W. D., *The Teacher's Philosophy*, 1910.
James, W., *Pragmatism*, 1907.
Kandel, I. L., *Comparative Education*, 1933.
Kilpatrick, W. H., *Philosophy of Education*, 1951.
———, *Education for a Changing Society*, 1926.
———, *Education and the Social Crisis*, 1932.
———, *A Reconstructed Theory of the Educative Process*, 1935.
———, *Remaking the Curriculum*, 1936.
Kluckholn, C., in *Foundations for Integrated Education, The Nature of Concepts, Their Relation and Role in Social Structure*, 1950.
Leighton, J. A., *Individuality and Education*, 1928.
Lippmann, W., *A Preface to Morals*, 1929.
Lodge, R. C., *Philosophy of Education*, 1937.
———, *The Questioning Mind*, 1937.
Lowell, A. L., *At War with Academic Traditions in America*, 1934.
McCallister, W. J., *The Growth of Freedom in Education*, 1931.
McGucken, W. J., *The Catholic Way in Education*, 1934.
Marique, R. J., *The Philosophy of Christian Education*, 1939.
Maritain, J., *Education at the Crossroads*, 1943.
Mayer, F., *History of Ancient and Medieval Philosophy*, 1950.
———, *History of Modern Philosophy*, 1951.
———, *Education for Maturity*, 1956.
Meiklejohn, A., *Education Between Two Worlds*, 1942.
Monroe, P., *Source Book of the History of Education*, 1901.
Moore, E. C., *What is Education?* 1915.
Morrison, H. C., *Basic Principles in Education*, 1934.
Mueller, G. E., *Education Limited*, 1949.
Nash, H. S., *The University and the Modern World*, 1943.

SELECTED BIBLIOGRAPHY

National Education Association, Educational Policies Commission, *Education and Economic Well-Being in American Democracy*.
————, *The Unique Function of Education in American Democracy*.
National Society for the Study of Education, 41st Yearbook, Part I, 1942.
Newman, J. H., *Idea of a University* (sixth ed.), 1886.
Nietzsche, F., *On the Future of Our Educational Institutions*, 1909.
Ogburn, Wm. F., *Social Change*, 1922.
Orata, P. T., *The Theory of Identical Elements*, 1928.
Otto, M. C., *Things and Ideals*, 1924.
Parker, F. W., *Talks on Pedagogics*, 1939.
Peters, C. C., *Foundations of Educational Sociology* (rev. ed.), 1932.
Pink, M. A., *The Defense of Freedom*, 1935.
Ragsdale, C., *Modern Psychologies and Education*, 1936.
Rugg, H., *Culture and Education in America*, 1931.
————, *Foundations for American Education*, 1947.
Russell, B., *Education and the Modern World*, 1932.
Scheler, M., *Die Stellung des Menschen im Kosmos*, 1928.
Schoenchen, G. G., *The Activity School*, 1940.
Smith, B. O., *Logical Aspects of Educational Measurement*, 1938.
Soares, T. G., *Religious Education*, 1928.
Spencer, H., *Education: Intellectual, Moral, and Physical*, 1861.
Thompson, G. H., *A Modern Philosophy of Education*, 1929.
Thorndike, E. L., *Human Learning*, 1931.
————, and A. I. Gates, *Elementary Principles of Education*, 1930.
Vieth, P. H., *Objectives in Religious Education*, 1930.
Wahlquist, J. T., *An Introduction to American Education*, 1947.
————, *Philosophy of American Education*, 1942.
Whitehead, A. N., *Aims of Education and Other Essays*, 1929.
————, *Science and the Modern World*, 1925.
Woelfel, N., *Molders of the American Mind*, 1933.
Wynne, J. P., *Philosophies of Education from the Standpoint of the Philosophy of Experimentalism*, 1947.

# Index

INDEX

Aaron, R. I., 39
Abélard, P., 122-124, 199, 200
Abolitionists, 53
Absolutism, 11, 32, 70, 75-77, 94;
   dangers of, 145
Abstraction, 69, 74, 88
Academy movement, 33
Activism, dangers of, 82
Acton, Lord, 3, 199
Actuality, 5, 6, 20, 115, 172
Adam, 27
Adams, H. B., 15, 25, 52, 199
Adams, J. T., 52
Adamson, J. W., 194
Adaptation, 70
Adler, M., 20, 76, 199
Administrators, 20, 81, 146-147, 156, 196
Aeschylus, 132, 199, 213
Agnosticism, 217
Agriculture, 33, 47
Aims of Education, The (Ortega y Gasset), 41-42
Albertus Magnus, 78, 199
Alberty, H., 164
Alcott, A. B., 53, 55, 199
Alexander, T., 156, 199
Alienation, 5
Allegory, 119

Allen, Ethan, 31, 199
Allport, G., 25
Aloneness, 102, 212
Altruism, 151, 217
American Friends Service Committee, 38
American Journal of Education, 54, 200, 215
American Philosophical Society, 33
American Psychological Association, 204
American revolution, 53, 208
American Scholar, The (Emerson), 55, 203
Anarchy, 48
Anaxagoras, 191, 200
Anderson, P. R., 39
Anselm of Laon, 123, 200, 220
Anthropology, 4
Anthropomorphism, 154, 157-158, 217
Anxiety, 147
Apologie de Raimond Sebound (Montaigne), 16
Aquinas, Saint Thomas, 78, 119, 199, 200, 220, 222
Aristippus, 218
Aristocracy, 47, 121

229

INDEX

Aristotle, 35, 43, 63, 85, 98, 123, 126, 131, 138, 155, 179, 199, 200, 218, 222
Arrowood, C. F., 52, 127
Arrowsmith, Martin, 82-83, 207
Art, 75, 103, 113, 116, 136, 161, 169-170, 172
Art as Experience (Dewey), 69, 79
Asceticism, 167
Ashley Montagu, M. F., 25
Astrophysics, 135
Atheism, 121, 205, 217; pitfalls of, 148
Athens, 11, 80, 120-122, 130, 131, 157, 160, 190 191, 200, 210, 213
Athleticism, 84
Atlantic Monthly, 125
Atman, 5, 217
Auguries of Innocence (Blake), 169, 200
Augustine, St., 5, 65, 107, 131, 200, 217
Augustinianism, 217
Authoritarianism, 7, 23, 44, 134, 154, 156-157, 217
Authority, 37, 95; education and, 48
Awareness, 5, 61; moral, 150, 151
Axiology, 218
Axtelle, G., 117

Babbitt (Lewis), 15-16, 25, 82, 83, 113, 179, 207
Bacon, Sir Francis, 6, 69, 132, 200
Bagley, W. C., 90, 117, 223
Barnard, H., 54, 200
Barrett, C., 105
Barth, K., 65, 131, 200
Beale, H. K., 223
Beck, L. W., 105
Behaviorism, 95, 210
Benne, K. D., 117

Bentham, Jeremy, 222
Beowulf, 87
Berdyaev, N. A., 131, 200
Bergson, H., 25, 117, 120, 127, 182, 200, 218
Berkeley, G., 88, 93, 200, 219
Berkson, I. B., 13, 184, 223
Bernal, J. D., 173
Bernard, St., of Clairvoux, 123-124, 200
Berto, G., 172, 200, 209
Bestor, A., 90
Bible, 28, 29, 31, 34
Biological activities, 63
Biology, 106, 129; mathematical, 135
Black, M., 117
Black Boy (Wright), 133, 150, 153, 215
Blake, W., 169, 200
Boas, F., 223
Bobbitt, J. F., 141
Bode, B. H., 13, 164, 184, 192, 200, 223
Boethius, A. M., 131, 201
Bogoslavsky, B., 223
Bondage, 126, 192
Bosanquet, B., 152
Bourne, H. R. F., 39
Bowles, P., 172, 201
Brahma, 57, 218
Brahman, 218
Brameld, T. B., 13, 78, 90, 105, 145, 184, 201, 221, 223
Brave Men (Pyle), 12, 14, 211
Breed, F. S., 184, 192, 201, 223
Breeding, 32
Bridgman, P. W., 171, 201
Briggs, T. H., 223
Brooks, Van Wyck, 66
Broudy, H. S., 13
Brown, F. J., 105, 223
Brown, H., 173

INDEX

Brownell, B., 25
Brubacher, J. S., 13, 165, 223
Bruce, W. C., 39
Brunner, E., 65, 201
Bruno, G., 55, 122, 201
Buchler, J., 184
Büchner, C. L., 93, 201
Buddha, 111, 159, 204
Buddhism, 101
Bureaucracy, 47, 208
Burnet, J., 223
Bury, J. B., 127, 223
Butler, J. D., 165
Butler, N. M., 223
Butts, R. F., 66, 141, 165

California Institute of Technology, 81
Calvin, J., 27, 28, 31, 65, 107, 201, 203, 218
Calvinism, 28, 30, 43, 65, 213, 218
Cambridge University, 199
Campayre, J. G., 127
Camus, A., 6, 201, 209
Canterbury Tales, The (Chaucer), 87, 202
Capitalism, 28, 31, 213
Capote, T., 149, 172, 201
Carlyle, T., 55, 201
Carr, P., 46, 201
Carroll, H. H., 141
Cartesianism, 97
Carthage, University of, 107
Cassiodorus, F. M., 131, 201
Cassirer, E., 25, 39, 62, 66, 201
Castle, The (Kafka), 178, 206
Catechism, 156
Categorical imperative, 149, 218
Catholics, 29, 38, 186
Causality, 57, 96, 170
Censorship, 29, 114
Centralization, 47, 48
Cervantes, M., 201

Chancellor, W. E., 223
Change, 5, 11, 17, 70, 71, 94, 124, 135, 144, 155, 205
Chapman, J. C., 223
Character, 32, 59
Charters, W., 223
Chase, S., 173
Chateaubriand, F., 88, 201
Chaucer, G., 85, 202
Cheating, 151
Chicago, University of, 103, 132, 199, 206, 209, 214
Childs, J. L., 78, 152, 184, 224
Chinard, G., 52
Choy, J., 224
Christ, Jesus, 34, 36, 43, 56, 111, 119, 144
Christianity, 43
Church of England, 34
Cicero, M. T., 35, 43, 202
Citizenship, study of, 160
City of God, The (St. Augustine), 5, 200
City of men, 5
Civilization, 3, 7, 9, 19, 32, 41, 55, 61, 68, 71, 87-88, 108, 131, 144; Egyptian, 130; Hebrew, 158; Oriental, 157; war and, 162
Clark University, 55
Classics, 33, 34, 73, 132
Clinton, De Witt, 54, 202
Coe, G., 141, 152, 224
Cole, P. R., 194
Coleridge, S. T., 55, 56, 202
Colet, J., 10, 131, 202
College, 15-16, 22, 166
Columbia University, 206, 207, 208
Comenius, J. A., 21, 103, 202
Commissar, 144-145
Common Faith, A (Dewey), 69, 79
Communism, 148, 208, 218

INDEX

Compassion, 159, 195
Competition, 168, 189
Comte, 221
Conant, J. B., 173
Condorcet, 43
Conference on the Scientific Spirit and Democratic Faith, 224
Confessions (St. Augustine), 107, 200
Conformity, 29, 32, 82, 119, 122, 124, 151, 156, 163
Congregationalists, 38
Conservatism, 44, 56
Contemplation, 11, 28, 44, 49, 85-86, 130
Contrast, 6
Convention, 86
Cooper, T., 93, 202
Cooperation, 44, 68, 73, 75, 108, 156, 168, 189, 207
Copernicus, N., 202, 209
Core work, 140, 193
Cosmological argument, 218
Counseling, personal, 168; skillful, 139; vocational, 169
Counts, G. S., 141, 194, 223, 224
Courtesy, 32
Cousin, V., 54, 202
Cousins, N., 124, 202
Creative thinking, 113-114
Creativity, 4, 19, 51, 57, 64, 83, 104, 110-115, 124, 126, 133, 172, 176, 177, 196, 210; nature of, 113; obstacles to, 110-111; teachers and, 112
Cremin, L. A., 66
Critique of Pure Reason, The (Kant), 5, 206, 221
Croce, B., 93, 136, 192, 202
Crow, L. D., 141
Cry, the Beloved Country (Paton), 150, 152, 210
Cubberly, E. P., 127

Culture, 35, 41, 58, 62, 64, 68, 88, 106, 112, 125, 158, 193; universal, 42
Cunningham, W. F., 13, 90, 224
Curriculum, *see* Subject matter
Curti, M., 25, 224
Cynicism, 6, 72, 208
Cyrenaicism, 218

Dale, E., 141
Dana, W. F., 66
Dante, 169, 202
Darkness at Noon (Koestler), 162, 207
Dartmouth College, 134
Darwin, C. R., 16, 70, 202
Darwinism, 213
Davis, A., 90
Days of Our Years (Van Paassen), 150, 214
Death, 5, 63, 64, 114, 121, 147, 159, 219
Decentralization, 47
Deduction, 218
DeHovre, F., 224
Deism, 31-35, 218
Deliberation, 32
Demiashkevich, M., 224
Democracy, 9-10, 11, 20, 21, 35, 45, 47, 53, 68, 156, 160, 185-192, 195, 197, 206; as a faith, 185-186; enemies of, 187; ideals of, 185-187
Democracy and Education (Dewey), 9, 13, 69, 79, 194, 202, 224
Democratic Vistas (Whitman), 53, 174
Democritus, 220
Departmentalization, 134
Depressions, 187
Descartes, R., 32, 96, 99, 178, 202, 220, 221

Desperation, 5
Determinism, 57, 218; economic, 20, 94; sociological, 9; theological, 27
Dewey, J., 5, 8, 9-10, 11, 13, 21, 49, 61, 68-79, 103, 115-116, 117, 133, 138, 152, 188, 192, 194, 202, 206, 219, 221, 224
Dialectic, 176, 218, 220
Dickinson, G. L., 127
Dickinson College, 202
Diderot, Denis, 160
Dignity, 32
Dillaway, N., 66
Dilthey, W., 136, 203
Discussion method, 109, 196
Divine Comedy (Dante), 169, 202
Dogmatism, 46, 59, 71, 77, 121, 145, 154, 158, 180; dangers of, 18-19
Don Quixote, 87, 201
Donne, J., 64, 203
Doob, L., 194
Doubt, 99, 122, 162, 163
Doughton, I., 224
Dreiser, T., 133, 203
Drever, J., 127
Drill, 59, 73, 157
Durant, W., 127
Durkheim, E., 203
Dyer, Sir Edward, 177, 203

Eaton, T. H., 165
Ebenstein, W., 194
Eby, I., 127
Echart, Meister, 176, 203
Eclectic, 202, 218
Education, adult, 197; advances in the 19th century, 54; American, 80; Athenian ideals and, 191; dilemmas of, 80-89; importance of, 11-12; inadequacies of, 80-89; as a creative process, 115-116; as a living faith, 164; as a way of life, 109-110; Athenian, 130, 190-191; athleticism and, 84; authoritarianism in, 48, 156; bigness in, 80; college, 15-16, 166; comparative approach in, 157; Deism and, 34-35; democratic vs. totalitarian, 189-190; democracy in, 9, 11, 20, 188; departmentalization in, 134; Dewey's views on, 71-72; direction in, 179-180; Egyptian, 81, 129-130; Emerson's views on, 56, 58-60; enlightenment in, 159-162; European, influence in U.S., 54-55; formal, 15-16; free universal, 12; general, 134-140; German, 55; goals of, 8, 21, 32, 33, 41, 42, 46, 59, 60, 86, 134, 154-164, 178; God and, 26-38, 131; good life, and, 166-167; Greek ideal of, 85-86, 130; history and, 10-12; humanistic, 132; ideal of, 134; ideal system of, 130; imagination in, 116; inspiration in, 127; integration in, need for, 85; Jefferson and, 44-47; lack of intensity in, 126; mass, 9, 45, 155; materialism and, 96; medieval, 131; moral values in, 143-151; mysticism and, 77-78; Nazi, 189; obstacles to, 154-158; of handicapped children, 49; physical, 45; power of, 59-60; professional, 85; progress and, 108-110; progressive, 51, 73-75, 95, 103, 109-110, 133, 199, 202, 221; public, 12, 54; Puritan, 28-31; Quaker, 36, 37-38; reconstruction of, 10, 96, 154; science and, 99-100, 171; scientific method in, 100; romantic view

INDEX

of, 103; social change and, 145; Spartan, 190; spirituality and, 61-62, 65; subject matter of, 129-134; task of, 20, 32; technology and, 81; television and, 139, 140; traditionalism in, 106 154-156; vocational, 73, 98, 130, 163-164; weaknesses in 83-89; wisdom and, 15-24
Education for Freedom (Hutchins), 23fn.
Education of Henry Adams, The, 15, 25, 199
Educational theory, teachers and, 21-22
Edwards, Jonathan, 26, 27, 31, 36, 145, 203
Effort, 73, 95
Egypt, education in, 81, 129-130
Einstein, A., 16-17, 158, 170, 203
El Greco, 87, 203
Élan vital, 218, 222
Eleatics, 11, 182
Eliot, T. S., 143, 172, 203
Emerson, R. W., 53-66, 82, 87, 93, 126, 203
Émile (Rousseau), 133
Emotions, 35, 78, 103, 187
Empiricism, 87, 218-219, 221; logical, 98, 211
Enlightenment, in education, 159-162
Epicureanism, 109, 146, 219
Epicurus, 43, 109, 147, 148, 191, 203, 219
Epistemology, 161, 219
Equality, 31, 47, 53
Erasmus, D., 10, 41, 131, 159, 203, 214
Essay Concerning Human Understanding (Locke), 32
Essay for the Recording of Illustrious Providences (Mather), 29

Essay on Man (Cassirer), 25, 62, 66, 201
Essays in Experimental Logic (Dewey), 69
Esthetic activities, need for, 168
Eternal recurrence, 219
Eternity, 126
Ethics, 36, 132, 212, 219
Ethics (Dewey and Tufts), 69
Ethics and Civilization (Schweitzer), 193
Eucken, R. C., 95, 203
Euclid, 203
Evaluation, 100
Everett, S., 224
Evil, 59, 101, 107, 172
Evolution, peaceful, 186-187; theory of, 17, 202
Existence, 17, 18, 20, 94, 97, 101, 150, 154; basic problems of, 100-103; human, 168; zest for, 167
Existential problems, 101-102
Existentialism, 50, 61, 201, 206, 208, 219
Experience, 5, 17, 18, 56, 70, 71, 77
Experience and Education (Dewey), 69, 79, 224
Experience and Nature (Dewey), 69
Experimentation, 122, 123; tradition vs., 120
Experts, need for, 187-188
Ezekiel, 123, 203

Facts, values and, 87
Fadiman, C., 125, 204
Faith, 11, 32, 34, 35, 37, 43, 44, 64, 65, 68, 76, 95, 96, 101, 107, 119, 122, 129, 147, 171, 185
Fanaticism, 32, 145, 158

INDEX

Farewell to Arms (Hemingway), 148, 152, 205
Fascism, 209, 210
Faulkner, W., 149, 172, 204
Faust (Goethe), 179, 204
Federalists, 53
Feuerbach, L. H., 93, 204
Ficino, M., 10, 131, 204
Finney, R., 165, 224
Firkins, O., 67
Fisch, M., 39
Fischer, L., 152
Fitzpatrick, E., 13, 165
Flaum, L. S., 90
Fleshman, A. C., 224
Folly, 159
Football, 81, 84, 125
Ford Foundation, 133
Formalism, 182, 219
Fox, George, 57
France, 59, 87-88
Francke, A. H., 88, 204
Frank, J., 90
Franklin, Benjamin, 31, 32-34, 35, 38, 39, 204
Frederick William III, 204
Frederick William IV, 156, 204
Free Man's Worship, A (Russell), 101
Freedom, 8, 9, 23, 30, 31, 37, 43, 46-51, 53, 57, 59, 75, 95, 124, 126, 150, 160, 163, 185, 186, 187, 197, 206; academic, 49; Jeffersonian view of, 51; meaning of, 48-49; scientific method and, 49
Freedom and Culture (Dewey), 69
Freethinkers, 29
French revolution, 53, 211
Freud, S., 7, 16, 158, 175, 204
Fröbel, F., 21, 73, 95, 103, 204, 224

Fromm, E., 25, 48, 90, 173
Futility, 5, 12, 19, 111, 159

Galileo, 99, 123, 158, 204
Gandhi, M. K., 111, 143-144, 204
Gates, A. I., 226
General Education in a Free Society, 133, 225
Genius, 59
Gentlie, G., 224
Germany, 7, 55, 59, 88, 122, 146, 148, 150, 156-157, 158, 166, 189
Ghiselin, B., 117
Gideonse, H. D., 224
Gilio-Tos, M. T., 224
Goals, of education, 8, 21, 32, 33, 41, 42, 46, 59, 60, 86, 134, 154-164, 178; of life, 5, 101
God, 10, 21, 43, 46, 50, 58, 60, 65, 71, 76, 94, 95, 98, 107, 110, 126, 143, 148, 160, 179, 212, 213, 215, 217, 218, 219, 221, 222; education and, 26-38, 131
Goethe, J. W., 55, 60, 88, 179, 204
Gogh, V. Van, 112, 204
Gomperz, T., 127
Good life, *see* Life, good
Goodness of man, 59, 108
Greece, ancient, 129; ideal of education in, 85-86, 130
Guidance, 139, 168-169

H. M. Pulham, Esquire (Marquand), 15, 25, 208
Habe, H., 157, 204
Habits, correct, 59
Hall, G. Stanley, 72, 73, 133, 204
Hamilton, A., 47, 185, 205
Hamilton, E., 127
Handicapped children, education of, 49

235

INDEX

Hardie, D. C., 224
Harper's, 125
Harris, W. T., 9, 69, 73, 95, 205
Hartshorne, H., 152, 225
Harvard University, 28, 55, 60, 133, 180, 210, 212, 213, 214
Haverford College, 206
Hayakawa, S., 117
Hedonism, 106, 108, 219, 221
Hegel, G. W., 69-70, 93, 95, 175, 177, 202, 205, 218, 219
Heidegger, M., 19, 50, 102, 205
Heine, H., 88, 205
Heisenberg, W., 135, 170, 205
Héloïse, 123, 199
Hemingway, Ernest, 4, 13, 112, 148-149, 152, 205
Henderson, J. C., 52
Henderson, S., 25, 165
Heraclitus, 11, 162, 205, 221
Herbart, J. F., 73, 205
Herbert, George, 37, 205
Heresy, 29, 76, 123, 146, 156, 163, 199, 203, 210
Hierarchy, 11, 71, 75
Hirst, F. W., 52
History, 3, 9, 17, 41, 42, 43, 46, 69, 71, 136, 149, 155, 208; American, 29, 53; education and, 10-12
Hitler, Adolf, 7, 48, 150, 158, 166, 203, 205, 209
Hobbes, T., 93, 94, 205, 220
Hocking, W. E., 105, 225
Hogben, L., 225
Holbach, P. H., 93, 205
Holmes, O. W., 67
Homer, 132, 146, 205
Honeywell, R. J., 52
Honor, 32
Honor system, 188
Hook, S., 79, 117, 225
Hope, 103-104, 111, 147, 172

Hopkins, L. T., 225
Horne, H. H., 13, 105, 128, 184, 191, 205, 225
How We Think (Dewey), 69, 79, 115, 117, 224
Howerth, I. W., 225
Human Nature and Conduct (Dewey), 69, 79, 224
Humanism, 10, 131, 202, 219
Humanitarianism, 38, 145
Humanities, 96-97, 136, 139, 162, 171
Hume, David, 35, 101, 206
Humility, 16-18, 37, 87, 111, 123
Husserl, Edmund, 212
Hutchins, R. M., 9, 11, 14, 21, 23, 90, 131, 134, 206, 225
Hutchinson, Anne, 30, 206
Huxley, Aldous, 217
Huxley, J., 225
Hyde, W. D., 225
Hygiene, mental, courses in, 161
Hysteria, 187

Idealism, 38, 77, 93-95, 200, 201, 205, 214-219; truth and, 177-178
Ideals, 3, 5, 8, 10, 48, 61, 68, 76, 161, 176; ethical, 188-189; moral, 33, 59, 61, 72; Puritan, 26-27
Ideas, 4, 5, 6, 7, 8, 9, 61, 71, 113, 124, 161; unorthodox, 29
Ideology and Utopia (Mannheim), 97, 208
Imagination, 116, 130
Immanence, 219
Immediacy, 180, 181
Immortality, 35, 64, 126, 130, 147, 211
Imperialism, 7
Indeterminacy, theory of, 205
India, 144

236

Indians, 37
Individualism, 43, 57, 59, 75, 82, 95, 134, 169, 177
Industrialism, 9, 143
Inquiry, freedom of, 187
Inspiration, need for, 125-127
Instrumentalism, 219
Integrity, 82, 83, 147
Intellectual life, 63, 109, 154, 176
Intelligence, 6, 72, 103, 116, 124; critical, 122
Intensity, need for, 126
Interest, 73, 95
Intolerance, 29, 145
Introduction to Metaphysics (Bergson), 182
Intuition, 55, 57, 219, 220
Inwardness, 56, 119; need for, 176-177
Iran, education in, 81
Irrationality, 7, 145, 178
Irresponsibility, 19, 48, 51
Isidore of Seville, 131, 206
Italy, 7

Jackson, A., 53, 206
James, W., 5, 10, 59, 70, 88, 95, 101, 119, 133, 192, 206, 220, 221, 225
Jaspers, Karl, 50
Jeffers, R., 149, 206
Jefferson, Thomas, 38, 41-51, 52, 53, 56, 61, 185, 187, 201, 205, 206
Jesus, *see* Christ, Jesus
Joad, C. E. M., 105
Johns Hopkins University, 55
Johnson, G., 25
Jones, H. M., 141
Jones, R. M., 144, 149, 206
Jones, W. T., 117
Joyce, J., 178, 206
Justice, 32, 36, 43, 62

Kafka, F., 178, 206
Kalamazoo case, 54
Kandel, I. L., 141, 225
Kant, I., 5, 17, 18, 55, 56, 102, 112, 133, 135, 149, 175, 201, 206, 218, 219, 220-221
Kaplan, O. J., 141
Kausalbegriff in der Physik, Der (Planck), 99
Khrushchev, Nikita, 163
Kierkegaard, S., 21, 206
Kilpatrick, W. H., 5, 8-9, 14, 70, 78, 79, 109, 112, 123, 140, 141, 184, 192, 206, 225
Kluckholn, C., 225
Knode, J. C., 105
Knower and the Known, The (Dewey and Bentley), 69
Knowledge, 6, 11, 21, 22, 32, 35, 36, 41, 44, 45, 54, 55, 59, 65, 69, 71, 76, 121, 132, 192; application of, 33, 43, 61, 132; factual, 87, 119, 134; limitations of, 16-19; social nature of, 71
Know-Nothing Party, 124
Koch, A., 52
Koestler, A., 144, 162, 165, 207
Köhler, W., 18, 207
Kohn, H., 194
Kokoschka, O., 86, 169, 207
Königsberg, University of, 206
Koran, 50
Korzybski, A., 154, 207
Kropotkin, P., 108, 207
Krutch, J. W., 125, 128, 207

Laissez-faire, 23, 48
Lamprecht, K., 136, 207
Langer, S., 62, 67, 117, 207
Langfitt, R. E., 184
Lao-tse, 222
Laski, H. J., 136, 194, 207
Last Puritan (Santayana), 26

INDEX

Laws, democracy and, 186
Leadership, 187-190
Leary, D. B., 165
Leibnitz, G. W., 55, 88, 135, 207, 221
Leighton, J. A., 141, 225
Leonardo da Vinci, 69, 160, 207
Lessing, G. E., 88, 207
Letters Concerning Toleration (Locke), 32
Lewin, K., 18, 207
Lewis, Sinclair, 15, 25, 82, 113, 133, 179, 207
Liberal arts, 85, 86, 130, 131, 136, 196
Liberty, 30, 48, 53, 82, 163
Lie, The (Raleigh), 182-183, 211
Life, education as a way of, 109-110; essentials of, 102; goal of, 5, 101; good, foundations of the, 166-170; quest for good, 166-172; intellectual, 63, 109; philosophy and, 110; task in, 168; zest for, 167
Lilge, F., 194
Lincoln, Abraham, 53
Lippmann, Walter, 108, 152, 207, 225
Locke, John, 32, 33, 34, 43, 56, 132, 185, 186, 208, 219
Lodge, R. C., 105, 184, 225
Logic, 71, 115-116, 132, 155, 200, 207, 210, 218; Aristotelian, 154-155
Logic (Dewey), 69, 115
London, University of, 85, 86, 214
Love, 36, 37, 56, 59, 94, 120, 159, 167
Lowell, A. L., 225
Lowenfeld, V., 117
Loyalty, 59, 113
Lucretius, 159, 208, 219
Luther, Martin, 57

Lynd, H. M., 29, 39, 208
Lynd, R., 29, 39, 90, 208

Mach, E., 18, 208
Machiavelli, N., 163, 208, 220
Machiavellianism, 77, 220
MacIver, R. M., 90, 136, 208
Madison, James, 47, 208
Mailer, N., 149, 162, 172, 208
Malraux, A., 117
Malthus, T. R., 208
Mann, H., 54, 208
Mann, T., 88, 208
Manners, 32
Mannheim, K., 97, 208
Marcel, G., 104, 208
Marique, R. J., 225
Maritain, J., 25, 76, 131, 208, 225
Marquand, J. P., 15, 25, 208
Marx, K., 93, 94, 208-209, 218, 220
Marxism, 50, 158, 205
Mason, R. E., 152
Massachusetts Institute of Technology, 81, 207, 215
Materialism, 3, 93-97, 180, 205, 220
Mathematics, 98, 100, 101, 115, 177, 181, 209, 210, 212
Mather, Cotton, 29, 209
Mather, Increase, 29, 209
Maugham, W. S., 114, 179, 184, 209
May, R., 173
Maya, 220; veil of, 5
Mayer, F., 39, 52, 90, 128, 173, 194, 225
McCallister, W. J., 128, 225
McGucken, W. J., 225
Mead, G. H., 192, 209, 221
Mead, Margaret, 49, 209
Medicine, psychosomatic, 135

Meiklejohn, A., 105, 225
Melby, E. O., 194
Meliorism, 72, 220
Memorization, 87, 106, 157
Mencken, H. L., 26, 209
Mental hygiene, courses in, 161
Mercer University, 123
Mercy, 36, 195
Metaphysics, 35, 94, 220
Methodism, 57
Methodists, 38
Methodology, 3, 8, 30, 70, 71, 85, 178
Middle Ages, 11, 71, 122, 131, 145, 212
Middletown (Lynd), 29, 88, 208
Middletown in Transition (Lynd), 29, 39, 88, 208
Militarism, 43, 190
Mill, John Stuart, 222
Mind in the Making (Robinson), 116, 211
Moderation, 35, 130, 147, 200
Modernism, 220
Mohammedans, 50
Moksha, 101
Monadology (Leibnitz), 135, 207
Monroe, P., 141, 225
Montague, W. P., 173
Montaigne, M., 10, 16, 17fn., 25, 87, 110, 131-132, 209
Montesquieu, Baron, 185, 209
Moore, E. C., 128, 184, 225
Morality, 33, 46, 151
Moravia, A., 172, 209
Morrison, H. C., 225
Morse, J. T., 52
Mosier, R. D., 67
Mueller, G. E., 14, 225
Muller, H. J., 128
Mumford, L., 14, 117, 141, 173
Murphy, G., 173
Mussolini, Benito, 7, 48, 163, 209

My Pedagogic Creed (Dewey), 9, 69, 79
Mysticism, 70, 77-78, 114, 124, 203, 206, 220
Mythology, 43, 106

Naked and the Dead, The (Mailer), 162, 208
Napoleon I, 53, 209
Narcissism, 7
Nash, H. S., 141, 225
National Education Association, 226
National Society for the Study of Education, 194, 226
Nationalism, 7, 50, 171
Native Son (Wright), 102, 215
Naturalism, 222
Nature, 34, 43, 45, 55, 58, 60, 61, 64, 69, 71, 86, 94, 95, 97, 98, 99, 100, 113, 115, 170, 181, 192, 222
Negativism, 56
Neoplatonism, 220
Neoscholasticism, 208
Neuroses, 7, 102, 161
Neutra, R., 128
New York Free School Society, 54
Newman, J. H., 142, 226
Nicholas of Cusa, 17, 209
Niebuhr, R., 65, 76, 131, 160, 173, 209
Nietzsche, F., 16, 18, 114, 133, 148, 169, 209, 219, 222, 226
Nihilism, dangers of, 148-149
Nineteen Eighty-four (Orwell), 51fn., 52, 144, 210
Nirvana, 101, 204, 220
Non-conformity, 57, 59
Northrop, F. S. C., 152
Noumenon, 220

Objectivity, 97-99, 144, 169
Ogburn, Wm. F., 226

INDEX

Ohio State University, 200
O'Neill, E., 149, 210
Ontological argument, 220-221
Open-mindedness, 10, 71, 192
Open Society and its Enemies, The (Popper), 97, 211
Optimism, 6, 72
Orata, P. T., 226
Oregon, University of, 214
Ortega y Gasset, J., 14, 41, 52, 135, 210
Orwell, George, 51, 52, 145, 210
Otto, M. C., 90, 226
Over-Soul, 55-56

Padover, S. K., 52
Paine, Thomas, 31, 34, 210
Palmer, G. H., 67, 152
Pantheism, 213, 219
Paralogisms, 5
Pareto, V., 19, 136, 175, 210
Parker, F. W., 226
Parmenides (Plato), 176
Parrington, V. L., 128
Particularism, 77
Pascal, B., 6, 87, 101, 105, 210
Pasteur, L., 112, 170, 210
Pater, W., 142
Paton, A., 150, 152, 210
Patrick, C., 116, 210
Pavlov, I. P., 95, 210
Pedants, 21
Peirce, C. S., 10, 70, 170, 210
Pennsylvania, University of, 202
Pensées (Pascal), 101, 210
Perennialism, 206
Perfection, 7, 23, 44, 58, 76, 95, 157, 179, 221
Pericles, 191
Permanence, 5, 6, 11
Peron, Juan, 163
Perry, B., 67

Perry, R. B., 26, 152, 210
Personalism, 221
Persons and Places (Santayana), 180
Pessimism, 72, 103, 172, 206, 212
Pestalozzi, J., 21, 54-55, 103, 210, 212
Peters, C. C., 25, 226
Pharisees, 119
Phenomenology, 212
Phidias, 160, 210
Philosophical Ideas in the United States (Townsend), 26
Philosophy, affirmative, search for, 172; basic, of general education, 135; classical, 55; consequences of, 19; creative, 4; decline of, 88; Dewey's, 68-78; educational, values of, 20-24; Emerson's, 55-62; existential, 21; humanization of, 161; importance of, 19; Jefferson's, 42-48; life and, 110; mature, 7, 11, 17, 21; meaning of, 5; medieval, 10, 69; mission of, 89; reconstruction of, 10, 32; traditional, 10
Philosophy in a New Key (Langer), 62, 67, 117, 207
Pico della Mirandola, G., 10, 210
Pink, M. A., 226
Pioneers, 31
Pisa, University of, 123
Plague, The (Camus), 6
Planck, M. K., 99, 170, 210
Plato, 5, 15, 34-35, 43, 44, 55, 69, 78, 85, 93, 94, 109, 132, 138, 146-147, 176, 210-211
Platonism, 43, 55, 146-147, 202, 204, 211
Play, 73, 74, 106, 167
Pleasure, 106, 109, 147, 203, 219, 221

INDEX

Plotinus, 55, 93, 104, 211, 220
Plutarch, 190, 211
Poetry, 106, 181, 193, 198
Poincaré, J. H., 17, 211
Politics, 80
Popper, K. R., 97, 136, 211
Positivism, 215, 221
Power, 3, 6, 9, 48, 77, 80, 148, 199; nature of, 80; of education, 59-60
Practicalism, 35
Pragmatism, 10, 69, 76, 192, 206, 209, 210, 219, 221; romantic, 192-193
Predestination, 43, 107, 218
Preface to Morals, A (Lippmann), 108, 152, 207, 225
Prejudice, 7, 159, 160
Premises, importance of, 93
President's Commission on Higher Education, 142
Pressure groups, 20
Priestley, J., 93, 211
Princeton University, 203
Progress, 159-160; education and, 108-110
Protagoras, 157, 211
Providence, 28, 34
Provincialism, 18, 197
Prussian Elementary School, The (Alexander), 156, 199
Psychoanalysis, 204
Psychology, 115, 155, 175; Gestalt, 136, 214
Psychosomatic medicine, 135
Public and Its Problems, The (Dewey), 69, 74
Puritanism, 26-31, 107-108, 146, 206, 209, 215, 218, 221
Puritanism and Democracy (Perry), 26
Puritans, 26-31, 38, 108, 186
Pyle, E., 12, 14, 211

Quakers, 29, 36-38, 57, 144, 186, 206, 215
Quest for Certainty, The (Dewey), 69

Rabelais, F., 10, 211
Rader, M. M., 117
Radhakrishnan, S., 93, 144, 211
Ragsdale, C., 226
Raleigh, Sir W., 182, 211
Ramus, P., 10, 131, 211
Randall, J. H., 152, 184
Rationalism, 221
Rationalists, 32
Ratner, J., 194
Raup, R. B., 117, 194
Razor's Edge (Maugham), 114
Read, H., 165
Realism, 181, 208, 213, 221
Reality, 5, 6, 35, 50, 56, 71, 95, 147, 172, 219
Reason, 35, 44, 46, 65, 86, 98, 100, 101, 103, 104, 107, 108, 120, 147
Reconstruction in Philosophy (Dewey), 69, 79, 192, 224
Reconstructionism, 221
Redlands, University of, 139
Reformation, 57, 107
Regression, 17, 145
Reichenbach, H., 98, 105, 211
Relativism, 11, 55, 75-76, 77, 221
Relativity, theory of, 135, 203
Religion, 103, 129, 132, 148, 171-172, 181, 202; basis of, 35; Dewey's views on, 76; Emerson's views on, 61-62; Jefferson's, 43, 45; traditional, 31
Renaissance, 10, 11, 110, 122, 131-132, 160, 202, 203, 204, 207, 208, 210
Report on the State of Public Education in Prussia (Cousin), 54

INDEX

Republic (Plato), 34, 138, 211
Responsibility, 160
Reuchlin, J., 10, 211
Revolt of the Masses (Ortega y Gasset), 41, 52, 210
Revolution, 162-163
Rhode Island, 30
Riesman, D., 112, 211
Righteousness, 32, 33, 121
Rise of Scientific Philosophy, The (Reichenbach), 98, 211
Robinson, J. H., 116, 211
Rogers, H. K., 184
Romanticism, 100
Rorschach, H., 100, 211
Ross, F., 90
Ross, J. S., 105
Rousseau, J. J., 73, 88, 108, 133, 210-211, 212
Royce, J., 184
Rubáiyát, 6
Rugg, H., 25, 152, 226
Rusk, R. R., 105
Russell, B., 6, 9, 14, 69, 88, 101, 115, 153, 181, 192, 212, 214, 226
Russell, P., 39, 67
Russia, 122, 158, 162-163

St. Francis, 7, 167, 212
Salvation, 7, 21, 27, 28, 43, 65, 71, 76, 129, 159, 167
Sanborn, I. B., 67
Sanity, 167
Santayana, G., 3, 10, 15, 18, 26, 118, 128, 150, 180, 212
Sarton, G. A., 30, 97, 212
Sartre, J. P., 50, 61, 88, 102, 172, 184, 205, 209, 212
Saturday Review of Literature, 125, 202
Scheler, Max, 4, 212, 226
Schiller, F. C. S., 221

Schilpp, P. A., 79
Schleiermacher, F. E. D., 35, 212
Schoenchen, G., 79, 226
Scholarships, 45
Scholasticism, 131-132
School and Society (Dewey), 9, 69, 79, 224
Schopenhauer, A., 18, 94, 133, 169, 172, 212
Schweitzer, A., 14, 42, 52, 144, 151, 153, 193, 212
Science, 30, 31, 32, 41, 42, 45, 49, 50, 55, 57, 71, 81, 86, 94, 96, 97, 98, 99, 103, 129, 131, 132, 135, 136, 143, 158, 162, 170-171, 201; education and, 99-100; empirical, 87; objectivity and, 99
Science and the Modern World (Whitehead), 62, 67, 87, 105, 226
Scientific method, 49-50, 71, 97, 99, 100, 155, 164, 171, 192, 198
Sectarianism, 46
Segregation, 36
Self, 101-102, 151; concept of, 5; understanding of, 168
Self-examination, 133
Self-expression, 23
Self-realization, 161, 221
Self-reliance, 151, 156, 157
Self-sacrifice, 59
Seneca, M., 35, 212
Sensitivity, 150-151, 156
Sheldon, E., 54, 212
Shelley, P. B., 94, 212
Sherrington, C., 118
Sic et Non (Abélard), 122, 199
Sidney, Sir Philip, 203
Skepticism, 6, 19, 45, 55, 103, 149, 163, 206
Skills, 41, 116

Skinner, C. E., 184
Slavery, 36, 37, 53, 98, 150
Slogans, 82
Smith, B. O., 117, 226
Smugness, 7, 119, 145, 195
Snows of Kilimanjaro, The (Hemingway), 4
Soares, T. G., 39, 226
Social activities, 63
Socialism, 148, 156, 157, 189, 205
Society, teachers and, 129-140
"Society for Establishing a Free School in the city of New York," 203
Society of Friends, 36-38, 110
Socrates, 41, 59, 78, 95, 110, 119, 120-122, 123, 191, 210, 212-213
Solipsism, 178
Some Thoughts Concerning Education (Locke), 32
Sophists, 121, 157
Sophocles, 132, 213
Sorokin, P. A., 14, 136, 213
Spain, 87; education in, 81
Sparta, 43, 190, 191
Specialization, 41-42, 135, 136, 137; dangers of, 41-42
Spencer, H., 133, 134, 153, 213, 217, 226
Spengler, O., 3, 19, 136, 143, 213
Sperry, W. L., 40
Spillane, Mickey, 125
Spinoza, B., 77, 98, 126, 170, 204, 213, 221
Spiritual life, 64
Spirituality, 61-62, 65, 82, 119, 167
Spoils system, 53
Sports, 33
Stalin, J., 48, 213
Stanley, W. O., 25, 142
States rights, 47

Steele, Sir R., 34, 213
Stellung des Menschen im Kosmos, Die (Scheler), 226
Stereotypes, 82
Stewart, D., 56, 213
Stoicism, 181, 221
Stowe, C., 54, 213
Stranger, The (Camus), 6
Street, Harry, 4
Students, philosophy of education and, 22-23; relationship between teachers and, 21
Study of History (Toynbee), 80, 90, 214
Sturm, J., 96
Subject matter, evolution of, 129-132; modern trends, 132-134
Subjectivity, 97, 99, 144, 169, 205
Success, 37, 82, 121; material, 83
Sullivan, H. S., 173
Summing Up, The (Maugham), 179, 184
Summum bonum, 221
Supernaturalism, 70, 76, 219, 222
Superstition, 7, 43, 96, 171
Survey courses, inadequacy of, 138
Symbolism, 55, 71, 119, 181

Taoism, 222
Tatler, 213
Tawney, R. H., 28, 136, 213
Teachers, 20-21; as optimists, 172; as prophets, 125; as spiritual guides, 65; authoritarian, 156-157; creativity and, 112; educational theory and, 21-22; Emerson's views of, 56, 58, 60; faith of, 64-65; inspired, need for, 84-85; mission of, 119-122; Puritan, 28-29, 30; relationship between students and, 21; society and, 129-140; status of, 81-82; task of, 134; truth and, 182

INDEX

Teaching, 104, 111, 138, 195, 196, 197; cooperative, 138-139; ideals of, 119-127
Tead, O., 174
Technology, 6, 7, 11, 80, 124, 133, 143, 154, 164; education and, 81
Teleological argument, 222
Televison, 139, 140, 171, 197
Temple, W., 174
Tentativeness, 71, 155
Terman, L. M., 100, 213
Tests, 8, 87
Thayer, V. T., 25, 40, 90
Theism, 222
Theology, 10, 31, 32, 36, 43, 50, 62, 71, 96, 101, 129, 131, 172, 217, 220; neglect of, 131
Thermodynamics, 210
Thinking, creative, 113-114; independent, need for, 122
Thirty Years War, 160
Thomas, E. D., 52
Thomas, W. J., 108, 213
Thomism, 222
Thompson, G. H., 184, 226
Thoreau, H. D., 53, 111, 143, 144, 213
Thorndike, E. L., 100, 213, 226
Thorpe, F. N., 40
Thucydides, 191, 214
Thurstone, L. L., 100, 214
Thus Spake Zarathustra (Nietzsche), 148, 209
Tillich, P., 131, 214
Time, 64
Tolerance, 33, 37, 38, 158, 186, 214
Tonne, H. A., 105
Totalitarianism, 19, 95, 146, 187, 192, 210, 211
Townsend, H. G., 26, 214

Toynbee, A., 18, 31, 80, 90, 135, 136, 214
Traditionalism, 33, 44, 71, 84, 120, 122, 154-156
Transcendentalism, 55-56, 203
Trial, The (Kafka), 178, 206
Trilling, L., 174
Trinity, 43
Truth, 5, 6, 30, 32, 34, 62, 71, 76, 95, 99, 116, 130, 131, 157, 175-183
Tsanoff, R., 118
Tufts, 69
Tuttle, H. S., 165
Two Sources of Religion and Morality, The (Bergson), 120, 127
Two Treatises on Government (Locke), 32

Ulich, R. S., 40, 52, 192, 194, 214
Ulysses (Joyce), 178, 206
Unamuno, M., 87, 214
Understanding, 38, 42, 77, 150, 158; scientific, 171
Uniformity, 57
Union Theological Seminary, 209
Unitarianism, 211
Unitarians, 38
United Nations, 158
Universalism, 36, 42, 77, 132
Unreality, 5, 12, 55
Upanishads, 5, 55, 101, 144, 217
Utilitarianism, 222
Utopia, 5, 6, 145, 146, 172, 210
Utopianism, 221

Valuation, 100
Value, 222
Values, sense of, 161; transvaluation of, 209, 222
Van Paassen, P., 150, 214

INDEX

Varieties of Religious Experience (James), 70, 206
Vedas, 222
Vice, 34
Vienna, University of, 204
Vieth, P. H., 40, 226
Virginia, University of, 45-46
Virtue, 31, 32, 33, 34, 47, 59, 121, 158
Vitalism, 222
Vives, J. L., 10, 214
Voltaire, 18, 59, 87, 160, 214
Voluntarism, 222

Wagner, R., 18, 214
Wahlquist, J. T., 79, 226
War, 36, 37, 48, 146, 162, 187, 189, 190, 209
Ward, H. H., 25
Warters, J., 142
Washburne, C., 153
Waugh, E., 130, 214
Wealth, 44
Weber, M., 136, 214
Welsh, M. G., 118
Welt als Wille und Vorstellung, Die (Schopenhauer), 94
Weltanschauung, 71
Wertheimer, M., 18, 214
Wesley, John, 57
Whitehead, A. N., 9, 41, 62, 63, 67, 87, 100, 105, 113, 115, 165, 214, 226
Whitman, Walt, 22, 53, 167, 174, 214
Wickman study, 139

Wiener, N., 214-215
Wild, J. D., 52, 105
Wilder, T. N., 132, 215
Williams, Roger, 30, 215
Williams, T., 149, 215
Wilson, E., 174
Wilson, H. E., 142
Wisdom, 32, 35, 45, 60, 77, 120, 121, 157, 158; education and, 15-24
Witchcraft, 29, 171, 209
Wittgenstein, L., 135, 215
Woelfel, N., 226
Woodberry, G. E., 67
Woodbridge, W. C., 54, 215
Woody, T., 40
Woolman, John, 36-37, 215
Wordsworth, W., 55, 115, 215
Work, 106; value of, 28
World as Will and Idea, The (Schopenhauer), 133
World-mindedness, 158
Wright, R., 102, 133, 150, 153, 215
Wynne, J. P., 14, 226

Xenophanes, 157, 215

Yale University, 23, 206
Yauch, W. A., 90
Yogi, 144

Zeitgeist, 18
Znaniecki, 213
Zoroaster (Zarathustra), 18, 148, 215

245

Date Due